The Rise of Socialist Fiction 1880–1914

Also by H. Gustav Klaus, published by *EER*:

The Literature of Labour. 200 Years of Working-Class Writing. Second edition with new Introduction. Available.

The Socialist Novel in Britain, edited by H. Gustav Klaus, Second edition with new Introduction. Available.

Voices of Anger and Hope. Studies in the Literature of Labour and Socialism. To be published in the autumn of 2018.

The author:
H. Gustav Klaus is Emeritus Professor of the Literature of the British Isles, Universität Rostock, Germany. He has also been a Visiting Professor at the University of Queensland; a Research Fellow at the Universities of Edinburgh and Aberdeen, and a Visiting Fellow at Corpus Christi College, Oxford.

The Rise of Socialist Fiction 1880–1914

Edited by
H. Gustav Klaus
Emeritus Professor of the Literature of the British Isles, University of Rostock, Germany

Second edition with new Introduction

EER
Edward Everett Root, Publishers, Brighton, 2018.

EER
Edward Everett Root, Publishers, Co. Ltd.,
30 New Road, Brighton, Sussex, BN1 1BN, England.
www.eerpublishing.com

edwardeverettroot@yahoo.co.uk

The Rise of Socialist Fiction 1880–1914
First published in Great Britain in 1987.
This second edition first published 2018.
© H. Gustav Klaus and contributors, 1987, 2018.
This edition © Edward Everett Root Publishers 2018

ISBN: 978-1-911454-92-2 Paperback
ISBN: 978-1-911454-93-9 Hardback

H. Gustav Klaus and the contributors have asserted their right to be identified as the authors of this Work in accordance with the Copyright, Designs and Patents Act 1988 and as the owner of this Work.

All rights reserved. No part of this publication may be reproduced, stored in a retrieval system or transmitted in any form or by any means, electronic, mechanical, photocopying, recording or otherwise, without the prior permission of the copyright owner.

Cover and Production by Pageset Limited, High Wycombe, Bucks.
Printed in Great Britain by Lightning Source UK, Milton Keynes.

Contents

	Notes on contributors	vii
	New Introduction to 2018 edition	xi
	Errata	xvii
	Introduction to 1987 edition	1
1	Citizens of centuries to come: the ruling-class rebel in socialist fiction *Kiernan Ryan*	6
2	Radicalism—feminism—socialism: the case of the women novelists *Brunhild de la Motte*	28
3	Tendencies in narrative fiction in the London-based socialist press of the 1880s and 1890s *Jack Mitchell*	49
4	The strike novel in the 1890s *H. Gustav Klaus*	73
5	Struggles of the past: brushing history against the grain *J. M. Rignall*	99
6	Anarchism and fiction *Graham Holderness*	121

7	French naturalism and the English socialist novel: Margaret Harkness and William Edwards Tirebuck *Ingrid von Rosenberg*	151
8	Allen Clarke and the Lancashire school of working-class novelists *Paul Salveson*	172
9	Henry Lawson's radical vision *Michael Wilding*	203
10	Tressell in international perspective *Ronald Paul*	231
11	Ethel Carnie: writer, feminist and socialist *Edmund and Ruth Frow*	251
	Chronological Table	267
	Index	273

Notes on contributors

Edmund Frow (1906–1997), toolmaker and trade unionist, started early collecting books, pamphlets and magazines about the labour movement, and was later joined by his wife **Ruth Frow** (1922–2008), teacher and equally a trade unionist and bibliophile, in building a legendary library, first housed in their home and eventually taken over by Salford City Council. They co-authored numerous articles, pamphlets and books about the history of labour struggles, among them *Strikes: a Documentary History* (1971) and *Manchester and Salford Chartists* (1996).

Graham Holderness, writer and critic, has published some fifty books, mostly on Shakespeare, and hundreds of chapters and articles of criticism, theory and theology. He is also a novelist, poet and dramatist. His latest publications are *Black and Deep Desires: William Shakespeare Vampire Hunter* (2015) and *The Faith of William Shakespeare* (2016).

H. Gustav Klaus is Emeritus Professor of the Literature of the British Isles at the University of Rostock, Germany. His several publications in the field of working-class writing include *The Literature of Labour* (1985), *Factory Girl* (1998), *James Kelman* (2005), and the edited collections *Tramps, Workmates and Revolutionaries* (1993), *British Industrial Fictions* (2000, with Stephen Knight) and *Ecology and the Literature of the British Left: The Red and the Green* (2012, with John Rignall). A collection of his more recent essays, *Voices of Anger and*

Hope, is in preparation for publication by Edward Everett Root Publishers in 2018.

Jack Mitchell (1932–1997) was a Scottish academic who had lived in the German Democratic Republic since 1956 and taught at the Humboldt University, Berlin. He published the first book-length study of *Robert Tressell and The Ragged Trousered Philanthropists* (1969), with a Foreword by Raymond Williams, and *The Essential Seán O'Casey* (1980). He was also a folk singer and in charge of the group Jack & Genossen [comrades]. After the collapse of the GDR he spent his last years in Ireland.

Brunhild de la Motte worked as a lecturer in English literature at Potsdam University in the GDR until 1988 when she moved to Britain. She continued her research for the Berlin Academy of Sciences, but with the demise of the GDR was obliged to change track. Working as a freelance journalist, she wrote political articles for the leftwing, German national newspaper *Neues Deutschland*, and later took up a position as a national negotiator with Britain's public services trade union Unison.

Ronald Paul is Professor of English Literatures at the University of Gothenburg, Sweden. His books include *Unruly Nations: A People's History of Britain* (2001) and *Dissonant Voices: Literature and Society in Britain from Chaucer to the Present Day* (1999). He has edited *The Other Half: British Working-Class Stories* (1994) and co-edited *Critical Perspectives on Pat Barker* (2005). More recently he has published essays on Ellen Wilkinson, Ethel Carnie Holdsworth, Edward Upward, Sylvia Townsend Warner and John McGrath.

John Rignall is Reader Emeritus at the University of Warwick. His publications include *Realist Fiction and the Strolling Spectator* (1992), *George Eliot, European Novelist* (2011), and as editor *George Eliot and Europe* (1997), and *The Oxford Reader's Companion to George Eliot* (2000). More recently he has co-edited with H. Gustav Klaus *Ecology and the Literature of the British Left: The Red and the Green* (2012).

Ingrid von Rosenberg is Emeritus Professor of British Cultural Studies at the Technical University of Dresden, Germany. She has published in a variety of fields ranging from women's writing to popular culture and postcolonial studies, with a special focus on Black and Asian British literature, film, photography and the visual arts. Her books on working-class writing include *Der Weg nach oben: Englische Arbeiterromane 1945–1978* (1980) and *Alan Sillitoe: "Saturday Night and Sunday Morning"* (1984).

Kiernan Ryan is Emeritus Professor of English Literature at Royal Holloway, University of London and an Emeritus Fellow of Murray Edwards College, University of Cambridge. His publications include *King Lear: Contemporary Critical Essays* (1993), *Ian McEwan* (1994), *New Historicism and Cultural Materialism* (1996), *Shakespeare: The Last Plays* (1999), *Shakespeare: Texts and Contexts* (2000), *Shakespeare* (3rd edition, 2002), *Shakespeare's Comedies* (2009) and *Shakespeare's Universality: Here's Fine Revolution* (2015).

Paul Salveson is a visiting professor at the University of Huddersfield and works in the railway industry. His books include *Socialism with a Northern Accent* (2011), *Railpolitik – bringing railways back to communities* (2013) and *With Walt Whitman in Bolton* (new edition 2016). He is an active member of the Hannah Mitchell Foundation which campaigns for regional democracy for the North of England. His website is www.paulsalveson.org.uk

Michael Wilding, English-born Australian writer and academic, has always been interested in the relationship of literature and politics. His literary studies range from writers in the English Revolution (*Dragon's Teeth*, 1987) to modern British and Australian novelists (*Political Fictions*, 1980; *Social Visions*, 1993; and *The Radical Tradition*, 1993). He has also published some twenty volumes of fiction, from the early short-story collection *Aspects of the Dying Process* (1972) to the mordantly witty observations on corporatist university life, *Academia Nuts* (2002).

New Introduction to 2018 edition

For the emergence of what we can now identify as a canon of working-class and socialist narratives, the late nineteenth and early twentieth century was a crucial period. It saw the spectacular rebirth of the labour movement and with it the formation of several socialist groups, whose organs would, like their Chartist predecessors, open their pages to creative literature. In personal terms, the period also witnessed again the fusion of writer and activist, a phenomenon that was to last at least until the 1930s, when writers left their desk to serve on the Republican side in the Spanish Civil War or, as with Lewis Jones, agitated for the cause literally until their last heart-beat.

The period brought forth not only the first landmark in the history of socialist fiction, Robert Tressell's *The Ragged Trousered Philanthropists*, but also the first female proletarian novelist, Ethel Carnie (who after marrying added Holdsworth to her name). Both are given prominent treatment in this book, Tressell's novel illuminatingly set in an international context of burgeoning socialist fiction, Carnie rescued from near-obscurity. Recovery and recirculation were always on my mind when I embarked on an exploration of a submerged and often radical tradition in British literature. Not that every forgotten text merits resurrecting, but some of the voices in these books still speak to us: those of the selfless fighters against social injustice, those of the losers of history, those who hold fast to their commitment in the face of overwhelming odds, those who are torn by inner conflict over the issue what constitutes an ethical way of life in a society that restricts the opportunity of a carefree existence and the attainment of personal liberty to a minority, and those of the narrators in these fictions and the authors behind them. This prompted me to conclude the original introduction with a call for a Library of Socialist Classics. It did not fall on deaf ears. Merlin Radical Fiction, presided over by John Lucas, reissued among other items Margaret Harkness's *Out of Work*; much later, Nottingham Trent Editions brought out Carnie Holdsworth's *This Slavery*. Both new editions came with useful contextualising introductions, the latter from Nicola Wilson, who has since become the general editor of the Carnie Holdsworth reprint series. And *The Ragged Trousered Philanthropists*, whose author has of late been increasingly studied and claimed as an Irish diasporic writer, has never gone out of print since the first unexpurgated edition of 1955.

But beyond the discovery of individual voices, to which might be added the names of Allen Clarke and W. E. Tirebuck, the importance of the closing decades of the nineteenth century resides in the social and intellectual ferment in which many movements, causes, schemes, concerns and faiths surfaced, flourished, overlapped and intermingled. Among these were the three radical movements of feminism, Socialism and Anarchism. Socialism, still a broad church, came in several variants – ethical, marxist revolutionary and gradualist constitutional – united only in their campaigning and educational activities for the ultimate goal. In the 1880s it consisted of small sects, and even by the turn of the century it remained in Britain, contrary to its Continental counterparts, of marginal political influence. But its strong commitment to a social cause – the material betterment of the downtrodden through a change in the property relations and the establishment of a truly participatory polity – combined with the vision of a whole new way of life, of universally liberated social relations, appealed to members from all classes of society and invested its adherents with an altruistic feeling of purpose and worth. The forward-looking, hopeful perspective of Socialism also made it attractive to a number of writers. Some of them shared concerns with feminism: from such a perspective the New

Woman could, for example, demonstrate her independence and commitment to social and political emancipation not only by seeking work and demanding the suffrage, but by 'going over' to the workers' side, the disaffected thus joining the dispossessed, as the eponymous heroine does in Tirebuck's *Miss Grace of All Souls'*.

However, writers of whatever socialist persuasion could also focus on industrial strife, thereby highlighting the upsurge of trade unionism, or settle on urban poverty, unemployment and vagrancy. Here the novelists crossed paths with the naturalist writers and the social explorers who in disguise descended into the darker reaches of the city. Inevitably, naturalism came to occupy a prominent place in the method of representation. It nurtured and sometimes merged with social realism. But first-hand accounts in the form of reportage or autobiography, sometimes employing fictional devices, also came into play.

What the present book and its two predecessors, *The Socialist Novel in Britain* (1982) and *The Literature of Labour* (1985), essentially attempted to do was stimulate interest in a chronically neglected area of Britain's cultural heritage and lay a foundation on which other scholars could build. To name but two major subsequent interventions in the terrain covered by this symposium, Pamela Fox, in her *Class Fictions* (1994), directly engaged with Tressell and Carnie Holdsworth and identified an 'aesthetics of resistance' in working-class novels, which she found anchored simultaneously in class 'shame', a feeling of social inferiority, and class defiance, both discernible even in the portrayal of female-inflected areas of working-class life such as the home, domestic work and family life. In the process she revalued romance as a gender-specific mode of opposition to the ruling patriarchal capitalist order. Ian Haywood, in his short history of *Working-Class Fiction from Chartism to Trainspotting* (1997), while dwelling on the naturalist writers of the period, also dealt with Clarke, Tressell, Carnie Holdsworth and Patrick MacGill. But in recent years the greatest service to students and scholars interested in the genre was rendered by Deborah Mutch's meticulously annotated five volumes of reprints of serial fiction from the labour periodical press, *British Socialist Fiction, 1884–1914* (2013), a corpus of works rich in generic and tonal variety that had never before been available in book format. Mutch clearly had taken the cue from Jack Mitchell's discussion of a portion of this fiction (chapter 3) with, at its centre, a closer look at 'A Working Class Tragedy', the work of a mysterious 'H. J. Bramsbury', which, Mutch assumes, is a pseudonym for H. M. Hyndman.

Eric Hobsbawm once wrote in a new preface to the reprint of one of his early publications: 'A volume of readings compiled today would naturally be somewhat different.' (*Labour's Turning Point 1880–1900*; 1948, 1974). This also applies to the present symposium. The most obvious absence is perhaps that of the tramp, for the period was the golden age of tramp literature. It produced the most famous tramp narrative of them all, W. H. Davies's *The Autobiography of a Super-Tramp* (1908), promoted by Bernard Shaw, and, already preceding it, a whole string of wander books by the prolific Bart Kennedy, who by rights should also have made it into the collection on the strength of his incendiary half-fictional, half autobiographical *Slavery: Pictures from the Depths* (1905). I have since made amends for this omission by including several tramp tales in an anthology of working-class short stories, *Tramps, Workmates and Revolutionaries* (1993), and recently by contributing an essay on the subject for the Cambridge *History of British Working Class Literature* (2017), 'On the Road: All Manner of Tramps in English and Scottish Writing from the 1880s to the 1920s', plus a portrait of Bart Kennedy for the journal *English Literature in Transition 1880–1920* (60:2, 2017).

Kennedy and Allen Clarke had Irish roots; Tressell and MacGill were born in Ireland. So a consideration of Irish diasporic writers in Britain more generally would be a welcome addition. Conversely, the attitudes of British socialist writers to the Empire, its effect on the working class, and to the issue of race would deserve an investigation. A new volume would certainly pay more attention to the utopian fantasy of the period in its socialist colouring by Edward Bellamy, William Morris, H. G. Wells and Robert Blatchford. It would also have to trace how the vibrant ecological imagination of late-nineteenth-century radicals infused the socialist vision in both fiction and prose. Looking in this context at the relevant writings of Morris, Edward Carpenter and Henry Salt would push or transgress the boundaries of fiction. But then the criticism of the 'literature in the age of transition', which witnessed transgressions and crossovers of all kinds including those of genres, should be able to accommodate such an excursion. If it is true, as Carpenter maintained retrospectively, that notwithstanding the numerical insignificance and fragmentation of Socialism into many groups and societies 'the general teaching and ideals of the movement have permeated society in the most remarkable way, and have deeply infected the views of all classes, as well as general literature' (*My Days and Dreams*, 1916), it is no less the case that the socialist press and literature in all its forms played their part in upholding and spreading the socialist ideal.

H. Gustav Klaus
April 2017

Errata

page and line

41:	22	for 'International', read 'Independent'
47:	7	for 'Gertude', read 'Gertrude'
95:	2	for 'Jospeh', read 'Joseph'
129:	26	for '1884', read '1894'
253:	14	for 'Barnett', read 'Burnett'

Introduction

> The validity of uniting knowledge and commitment is demonstrated through a dialectical practice which reconstructs that which has been suppressed out of the historical traces of its suppression.
>
> Jürgen Habermas[1]

This book continues the enquiry opened with *The Socialist Novel in Britain*. Like its predecessor, it is a collaborative effort, bringing together the research of scholars who work in many different contexts and countries, but who share a concern for a neglected literary tradition whose contours are at last visible in outline now that the veil of silence covering it is being lifted.[2]

One difference from the earlier project is that the present collection of essays, all specially commissioned for this volume, focuses on a clearly defined period. This allows not only ampler treatment of genres, authors and themes, but also the occasional contrasting analysis of working-class and middle-class attitudes to the same subject, and the probing into the relationship between socialist fiction and the mainstream. And it furnishes the space to look beyond the boundaries of English literature: by establishing the status of Zola's *Germinal*, and the impact of that remarkable text on a number of English novelists (see chapters 6 and 7); by introducing the prose of Australian-born Henry Lawson, whose powerful sketches and short stories enjoyed wide English distribution and recognition at the turn of the century and who came to live and write in

Britain for a couple of years (see the contribution by Michael Wilding); and, most importantly, by taking stock of the almost simultaneous international breakthrough of the socialist novel in the 1900s, in the works of Andersen Nexö, Maxim Gorky, Upton Sinclair and Robert Tressell (see the essay by Ronald Paul).

The main emphasis of the volume rests naturally on fiction from the British Isles. But here too there is a significant shift away from an exclusive concentration on the slum fiction of the metropolis, which has dominated most accounts of the late-Victorian 'social' novel. Margaret Harkness set three of her novels in the East End, but her *A Manchester Shirtmaker* and W. E. Tirebuck's *Dorrie* situated in Liverpool (both featured in Ingrid von Rosenberg's contribution) remind us that there is a similar, less well-known range of fiction exploring the working-class environment and poverty in the provincial cities.[3] What is more, Lancashire can claim an entire school of working-class novelists of its own, growing out of a strong regional socialist culture and gathering round the once immensely popular figure of Allen Clarke. Their achievement has altogether passed out of the literary historians' sight, and Paul Salveson does much here to retrieve this unique moment in the history of English socialist literature.

To see the interest of this line of socialist narratives merely 'in the illumination it casts on the mainstream of English fiction',[4] as has been suggested, is to miss its essence, which is its radical otherness. This quality is embodied in a set of values often at odds with, and sometimes diametrically opposed to, most middle- and upper-class attitudes. But it can also be located in the re-working of many structural elements of the novel in the process of its critical appropriation by socialist practitioners. This difference extends to the channels of distribution (note, for example, how many of the works discussed here, starting with Shaw's *An Unsocial Socialist* and Morris's *Pilgrims of Hope*, were first and sometimes only serialised in the labour press), and often involved modes of reception quite different from the isolated act of reading.[5] As the British working class of this period led (in Standish Meacham's phrase) 'a life apart',[6] so the socialist fiction of the time represents a world of its own, by which, of course, I am not implying that it was in any way autonomous or self-determined.

There is no need here to repeat the full argument for the use of the term 'socialist novel';[7] if it does nothing else, the present volume at least provides fresh evidence for the view that there is a substantial area of writing worthy of this name, and that it emerges conspicuously in our period. But it may require pointing out that, as socialism got under way in Britain in the 1880s and 1890s, a variety of rival notions and doctrines was being negotiated in the movement, including powerful strains of a Christian-inspired and ethically oriented socialism, which successfully infiltrated imaginative literature. The novels of William Edwards Tirebuck, analysed here from three different angles (see chapters 1, 4 and 7), are a case in point. Yet though we may be rightly sceptical of some of the more abstruse variants of this 'religion of socialism', it will not do to evaluate the socialist perspective of a particular work without a proper understanding of the cultural and ideological texture that shaped it. As Stephen Yeo has shown,[8] this exciting phase of practical socialism dedicated to brotherhood and sisterhood had strengths as well as weaknesses; and when it finally exhausted itself and gave way in the mid-1890s under the pressure both from outside forces (as new leisure industries and means of communication transformed recreational patterns) and from internal reorientations (towards parliamentary party politics), a whole lived culture vanished in its wake.

It is hardly incidental that the conjunction of feminism and socialism, examined here by Brunhild de la Motte, found its strongest fictional expression in those early years of the movement, when many issues were far from sealed. Feminist criticism (and publishing) has yet to rediscover its socialist mothers of the novel. So far the current vogue of reprints has bypassed the works of Clementina Black, Emma Brooke, Ethel Carnie, Gertrude Dix, Margaret Harkness, Constance Howell and others. Considering that even for specialists of the period most of the authors dealt with in the following pages will be unfamiliar, this comes as no real surprise. During the thirty-year run of the academic journal *English Literature in Transition 1880-1920* only one or two forlorn articles have treated socialist narratives.[9] So much for the selective critical consensus which has assigned our authors to the graveyard of the justly forgotten.

I would suggest that a number of them deserve better, not only the above-mentioned women novelists, but also Allen Clarke and some of his fellow writers from Lancashire (such as Arthur Laycock and Fred Plant), Frank Harris, W. E. Tirebuck and the writers' duo D. F. E. Sykes and G. H. Walker. Where is that Library of Socialist Classics which will help to recirculate and reclaim their stories, romances and novels; facilitate additions to syllabus lists; enable irritated critics to fault our readings; give general readers a chance to judge for themselves on the merits and flaws of these works; and offer the historian and the socialist an imaginative insight into the aspirations and struggles of those forerunners 'who strove . . . not merely to rend the chains of the prisoners, but had to achieve the more difficult task of convincing them that they would be happier if they were free'?[10]

NOTES

1. Jürgen Habermas, *Technik und Wissenschaft als 'Ideologie'* (Frankfurt, 1968), p. 164 (my translation—HGK).
2. Since 1982 there has also been Jeremy Hawthorn's valuable collection *The British Working-Class Novel in the Twentieth Century* (London, 1984) and my own *The Literature of Labour. Two Hundred Years of Working-Class Writing* (Brighton, 1985).
3. For a discussion of the Manchester-based fiction of this kind see T. Thomas, 'Representation of the Manchester working class in fiction, 1850-1900', in Alan J. Kidd and K. W. Roberts (eds.), *City, Class and Culture. Studies of Social Policy and Cultural Production in Victorian Manchester* (Manchester, 1985), pp. 193-216.

4. P. J. Keating, *The Working Classes in Victorian Fiction* (London, 1979; first pub. 1971), p.245.
5. See Stephen Yeo, 'A new life: the religion of socialism in Britain 1883-1896', *History Workshop*, 4 (Autumn 1977), pp.5-56, for an account of the function of readings and songs in meetings, and of the spell-binding effect of declamations from *News from Nowhere* on audiences; and Peter Miles, 'The painter's Bible and the British workman. Robert Tressell's literary activism', in Hawthorn (ed.), *op. cit.*, pp.1-17, for an account of the uses made of *The Ragged Trousered Philanthropists*.
6. Standish Meacham, *A Life Apart. The English Working Class, 1890-1914* (London, 1977).
7. Cf. *The Socialist Novel in Britain* (Brighton, 1982), pp.1-3; and *The Literature of Labour, op. cit.*, pp.xi-xii, 107-9.
8. Yeo, *op. cit.*
9. See for example James G. Kennedy, 'Voynich, Bennett, and Tressell. Two alternatives for realism in the transition age', XIII (1970), pp.254-86; and Suzanne Rahn, 'The Story of the Amulet and the socialist Utopia', XXVIII (1985), pp.124-44, which deals with Edith Nesbit.
10. Mark Rutherford, *The Revolution in Tanner's Lane* (1887), ch. VIII. For a discussion of this novel see chapter 5 by J. M. Rignall.

· 1 ·

Citizens of centuries to come: the ruling-class rebel in socialist fiction

KIERNAN RYAN

> The age is not yet ripe for my ideal. Meanwhile I live, a citizen of centuries to come.
>
> Schiller[1]

The conversion to socialism of men and women of the middle and upper classes was a crucial factor in the struggle to establish the movement in Britain in the closing decades of the nineteenth century. As Stanley Pierson has pointed out:

> The inner dynamic of socialism was supplied in large part by those adherents who had been loosened from conventional interests; a deep commitment to socialism presupposed, as Marx had recognised, a strong sense of social and cultural disinheritance. But such a condition was more characteristic of marginal members of the middle classes than it was of working class leaders.[2]

Certainly the early recruits tended to be people who were 'seeking to overcome a painful social and psychological condition' resulting from the fact that 'traditional institutions and value systems had ceased to provide any satisfactory orientation to life'.[3] For such people the commitment to socialism possessed a special intensity dictated by their drive to resolve the urgent inner conflict between their old selves and their emerging new identities. Hence it came about that 'the Socialist movement drew much of its initial vitality as well as its continuing force from individuals who were suffering from an acute sense of self-division', from 'the social estrangements and the ontological anxieties of marginal individuals and their struggles to find a "new life" '.[4] And nowhere were these estrangements and anxieties more sharply felt than by those who had defected from the ruling classes, not only to help forge a juster socialist society, but to invest their lives with a feeling of purpose and worth, which their complicity in the injustice of capitalist society had hitherto denied them.

Such figures exercised an understandable hold over the imaginations of socialist novelists during this seminal period, not least because the authors no doubt found in them ways of voicing and probing versions of their own lived predicaments and political longings. This essay looks at several of the more interesting novels written on this theme between 1880 and 1914. All of them deal with men or women who have made, or are making, the lonely and difficult journey from the culpable security of a bourgeois or even aristocratic way of life to the rootless and thankless uncertainties of radical commitment in a world with little appetite for emancipation.

Between them the protagonists of these novels undergo conversion to a range of creeds and standpoints, reflecting the complex spectrum of secular and Christian variations on the socialist vision with which the dissident mind was obliged to wrestle around the turn of the century.[5] In most of the narratives, however, the representation of the convert's experience instils in us no sense of having arrived at some absolute conviction or conclusive solution. On the contrary, what come through are feelings of permanent dislocation and restlessness, an endless striving to surmount irresolvable contradictions, and the enduring ache of unrealised aspirations. Stranded in a social limbo between their own class and the proletariat, marooned in the gulf of time which persistently divides their utopian visions from historical reality, the central characters of these fictions inevitably tend to be isolated, awkwardly singular individuals, who resist easy or complete absorption into any of the prevalent political definitions.

But that recalcitrant individuality and visionary intransigence, which at times makes these mavericks so impossible for the immediate practical purposes of a disciplined mass movement, is the source of their value to the socialist novelist as a means of keeping the spirit of creative dissatisfaction constantly alive. All the protagonists considered here are at some level variants of the wise fool or the holy fool, inspired eccentrics and prophetic misfits living as internal exiles in their own society, and thus ideally situated to be used by the author to subvert the ruling-class world from within by insistently exposing what it takes to be normal and desirable as outrageous and intolerable. Yet at the same time, without leading the novelist to relax the grip of his commitment, these figures can also serve to illuminate what is limited and questionable about the alternative ways of living and thinking, and so sustain a salutary awareness of the human need for more than the available manifestations of socialism can yet imagine or supply.

The fictional possibilities of the ruling-class recruit are already brilliantly exploited in the earliest and best-known of the novels I wish to bring into focus, George Bernard Shaw's *An Unsocial Socialist* (1884). The title-role belongs to the bizarre Sidney Trefusis, the scion of a wealthy, self-made manufacturer and an aristocratic mother. Trefusis' privileged education and inherited fortune have only succeeded in furnishing him with the intellectual and financial means to occupy his life 'partly in working out a scheme for the reorganisation of industry, and partly in attacking my own class, women and all' (p.208).[6] The novel's skeletal romantic plot provides, indeed, little more than a series of shameless pretexts for his virtuoso assaults on the social and sexual order of the day.

Trefusis is unapologetic about being a vociferous socialist while remaining an abundantly propertied capitalist. He is marvellously free of moralising guilt about the origins and advantages which have made him literally his own worst enemy, and has no illusions about the futility of seeking moral salvation by renouncing his wealth and power:

I was made a landlord and capitalist by the folly of the people; but they can unmake me if they will. Meanwhile I have absolutely no means of escape from my position except by giving away my slaves to fellows who will use them no better than I, and becoming a slave myself; which, if you please, you shall not catch me doing in a hurry. (p.77)

The explanation displays the disarmingly frank impudence of the clown, whose licence Trefusis adopts as a way of thriving on the radical contradictions in his situation and distancing himself ironically from the conflicting selves which he slips in and out of at will: 'I am just mad enough to be a mountebank . . . With my egotism, my charlatanry, my tongue, and my habit of having my own way, I am fit for no calling but that of saviour of mankind—just of the sort they like' (pp.106-7).

As that self-mocking allusion to messianic fantasies might suggest, Trefusis' protean fooling creates valuable opportunities to burlesque the stereotyped postures lying in wait to trap the otherwise progressive mind in bourgeois illusions. Thus Trefusis' attempt to conceal himself behind the ludicrous persona and stage-rustic's dialect of the 'sham labourer',[7] Jeff Smilash, humorously underlines the distance which separates the upper classes from the actual labouring man, and the absurdity of disaffected members of those classes trying to turn themselves into proletarians. Even more central to the novel is Shaw's sabotaging through Trefusis of 'the sham lover of middle-class romance'[8] as part of the wider endeavour to dismantle the dominant sexual ideology, a task Shaw considered indivisible from the undermining of capitalism.

This disjunctive framing of accustomed modes of perception expands to embrace a parodic guying of the romantic conventions of the novel itself, as when Trefusis and his female counterpart, Agatha, brazenly discuss their fictional fate as the hero and heroine about to wind up the plot through the inexorable device of their own marriage (pp.225-5). The novel's baring of its devices, in order to expose and unsettle the stultifying assumptions they would normally smuggle through unseen, culminates in the remarkable 'Appendix' which Shaw added as an integral part of the text in the 1888 edition. The 'Appendix' purports to be a letter from the 'real' Trefusis to the author, whom he takes to task for his craven submission to the 'romantic system of morals' (p.257) which the largely female readership of novels dictates, and the consequent 'acceptance of the infatuation of a pair of lovers as the highest manifestation of the social instinct' (p.258). And Shaw's parting shot to himself in the guise of this fresh incarnation of Trefusis is: 'allow me to express my regret that you can find no better employment for your talents than the writing of novels' (p.262). The effect is to open to playful questioning not only the implications of the form but the authority of both the hero and Shaw himself.

In the complex, volatile figure of Trefusis, Shaw finds the perfect candidate for the part of 'incorrigible mountebank', licensed to scandalise his class with 'his terrible truth-telling'.[9] Even the bereaved and grieving parents of his own recently deceased young wife are not spared an acid reminder that 'plenty of people are starving and freezing today in order that we may have the means to die fashionably' (p.127). Trefusis' systematic violation of conventional expectations is what renders him an 'unsocial' socialist. But since indeed 'what is now called "society" ' is not 'society in any real sense' (p.258), to be unsocial is inescapable for the truthful socialist, who appears callous and heartless only to those who define their humanity in terms of the hypocritical moralism and shallow sentimentality of class society.

Shaw's casting of the capitalist convert as clown equips him with an arresting means of arguing an angrily engaged point of view while flaunting the blatant inconsistencies and ambiguity of the position from which it is being argued. The bare-faced fictionality of Trefusis and the novel's reflexive profiling of its own devices hold us sufficiently detached and alert throughout to prevent an unqualified acceptance of the perspectives it promotes. Instead the novel keeps these perspectives in solution, mindful of their own provisionality and thus reluctant to congeal into incontestable doctrine. In *An Unsocial Socialist*

Shaw turns the potentially tragic dilemma of a divided self into a wily and exuberant fighting virtue.

Grant Allen's *Philistia* (1884), on the other hand, revolves around an altogether more tormented experience of enlistment in the cause. Ernest Le Breton, an aristocratic but impecunious young intellectual, is undoubtedly cast in the mould of the holy fool rather than the wise fool, and the novel charts this socialist pilgrim's bleak progress to the understanding possessed by Shaw's more worldly-wise Trefusis from the start. It's the dismaying realisation that

> if he was going to live in the world at all, he must do so by making at least a partial sacrifice of political consistency. You may step out of your own century if you choose, yourself, but you can't get all the men and women with whom you come in contact to step out of it also just to please you.[10]   (II, 151)

Le Breton is obliged to learn that uncompromising idealism and selfless devotion to the socialist dream are not rewarded by a personal sense of moral absolution and political salvation. It is here that the irrepressible analogies between the socialist convert and the Christian convert are most prone to break down completely. The novel is centrally occupied, in fact, with the complicated relationships between contemporary socialist experience and the narratives of religion.[11] The title, *Philistia*, signifies the land of the uncivilised bourgeoisie, the class-divided England in which the socialist chosen people, the 'Children of Light' (p.1), find themselves in bondage, fighting to keep their faith alive. Through an external framework of chapter headings, such as 'The daughters of Canaan' and 'The Philistines triumph', as well as through a whole internal network of religious allusions, a mock-epic effect is created, whereby the heroic realm of biblical legend maintains a running ironic commentary on the incongruity of its imputed parallels with the social and political realities of upper-class Britain in the late nineteenth century. Built into the basic idea of the novel is a sympathetically critical endeavour to prise contemporary socialism away from the delusively providential and redemptive terms in which its identification with religious experience, however involuntary, commonly led it to be perceived. Not to recognise the difference, as Ernest Le Breton discovers, can be soul-destroying, especially when one's confidence in the power of moral and religious sentiments over objective social forces is repeatedly proved extravagant.

Ernest looks to socialism to still above all the profound moral and existential anxieties which have seethed within him since he first understood himself to be nothing more than a useless parasite on the labour of the proletariat:

> The thing that troubles me is not so much how to reform the world at large as how to shape one's own individual course aright in the actual midst of it . . . The great difficulty I myself experience in this, is that I can't discover any adequate social justification for my own personal existence. (I, 99)

As this might suggest, Ernest is the kind of intense and humourless ethical socialist who lacerates his conscience constantly. Like Shaw's Trefusis, he can be relied upon at every occasion, however innocuous, to remind everyone that 'others are dying of sheer want, and cold, and nakedness' (I, 84) while they themselves indulge in meaningless frivolity. Unlike Trefusis, however, Le Breton has no other acts up his sleeve, certainly none that would raise any laughs, and Allen does not disguise how insufferable such a remorselessly moralistic socialist can be, not least to other socialists. As the daughter of Ernest's political mentor, the emigré Max Schurz, remarks: living with Le Breton 'would be like living with an abstraction', and a woman 'might just as well marry Spinoza's Ethics or the Ten Commandments. He's a perfect model of a Socialist, and nothing else' (I, 199).

Yet it may be these very qualities which give such a man his special value to a militant young socialist movement. As Max Schurz points out to his daughter in defence of Ernest, as far as sheer selfless dedication to the good of others is concerned there is much to be said for the argument that 'the best socialists never come from the *bourgeoisie,* nor even from the proletariat; they come from among the voluntarily *déclassés* aristocrats' (I, 200).

On the other hand, Le Breton's refusal to compromise his principles in the slightest, even where the most scrupulous would concede there to be no other option, loses him job after job as a teacher and then as a journalist, and brings himself, his wife and their baby to the point of penniless starvation. And only the secret offices of good friends with money and influence finally save this infuriating absolutist from himself, making it possible for him to end up the editor of an influential new Radical periodical, *The Social Reformer*, whose success restores his guttering health and solves all his family's financial problems.

Even this welcome change in his fortunes, however, leaves Ernest at heart no more contented than before, no less reluctant to come to terms with the world as it so far stubbornly remains. The harrowing disillusionments he has suffered have, indeed, brought him to fear that there may be 'no fitting feeling for a social reformer except brave despair' (III, 272). Yet nothing can quite kill the 'pure idealistic Utopian philanthropy' (III, 30) which drives him, and by the close of the novel it becomes hard to withhold an exasperated respect for a spirit so resolutely intolerant of things as they are that nothing short of escaping completely from the mire of history could satisfy his craving for innocence and integrity. The novel, at any rate, leaves him the last word:

> As things are constituted now, there seems only one life that's really worth living for an honest man, and that's a martyr's. A martyr's or else a worker's. And I, I greatly fear, have managed somehow to miss being either. The wind carries us this way and that, and when we would do that which is right, it drifts us away incontinently into that which is only profitable.
> (III, 287-8)

The exploratory complexity of both Shaw's and Allen's novels is highlighted by turning to Constance Howell's *A More Excellent Way* (1888). This is a narrower, far less troubled narrative, whose hero's conflicts and setbacks never gain enough weight to pose a real threat to his convictions. But it does furnish an illuminating chronicle of the intellectual and psychological process of conversion from complacent bourgeois into embattled advocate of socialism.

The subject of this chronicle is the unfortunately named Otho Hathaway, the Harrow-educated offspring of a colonial administrator and a covertly feminist, Freethinking mother, who sows the first seeds of intellectual dissent in her adult son's mind and entrusts to him the task of taking her own ideas and struggle further. The catalytic event occurs, however, some time after his widowed mother's death, when Otho, now a footloose and financially independent young man in his late twenties, and vaguely Radical in his sympathies, witnesses a march of the unemployed from a window at his friend's club. He is overcome by disgust and shame at the callous boorishness displayed towards the marchers by the upper-class yobs around him, and by the realisation that 'it is my own class that are the brutes' (p.118).[12] His first encounter with real, livid class-hatred leaves a searing impression on his mind and sets him on the road to discover its source and the solution: 'Nothing could be again as it had been. The condition of the masses was no longer an abstract thought to him . . . His political faiths were breaking up, and he could not rest until he had a new faith' (p.133).

His outrage at the spineless response of the Liberals, the Freethinkers and the Radicals to the rigged trial of the group of Socialists who had led the march makes plain to him in what direction he must look. He gives his bookseller a huge order and settles down to a crash course in Marx, Engels, Lassalle, Bebel, Gronlund, Kropotkin, Elisée Reclus, Hyndman, Morris and Belfort Bax. The theory of 'Collectivist Socialism' which emerges from these works is 'a revelation to him' (p.138). But the clinching shock is its moral bearing on himself as 'one of the idle classes who, by their very existence, are oppressors. It was he who helped to cause the degradation of the poor' (p.139). Stricken with guilt and indignation, Hathaway joins the National Socialist Federation and embarks on a lifetime's work as a labour organiser and public speaker for the movement.

Meanwhile, on the romantic front, Hathaway's political development has brought him into increasingly acrimonious conflict with the expectations of his fiancée Evangeline and her family, who are desperately hoping that he will outgrow this faddish socialist nonsense once he assumes the burdens of respectable married life. Otho finds himself bewilderingly divided:

> He was leading two lives, with two different sets of companions, witnessing the most opposite scenes, and hearing the most opposed sentiments. And as the one life attracted him more and more, the other became repugnant to him. And yet he was of the middle class; by blood and education and tastes, he was bound to it; he could not throw in his lot with the members of the working class, for he did not belong to them'. (p.196)

To his middle-class friends, moreover, he scarcely appears to be inhabiting the same temporal dimension: ' "Mr Hathaway is so strange," thought Agnes Champneys; "he seems to stand aside, and view the present time as if he did not belong to it" ' (p.160).

Nowhere is this clearer than when Otho is genuinely surprised at the selfish and worthless Evangeline's refusal to sacrifice all in order to become the wife of an itinerant activist, living on a fraction of the income whose bulk Otho has given away to assuage his guilt. But such trustful naïveté is perhaps only to be expected from one who confidently predicts the arrival of 'a rationally-ordered community' (p.228) by the end of what he regards as this 'wonderful century' (p.253). It's not so much that Otho's prediction, certainly as far as Britain is concerned, has proved unduly optimistic, or that he may not ultimately be right to maintain that 'it must come right in the end. The solidarity of the working class is no forlorn hope. Socialism is a certain success' (pp.270-1). It's rather that the authority of his conviction suffers from not being plausibly tested by the sort of demoralising reversals which Allen's Ernest Le Breton is forced to survive.

Hathaway's unrewarding attempts to organise the hoppickers in his area do cause him to reflect on the inconvenient apathy and frequent rank conservatism of the working man. But his consternation at the fact that the workers 'do not stretch out their hands to welcome this thing which will be their salvation' (p.277) is swiftly eclipsed by his resolve simply to switch his theatre of operations and henceforth make it his mission 'to recommend socialism to the professional and upper classes' (p.262). The author allows herself to voice a mild qualm about Otho's 'great faith in his class' being 'more faith than it seemed they merited' (p.271), and gives his benignly sceptical uncle just enough room to wonder, 'Is that a clear view he has into the future, or is it a mirage?' (p.271). But even these few notes of quiet reservation are drowned out by the grand, self-inflating chord on which Hathaway is left to conclude the novel:

> If I were giving the workers my life in another way, if I were fighting by their side, shedding my blood, under the red flag, that would be a glorious death to die! And yet this must be better, because it is more useful. The time has not come yet to give my life for the people. I will give my life to the people.
> (p.278)

In Howell's novel the private world of love and the public realm of political commitment prove irreconcilable, and it is part of the protagonist's heroic sacrifice that he forgoes the former for the sake of the latter. In W. E. Tirebuck's *Miss Grace of All Souls'* (1895), by contrast, the heroine succeeds in uniting the personal and the political through a truly heroic marriage, which cuts across class divisions and convincingly prefigures the real human possibilities beyond them in a manner unparalleled by the other novels dealt with here.

Grace Waide is the daughter of the vicar of Beckerton, a Yorkshire mining village. When the narrative opens she is facing the prospect of an engagement to Harry Brookster, the son and heir of the local coal magnate. But she has begun to find herself drawn to the young miners' leader Sam Ockleshaw, whose family she regularly visits and has come to care deeply for. The injustice of the wretched conditions under which they and the other mining families live and work becomes unbearable to her. And this in turn makes even more excruciating the contradiction between what the Christian gospel preaches and what the Church permits to proceed with its blessing. Her own tacit complicity in this hypocrisy compels her one day early on, as she leaves the Ockleshaws' home, to pledge to herself that 'henceforth she would be true to the logical interpretation of the Gospel according to the light of God in her soul, rather than according to the lights of man in treaty with the ways of the world' (p.39).[13]

The moment marks the beginning of an exhausting endeavour to swim against the tide of social expectation and some of the deepest currents of feeling within herself. The first open rebellion is her refusal of Harry Brookster's proposal, which brings her into violent conflict with her father, the Reverend Egerton Waide. She explains to him that she does not want to marry Brookster because her political sympathies are on the side of the workers whom he and his father exploit. Moreover, to take the part of the working class, she argues, is surely the only course for a true Christian, who should condemn the Church's collusion with 'land, property and wealth' as 'against both the spirit and the letter of the Church's own Scripture' (p.53). Her father, who has himself, she now perceives, 'become entangled in the world' (p.53) beyond redemption, is left 'staring at her as if she had become a stranger' (p.55), which is exactly what she has become. As she painfully sheds the 'false ideal of her father, of the Church, and of society' (p.97), everything she has been brought up to regard as normal and familiar appears now as alien and remote as if it belonged to some other age. Yet to slip the shackles of her old self altogether and forge a fresh identity is as yet beyond her. As Sam's mother Nance shrewdly observes: 'There's a some'ut, Sam, i' yon vicarage lassie's look as if her mind wor tryin' to get out i'to somebody else's, an couldn' ' (p.122).

When the appalling deprivation of the 'Coal War' hits Beckerton, Grace's relationship with Sam grows closer and deeper as they work tirelessly together to meet the needs and maintain the morale of the strike-bound miners and their families. But once the battle has been won and the urgencies of the strike recede, family obligations and the returning pressures of convention conspire to push them apart again; and Grace needs all her resources to endure the isolation and despair which threaten to engulf her as the social and psychological barriers to the union they both inwardly desire—that 'plighted troth of the most daring kind' (p.305)—press in upon her mind:

> She was alone, estranged. The old anchorage had gone, and she wanted new. Nay, she had new anchorage already . . . and yet all the world seemed to push between, calling, 'You'll cast yourself away. You'll break your "father's" heart!' (p.295)

But when Harry Brookster calls to try his luck with Grace again, a sudden rush of courage spurs her to reveal not only that her heart is elsewhere engaged, but that 'it is one of your own poorly-paid men, Harry' (p.323). And she proceeds to spell out to the dumbfounded Brookster the radically different social and sexual perspective she can now boldly profess:

> You will forget that I still look at things from the point of view of the equal value of all labour, including the labour of the master . . . I would be proud to be the means of lifting up one of that class—understand me—not to a better kind of work, but to a better kind of life in connection with that work, however so-called humble or so-called mean, than to simply repeat the old, old kind of marriage with one's so-called superior, and fail to reach any justifying motive either in love or life. (p.320)

After this breakthrough, Grace feels 'quite equal to both the romance and the reality of her recent life' (p.349), and in the novel's closing scene it is she who goes alone to Sam's home to resolve the deadlock between them. As they walk out together in silent understanding, climbing over a stile into the open fields in an image charged with symbolic promise, the novel achieves a real sense of possible emancipation, a sense that new ground has been cleared within the bounds of personal accomplishment, but with no illusions about the difficulty that remains of cultivating and extending that terrain.

The eponymous hero of James Adderley's strange little novel, *Stephen Remarx. The Story of a Venture in Ethics* (1893), desires even more passionately than Grace Waide to preach and to practise the socialist vision which he sees at the heart of Christ's gospel. But the path which he follows in pursuit of his ideal, leading him as it does to become 'like a second Baptist . . . a "Voice" solemn and alone, crying in the wilderness of London society' (p.65), is quite extraordinary.[14] The novel offers in effect an imaginary biography of a Christian Socialist saint and martyr (as his name itself intimates), complete with invented newspaper reports, letters and reconstructions from contemporaries' notebooks to lend the fantasy a flavour of historical authenticity.

Stephen is an orphaned aristocrat, the son of Lord Remarx of Balustrade Abbey. After Eton he goes on to Oxford, where he comes under the influence of a progressive don, Frederick Hope. It is Hope's advanced ideas on social and theological questions which prove decisive in bringing about Stephen's conversion and subsequent ordination as a radical Anglican priest who believes in Christ as 'the One True Liberator' (p.6) and in his own duty to preach, to the rich above all, 'a divine discontent' (p.19).

Stephen's first curacy, however, is in the working-class parish of Hoxton which, thanks to the neglect of its idle and self-centred vicar, has become 'a hotbed of Secularism' (p.22). He joins the radical clubs to 'show them that so far as their ideals go, they are the right and true ones, because they are the ideals of Christ', and that, essential as the economic demands of the labour movement are, 'something more was wanted than material improvement for the masses' (p.28). But he is brought up short one day by a socialist lecturer's unanswerable attack on 'these so-called Christian Socialists who talk about Christ, the poor working man, who had not where to lay his head, while they themselves, who claim to represent Him, have never been without a comfortable bed in their lives. Let them show us what He was like, and then, perhaps, we may listen' (pp.36-7).

Stephen's attempt to respond to this challenge occupies the rest of the novel. The question of how far one can really understand and identify with the experience of a class which is not one's own is of course a thorny one for all ruling-class socialists, especially as it opens the moral authority of their socialism to serious question. For John Oxenham, one of the leaders of the great Dock Strike whom Stephen eventually converts, the answer is clear: 'Nobody can sympathise unless he has really experienced the sufferings of those whom he proposes to compassionate' (p.54). Convinced of the truth of this, Stephen astounds the wealthy congregation of his new West-End parish by announcing his foundation of a special religious community for those of them brave enough to take Christ's gospel literally and practise at last what they profess to believe. To the landlords, bankers, businessmen, lawyers and the like sitting stupefied before him he makes a heartfelt appeal that they surrender the sources of all their comfort and luxury 'to what is right and good' (p.108), since 'a man clothed in soft raiment and living in king's palaces cannot be a prophet' (p.110). The announcement of this utopian experiment in Christian Socialism, the 'venture in ethics' of the title, provokes outrage in upper-class circles and ridicule from the press, which derides the 'Remarkables' (as Stephen's followers become popularly known) as 'Lunatics, Jesuits, Jumpers, Vagabonds, and Anarchists' (p.128).

Needless to say, there is no stampede to join the tiny band of Remarkables and vow with them 'to keep Christ's law in the midst of this wicked world' (p.124). The testimonies of the few who do make the grade afford, however, excellent occasions for mordant satire on the consequences of actually living up to that vow. A reformed priest, who has been ostracised by his own family, confesses to having never understood till now 'why it might be necessary to hate one's father and mother' (p.133). While the converted stockbrokers are driven to despair by the fact that 'their life in the light of an earnest following of Christ appeared to be made up of ghastly fictions and unreal bargaining' (p.134).

The community's blatant lack of success in securing 'the triumph of Religion over Belgravia' (p.132) leaves Stephen undismayed. Being publicly hated, mocked and spat upon simply confirms his confidence in their role as a necessary thorn in the overfed flesh of the ruling class. Besides, as he points out, 'it is against our rules to trouble ourselves about results. We must be content to go on until we die, even if nothing substantial seems to come of it' (p.127). And in fact Stephen's own death arrives with indecent haste in the shape of a stupid street accident triggered by the aggression of a couple of upper-class thugs, infuriated by the sight of 'that canting idiot, Remarx' (p.147).

Adderley's abrupt resort to a bathetic fantasy of martyrdom, with the dying Stephen explicitly identified on the final page with the saint whose name he bears, only underscores, of course, the wild futility of the whole utopian venture from any realistic political viewpoint. If the social revolution has to wait upon the voluntary moral reformation of the rich and powerful, it will be quite a wait. Yet in his very absurdity there remains something haunting about the yearning, unworldly Remarx, whose quixotic experiment retains its inseparable imaginative virtue as a measure of the still monstrous gap between the allegedly Christian values and the brutally unchristian realities of capitalist Britain.

Although caustically critical of religion, Wargrave Lincoln, the dour middle-class militant featured in Olive Birrell's *Love in a Mist* (1900), would agree with Stephen Remarx on the need for would-be socialists from the bourgeoisie and above to 'come down to the common level of humanity' because 'until you have been poor you do not know what sorrow is' (p.53).[15] He himself claims to have 'never understood how poor men feel until I had brought myself to actual starvation' (p.53). But this deliberate self-impoverishment in the interests of ideological integrity gets a much rougher ride from Birrell's all too plausible, starkly disillusioned perspective. Her novel is a scathing but bracing exposure of the human cost of a lifetime's dedication to a rigid misconception of what socialism should mean.

Over the years Lincoln has given away almost all his money to the poor or lost it in nobly conceived but catastrophic co-operative projects. We learn that both his wife and his first son died as an indirect result of his calculated impoverishment and neglect of his family. The action of the novel discovers him living on the shabby verge of penury with his grown-up daughter Sibylla and his second little son Pippin, to whom Sibylla is devoted. It is no surprise that life with this nomadic father, so dispassionately egalitarian in his love of humanity at large that he can spare no special affection for his own children, has alienated Sibylla completely from his world. Indeed she has been driven into the arms of Keith Hamilton, a man who may be a bourgeois capitalist, but who is at least capable of elementary human kindness and emotional warmth. As Hamilton observes in outrage at Lincoln's 'strange obliquity of sight': 'Sibylla had been dragged out of her natural sphere, placed on the level of the people her father professed to pity, deprived of the very things he pronounced the birthright of each human being' (p.313). In tracing a young woman's rebellious marital return to the middle class from the clutches of a drab proletarian existence, artificially enforced by her father's abstract principles, the story of Sibylla entails a telling reversal of the route followed by Grace Waide in Tirebuck's novel.

At the heart of the book is Sibylla's unavoidable showdown with her father over her desire to leave and marry Hamilton. Reproved by him for lacking the sympathy with his cause which would have led her to consider such a marriage 'repulsive' (p.135), she replies, 'I have sympathised with you more than you think . . . only I see there are mistakes. We help the poor by lifting them up to our own level, not by sinking to theirs' (pp.136-7). In Lincoln's view, Sibylla's special love for Pippin and for Hamilton are symptoms of the bourgeois disease he is trying to cure: 'It is that inspired selfishness you call love which has wrecked our social progress' (p.139). For Sibylla, in contrast, her father will never achieve anything for 'the whole of humanity' (p.139) until he has learned how to love another individual: 'You do not know that love is, and yet you hope to save the world' (p.144).

It is not long after Sibylla has left him that the truth of her words comes home. At the age of only fifty-one the physical and emotional strain of his unflagging fight for socialism finally takes its toll and his health collapses. Reviewing his life's labour, he perceives only 'a long history of disappointment' (p.237). He suffers agonies of remorse for his dead wife and his neglect of the children she entrusted to him. And in the end he succumbs to a terrible despair:

> During the greater part of his life he had been in love with an idea, and believed in it, worshipped it, sacrificed all the things men usually value to promote its growth. Now in these dark moments, when strength was fast slipping away, for the first time the chilliness of doubt invaded the sanctuary where it lay enshrined. Like Joan of Arc in her dungeon, he began to question the reality of his visions: 'It is true, it is true, I heard the voices!' He, too, had heard voices, and they had guided him, as it now appeared, straight to destruction.   (pp.244-5)

His dying hours do bring him reconciliation with his estranged daughter, who has come to understand and forgive this man who 'was never on speaking terms with the world' (p.314) and 'his fierce determination to carry out one great idea, regardless of the torture he inflicted on those who should have been dearer to him than the whole earth' (p.276). But the feeling that the 'one great idea' may well have been an illusion stays with Sibylla and with us until the last page of the novel, where only a determined intervention by the author herself has the power to reverse the current of dismay and transform Lincoln's tragedy by placing it in the wider and longer perspective to which the characters within the narrative are blind:

> It seemed to her that his sacrifice had failed of its purpose. He had vanished, and this dark old earth, which has witnessed the fall of so many monarchies, the destruction of such countless hopes and ambitions, rushed through immensity with her burden of human sorrow quite unchanged. Sibylla was mis-

taken, though. Her father's spirit still lived and energised, through herself, through Hudson, through many others who had caught the fire of his great enthusiasm, and added to it a power of loving he had never known. (pp.326-7).

A similar process of isolation and disenchantment is undergone by the protagonist of the last novel I want to look at, *George Eastmont: Wanderer* (1905) by Margaret Harkness. But the experience is turned to more positive ends because of what Eastmont learns about himself and his relation to the socialist movement and to history. To a degree unmatched by the other novels, *George Eastmont* grasps and lays bare the ironic double-bind inherent in the predicament of the bourgeois socialist: the fact that the very individualism which fuels his rebellion against his own class and his single-minded drive for a different world is what keeps him in thrall to the divisive, alienating reality he seeks to escape, laying him wide open to disappointment and disillusionment every time the limits of his individual powers are inevitably exposed.

The problem emerges right from the start of Eastmont's conversion. Eastmont is a Sandhurst-educated soldier, whose 'baptism of fire' butchering 'poor savages' (p.12)[16] in Africa pitches him into a slough of self-loathing and brings on a nervous breakdown. While convalescing on his aristocratic grandfather's estate in Ireland, he reads by chance Adam Smith and from there runs rapidly through Ruskin, Kingsley, Maurice and more, until at last there is no resisting the seductive revelation which strikes him: 'A saviour of the masses was wanted, someone who would go amongst them and show them how to help themselves, rouse them out of their apathy and ignorance, and give them hope. Where was the man?' (p.15).

It takes bitter experience to teach young Eastmont the folly of casting himself in this glamorous, self-gratifying role. At first the sheer exhilaration of his success as a passionate speaker at mass rallies leads him to fantasise that 'possibly the chasm that now yawned between the masses and the classes might be closed by himself, who like the Roman of old would leap into the yawning cleft' (p.21). But his attempt to bridge that chasm, by the calculated 'experiment' (p.23) of a theoretically desirable but loveless marriage with a woman of 'the People', is disastrous and ends with the wretched woman's death from an accidental overdose of the drugs she has taken to alleviate her misery. Eastmont's remorseful realisation of his callous stupidity marks the culmination of a series of incidents which have begun to undermine his previously unshakeable confidence not only in himself but in the political will and wisdom of the masses.

Thus by the opening of Part II of the novel he has lost faith in the ballot and the bullet alike, and is unsure of his direction. The messianic fantasies have given way to a more sober, if somewhat jaundiced assessment of what is needed and what is possible:

> It is useless to pretend that our ideas have taken hold of the masses . . . Our social system is a sham, a gross injustice, but it will go on until working men learn to help themselves. I want to understand working men in order to work with them. I wanted to be one of them once, now I am not so ambitious.
> (p.118)

His arrogant assumption that the workers are at present irremediably apathetic is proved howlingly wrong when the great Dock Strike breaks out as if from nowhere to 'upset all his calculations' (p.130) and teach him another timely lesson. But the fact that the workers reveal themselves to be not yet strong enough to clinch the victory without ruling-class allies soon has him brooding and searching again for a more satisfactory course of action in the aftermath of the strike. He has no faith in trade unionism, and refuses a job as an organiser because 'I will not bind myself to think as others think on any subject, I must be free to hold my own opinions' (p.165). His reply to the union man who urges that now is the time for them all to pull together is: 'The strongest man is he who stands alone' (p.167).

But he must pay a price for the luxury of that creed. 'Cut off from his own people, and also from the people for whose sake he had given up his friends and relations' (p.168), henceforth 'he must go on by himself, and that meant isolation and loneliness' (p.169). Eastmont's stubborn self-sufficiency, combined with his frustration at the refusal of history and utopia to converge forthwith in a 'coup-de-théâtre' (p.175), threaten to lock him into a cynical dismissal of the whole labour movement as 'a thing that had now begun to pall on him' (p.183). But he swerves away from the edge of recantation to reaffirm that:

> He was a Socialist, although he did not see how to put his ideas into practice. Things were moving, he felt sure of that, only they did not move fast enough. He would never be a reactionary, but keep an open mind, and strike wherever a blow would be really effective. (p.189)

After a *Wanderjahr* spent in Australia, first as a clerk in a desolate labour-settlement and later as a newspaper editor grappling with the politics of the Land Question, he returns to found an experiment in communal ownership on the estate which his grandfather has left him in Ireland. With the prospect of this specific, practical and consciously provisional task he is, for the moment, as content with himself as such a man in such a plight can be. For he has come to terms not only with the compulsively nomadic loner whom his origins and history have conspired to turn him into, but with the limits of what any committed individual can expect to accomplish within the constraints of his moment in time:

> He must go on; only death could put a stop to this onward movement. Always on, and on, and by himself, to a goal he could not see, for he had long ago given up the hope of doing anything definite in the work he had set himself. He had learnt that he was only one with the rest. (p.238)

In somehow holding fast to his commitment despite himself, despite the evidence of the present, and despite the deep shadow of uncertainty cast by an unknown future, Eastmont has perhaps found a way of being heroic after all, from which those who still face the quandaries of these ruling-class rebels may have something to learn today.

NOTES

1. *Don Karlos*, ed Paul Böckmann (Stuttgart, 1974), lines 4432-4 (my translation).
2. Stanley Pierson, *British Socialists. The Journey from Fantasy to Politics* (Cambridge, Mass., and London, 1979), p.349.
3. ibid., p.1.
4. ibid., pp.2, 347.
5. For an invaluable survey of this spectrum, see Stanley Pierson, *Marxism and the Origins of British Socialism. The Struggle for a New Consciousness* (Ithaca and London, 1973).
6. George Bernard Shaw, *An Unsocial Socialist* (London, 1888). The most stimulating criticism on the novel is to be found in Alick West's superb study of Shaw, *A Good Man Fallen Among Fabians* (London, 1950), ch. II, and more recently in Eileen Sypher's ' Fabian anti-novel: Shaw's *An Unsocial Socialist*', in *Literature and History*, xi, 2 (Autumn 1985), pp.241-53.
7. Shaw quoted in Michael Holroyd's (unpaginated) Introduction to the Virago edition of *An Unsocial Socialist* (London, 1980).
8. Shaw, *ibid*.
9. Shaw, *ibid*.
10. Cecil Power [Grant Allen], *Philistia*, 3 vols (London, 1884).
11. For an excellent historical account of this whole question see Stephen Yeo, 'A new life: the religion of socialism in Britain, 1883-1896', in *History Workshop*, 4 (Autumn 1977), pp.5-56.
12. Constance Howell, *A More Excellent Way* (London, 1888). The novel is also discussed in Brunhild de la Motte's contribution to this volume and in P. J. Keating's *The Working Classes in Victorian Fiction* (London, 1971), pp.241-2.
13. William Edwards Tirebuck, *Miss Grace of All Souls'* (London, 1895). See also the accounts of Tirebuck and *Miss Grace* in the essays by H. Gustav Klaus and Ingrid von Rosenberg elsewhere in this volume.
14. James Adderley, *Stephen Remarx. The Story of a Venture in Ethics* (London, 1893).
15. Olive Birrell, *Love in a Mist* (London, 1900).
16. John Law [Margaret Harkness], *George Eastmont: Wanderer* (London, 1905). On the fiction of Margaret Harkness (excluding *George Eastmont*) see John Goode's fine essay, 'Margaret Harkness and the socialist novel', in H. Gustav Klaus (ed.), *The Socialist Novel in Britain* (London, 1982), pp.45-66.

· 2 ·

Radicalism—feminism—socialism: the case of the women novelists

BRUNHILD DE LA MOTTE

During the 1880s and 1890s the British book market saw a flood of novels dealing in one way or another with problems of the working class. The growing conflict of developing monopoly capitalism and the resulting polarisation of the classes led, on a sociological-ideological level, to a general politicisation of the working people and, on a moral level, to attempts by middle-class people to solve the conflict by concepts of humanist transcendence. Both, the political and the humanistic aspects were reflected in the literature of the period. Yet, whereas in the 1840s the general trend of the 'social-problem novels' by middle-class authors was a humanitarian concern for fellow citizens linked with the liberal hope to reduce the gap between the two classes by reforms, the perspective presented in the slum novels and Cockney-school novels of the 1890s indicated that a simplified solution in this direction was no longer possible. And when it was presented, as in Walter Besant's *All Sorts and Conditions of Men* (1882) or Robert Blatchford's *Julie* (1900?), the picture of the benevolent bourgeois or 'corrigeable' worker expressed a point of view that by the end of the century had become conservative. In contrast, the representation of working-class life by Arthur Morrison and George Gissing characterised poverty as a social evil and thus shook the confidence of the bourgeois reader in a 'unified' world; however, their novels were a curious mixture of pity and disgust as well as frustration.

There were, however, a number of novels that did not just present the problems of the working class but put them in a political context and tried to communicate the spirit of socialism spreading at that time, that is they showed a solution to the problem of poverty and human degradation in the transformation of the social system. Not surprisingly, many of these novels came from writers who were born into the working class, for example, H. J. Bramsbury, Allen Clarke and W. E. Tirebuck. It is, however, a striking phenomenon that their voices were joined by middle-class women who unreservedly sided with the working class and with the struggle for socialism. I would name here Constance Howell with her novel *A More Excellent Way* (1888), Clementina Black with *An Agitator* (1894), the novels by Margaret Harkness, especially *Out of Work* (1888) and *George Eastmont: Wanderer* (1905), Emma Brooke's *Transition* (1895) and Gertrude Dix with her novel *The Image Breakers* (1900).[1] By showing problems and consequences of political actions in the form of a narrative, these novelists took part in the public discussion about socialism. Of importance is the fact that the fictional heroes of these novels, despite the difficulties they face, basically retain their socialist conviction and do not withdraw into isolation at the end. The awareness of social confrontation and the necessity of taking sides and assuming an active part in social change is, in varying degrees, a predominant feature of these novels. Throughout they are characterised by a conviction that the situation of the working class can only be changed by political action. Thus these novels stand, in ideological terms, as P. J. Keating says, 'completely apart from the mainstream of late-Victorian urban working-class fiction'.[2]

Examining more closely these socialist novels by women we are not surprised to find that in most of them the Woman Question—as it was then called—played a significant part. This fact suggests a connection between the specific problems women faced in Victorian society and their political commitment. That there is a connection is confirmed by the simultaneous occurrence of vigorous feminist novels by writers such as Sarah Grand, Olive Schreiner, Mona Caird and George Egerton.[3] Presenting the psychological torments and sufferings of women forced into a gender role that made any development outside home and the family impossible and showing the devastating results of sexual ignorance, their novels are not just individual tragic stories—though this is the form all these writers chose as a contrast to the Victorian 'happy ending'—but point to the social sources of this situation. Attacking the patriarchal family and its attendant ideology, these novelists, by implication, threatened the bourgeois system which had incorporated patriarchy as one of its ideological pillars.

We find, then, during the 1880s and 1890s novels that criticise both class and gender role as two aspects of the bourgeois social system, that is, a combination of socialist commitment and feminist concern. This conjunction suggests that there is an objective factor at work which makes women more aware of the oppressed in society. And when we look at the novels written by women over the centuries we discover that not a few among them take sides with the underprivileged: for example, the anti-slavery novels of Aphra Behn (*Oroonoko*, 1688), Charlotte Tonna (*The System*, 1827), Harriet Beecher Stowe (*Uncle Tom's Cabin*, 1852) and Elizabeth Browning (*Aurora Leigh*, 1856); or the social novels of Maria Edgeworth (*The Absentee*, 1812) Elizabeth Gaskell (*Mary Barton*, 1848) and Charlotte Brontë. Numerous women in the past have presented with insight and partisanship the plight and, partially, the struggle of the oppressed—whether victims of class, race or sex discrimination.[4]

It is characteristic of the social status of women in class society that though divided by class they are linked by a common lack of rights. Although there clearly is a difference between a bourgeois woman and a proletarian, a white lady and a black slave, it is nevertheless true that, within her class and race, woman has a more inferior status than man. This situation is the result of private property either as material fact (in the property-owning classes) or as ideological orientation (in the oppressed classes) which forms the basis of man's dominance and causes the dependence of woman. It is this relationship of dominance and submission that provokes some feminist sociologists to see women as a class. Others consider them in terms of a 'caste' since women very often accept their position and perpetuate it by adapting to it. Or women's status is compared with that of a minority because of their marginalised position in society and the impossibility of escaping from this identity. Gerda Lerner repudiates these positions, in my view, most convincingly:

> Women are not a minority in any sense. Women are a sex. They have experienced educational, legal, and economic discrimination, as have members of minority groups, but they unlike truly marginal groups, are distributed through every group and class in society . . . Women are more closely allied to men of their own group than they are to women of other classes and races. Finally, women have always indoctrinated their children of both sexes in the very values by which they themselves have been doctrinated to subordination . . . Yet woman's position, whether as a member of the oppressed lower classes or as a member of the ruling elite, was always different in essentials from that of the male of her group.[5]

For a working-class woman the sex difference expressed itself not through her absence from work but rather through the quality of the workplace and the character of her work. As against male workers, the majority of women did not work in factories but in sweatshops and as servants[6]—which meant that there was a big difference in wages. Moreover, even when a woman did the same work as a man under the same circumstances she got paid less, since her work—according to patriarchal ideology—was additional to the income of her husband or father. Again, woman's existence was seen only in relation to and dependent on man. A woman from the working class, too, was expected to marry—yet, for her, this meant additional (unpaid) labour at home. Furthermore, the numerous pregnancies that usually followed in many cases ruined her health since she was forced to continue to work despite her condition because of the poor wages in general. If she did not get married she risked the possibility of being seduced and left with an illegitimate child for which she alone was responsible and which therefore shaped (and very often destroyed) her whole life, or she faced the harsh alternative of having to earn (extra) money by prostituting herself, thus, again, being dependent on men. All of this indicates that the situation of the working-class woman was in practice determined by her class *and* sex, which put her at a disadvantage in comparison with male workers. This situation was complicated even more by the rigid laws of capitalist exploitation which enforced competition between men and women on the labour market, for a woman would be hired at a lower wage—a fact for which women were blamed and which caused male workers to insist of gender roles, namely 'public' work for men and 'private' occupation for women in accordance with patriarchal ideology.

This contradictory situation illustrates the problematic nature of the interests of class and sex, namely that they are not automatically identical. Depending on the issue, working-class women could form alliances either with men from their own class to achieve class goals, or with women from other classes to fight for their rights as a sex, or, in fact, with both at the same time. In other words, although women like men are divided by class interests, they have a common interest in the achievement of equality. Therefore, women are not only linked with their own class but also across class lines to fight for legal, educational and political rights. By its very nature—since women's subordination is part of bourgeois ideology determined by private property *and* patriarchal ideology—this fight is ultimately a threat to bourgeois society and has therefore a potential link with the fight for socialism.[7] Moreover, there is an objective connection between the woman's cause and the socialist movement which was pointed out by Eleanor Marx and Edward Aveling: 'The truth is that she [woman], like the labour-classes, is in an oppressed condition; that her position, like theirs, is one of unjust and merciless degradation.' And they stressed that neither for women nor for the working class was a solution in sight unless the condition of society was changed, and that the emancipation both of women and of the working class needed to be carried out by their own forces.⁸

With the growing integration of women into the work process during the course of the nineteenth century—and this was true for women from the working class who were forced to work outside the home as a result of the industrial revolution, as well as for women from the middle class who finding themselves without sufficient parent capital or husband had to support themselves by work—their politicisation increased. Middle-class women especially, who were forced to become active in the fight for opportunities to work, including the education necessary for that work, and who found themselves confronted with barriers and restrictions on the basis of sex in practically all the professions, became conscious of their suppression as women. It is this context that made them take an interest in the conditions of women from the working class. Due to their own involvement in work, this interest took less the form of charity activities, as was predominantly the case in the 1840s, than of active participation: women produced studies about the conditions in factories and sweatshops and enforced some basic health regulations; they fought against the 'white slave traffic' and the Contagious Diseases Acts, which in practice were mainly directed against working-class women. In a somewhat different category were women who rejected their class background and threw their lot in with working women by supporting strikes, helping to organise trade unions (most prominently Emma Patterson and Clementina Black) and by forming women's associations, of which the Women's Co-operative Guild was the most important.⁹ Barbara Hutchins, a political activist of this period, describes the mutual stimulation of both the women's and the labour movement:

> As the women's movement draws towards the labour movement, as it is now so rapidly doing, it tends to lose the narrow individualism derived from the middle-class ideals of the last century. Mere freedom to compete is seen to be a small thing in comparison with opportunity to develop. The appeal for fuller opportunity is now stimulated less by the desire merely to do

the same things that men do, more by the perception that the whole social life must be impoverished until we get the women's point of view expressed and recognised in the functions of national life. On the other hand, the women Unionists, who have long been taxed with apathy and lack of interest in their trade organisations, are drawing from the women's movement a new inspiration and enthusiasm.[10]

But there was not only mutual stimulation but also a concern by activists with both socialist and feminist problems. Thus Annie Besant, member of the Social Democratic Federation (SDF) and the Fabian Society, was also active in the birth-control movement.

Without trying to argue that all feminists became socialists—the ideological divisions between bourgeois feminists, women conservatives and socialists were very often considerable when their class concerns rather than the general liberation of all women were stressed—it is legitimate to say that practically all leading women within the socialist movement (and it is from them and not from the rank-and-file members that we have the records) were feminists as well. This was an international phenomenon as becomes clear with Clara Zetkin in Germany, Eleanor Marx in England, Alexandra Kollontai in Russia, Anna Kuliscioff in Italy and Florence Kelley in the USA. Therefore, the conclusion seems justified that this conjunction is due to the dialectical relationship between the liberation of the working class and of women.[11]

However, although the Second International at its foundation congress in 1889 had adopted a paragraph in its programme stressing that the equality of women was to be a leading principle for all member parties, the conjunction of socialism and feminism was in practice not without its problems. On the one hand, women's issues were often underestimated because of a mechanistic understanding of Marxism resulting in reductionist attitudes about class as well as patriarchal views on gender among labour leaders; and, on the other hand, some women overestimated the immediate importance of their own problems in relation to the class struggle. However, as a whole, this conjunction strengthened both the women's cause and the labour movement; for it meant that talented middle-class women supported a socialist perspective.

Given this background, the phenomenon that some of the most radical novels of the 1880s and 1890s were written by middle-class *women* who had become politicised, is hardly accidental. These authors combined their interests as women with the socialist perspective available through the political movements of the period, which meant that they identified with the fight of the working class rather than viewing it from a distance.

CONSTANCE HOWELL, *A MORE EXCELLENT WAY* (1888)

Constance Howell's novel begins with a feminist issue: a woman of thirty, married to an officer in India, feels isolated and lonely. The cause of this unhappiness is a very common one among women of middle- and upper-class background: she did not really know her husband before the marriage; for, within the conventions of bourgeois match-making, a woman did not have much of a chance of getting to know the man she was to marry, further than that he was good-looking, had excellent manners and a secure position in society. The result was that the woman was often literally trapped in marriage and found herself confronted with a husband whom she could not warm to; it often happened that they were totally different in character and disagreed on moral, educational and political issues. This conflict is a frequent subject of feminist novels of the period, for example in Sarah Grand's *The Heavenly Twins* (1893) and Mona Caird's *The Daughters of Danaus* (1894). Constance Howell develops it in a political way by pointing out that the gender role of women (being submissive, superficially educated, religious) serves to maintain bourgeois society. This point is made apparent in the novel by the heroine's insight into the political function of religion. Reading in her husband's library Agatha Hathaway begins to doubt her religious belief and finally renounces Christianity altogether. This decision brings her into conflict not just with her husband, who though himself an agnostic sees his public position threatened, but also with the norms of a society which has incorporated religion into its ideology. The kind of opposition Agatha faces makes clear that this religiosity is to be carried mainly by women, almost as a substitute for the education granted to (middle-class) men, and by the poor who are thus made to accept their place in society. By making this connection between women and the poor explicit, Howell indicates the potential link between the emancipation of women and that of the lower, the working class. Howell does not make her protagonist into an active feminist, but she allows her to see the unfair chances for women in personal and professional life. And when she talks about equality and the causes for the 'weak' female character she is strategically using the arguments of Mary Wollstonecraft and John Stuart Mill. Agatha sympathises with the people because she sees that they are indoctrinated with falsehood (Christianity). Since she has no contact with the people, her solidarity with them grows out of her general sense of justice, and it is this sense of justice that 'made her champion them as a class'.[12]

It is Agatha's son who, influenced by her, takes the next step and actively sides with the people in their fight against capitalist exploitation. In Otho Hathaway Howell creates a character who throughout the novel is a passionate, optimistic fighter for socialism, giving everything for the cause—his money, his profession, his private life. Coming from a middle-class background with the financial security, education and culture that go with it, he is converted into an atheist through his mother, and turned into a socialist through studying not just the conditions of the poor but through analysing the causes of poverty. As a converted socialist he gives speeches and lectures and tirelessly meets the prejudices and arguments of his rich relatives.

Howell uses an omniscient narrator who adopts temporarily the perspective of Agatha and Otho. We are thus shown the process of their conversion to atheism and socialism. The context in which the conversions take place is skilfully established so as to show that learning the social facts involves an inner confict as well as, in the end, a conflict with one's own class. Agatha faces the problem that although she herself no longer believes in God, she is forced to have her son brought up as a Christian because according to the moral standards of her class a child would be taken away from its mother rather than denied a religious education. Howell's narrative strategy aims at the disclosure of the mechanism of bourgeois ideology whose proclaimed freedom proves to be a lie for women and the poor.

Otho's conversion to the cause of socialism happens as the result of experiencing the contrast between the 'mob' in the streets (the Trafalgar Square riots of 1886) and the contented, sneering members of his own class who watch the battle from a safe distance. In terms of narration we find a strategy similar to that described above: the basic conflict between the classes is named and then an analysis of the causes of this situation offered. This is supplemented by a summary of Otho's reading of socialist literature (including Marx, Lassalle, George) so that we have a political 'lecture' that at the same time functions as a report about Otho's learning process. At that stage of the novel, it is still the narrator who undertakes the political analysis, which includes a clear-sighted evaluation of the existing socialist groups of that period. But soon the narrator's comments are replaced by Otho's voice in the political process, that is, the political discussion now becomes part of the character's life. Otho gives his first speeches and, still predominantly moving in circles of his own class, has numerous discussions where he opposes the common arguments against socialism. These are the most successful parts of the novel because the arguments are sharp, witty and to the point—as no pamphlet could have been. By putting the socialist argument in the context of standard middle-class prejudice and tiresome clichés about the working class, Howell is able to show both the strength of socialist theory and the process of change in people coming to terms with it. Thus, through the confrontation of characters, the rational argument is complemented by emotional involvement, which makes the reader's identification with the presented problem easier. But more than that, the drama of the arguments, the wit in rebuttal, the inanity of the bourgeois arguments about socialism give the novel an aesthetic dimension.

The novel is structured in such a way that, on the one hand, the disastrous economic consequences of capitalism for the masses are shown mainly through direct speech; on the other hand, the effect capitalism has on the individual is indicated through characterisation. Thus Mrs Fleming, a minor character in the novel, is described as follows:

> Mrs. Fleming, who kept the boarding-house, was a type of the woman whom a capitalistic system produces . . . The struggle for life had hardened and narrowed and spoilt her. Her whole being was absorbed in the effort to keep herself and her children in a certain station; and in her desperate fear they should fail and sink below it, all the evil of her nature was rampant against her fellows.[13]

The park keeper who stops Otho distributing leaflets is characterised as a conservative working man whose selfish contentment in his job blinds him to the interests of his class. Dr Hathaway, a freethinker sympathising with the poor, remains conservative for convention's sake in order to keep his position as a recognised medical man.

The novel ends with Otho's optimistic faith in an early victory of socialism, expressed in a tone that is almost unique in the literature of that period—without however giving the impression that the fight will be an easy one. Howell shows that the conversion of middle-class people to the socialist cause means a separation from friends, relatives and even lovers. (Otho has to give up the idea of a marriage with an apolitical girl from his class whom he passionately loves but who cannot understand his conviction and is unwilling to give up her way of life for it.) Howell makes no secret of the fact that a socialist activist like Otho is slandered by the upper class, scorned by the middle class which fears losing its position in the social hierarchy, and misunderstood by a working class that is divided by the complacency of those who have jobs and the discontent of those who do not—in other words, who is opposed by the full impact of bourgeois ideology and working-class antagonism. Yet, in presenting Otho as a sympathetic character who analyses the reasons for these reactions by putting them into a wider political context, she makes this very contrast the basis of her social critique. Moreover, she creates a figure whose commitment and political knowledge anticipates many future heroes of socialist novels.

EMMA BROOKE, *TRANSITION* (1895)

Emma Brooke's work illustrates the interrelation of feminism and socialism in a remarkable way. Her first novel, *A Superfluous Woman* (1894), is a typical feminist work of the 1890s while her next novel, *Transition*, is clearly socialist-orientated. The first is a psychological study of an aristocratic woman who in accordance with the conventions of her class is reduced to meaningless activities illustrating merely a flamboyant life style. In her heroine Brooke demonstrates the ultimate connection between enforced passivity and a state of invalidism and neurasthenia. She has thus created a character which challenges a prevailing opinion in the nineteenth century that the fragile health of a 'lady' was a result of the weakness of the female sex. Brooke makes her heroine leave her family and seek experience outside her overprotected golden prison where she had withered away out of sheer boredom. In the countryside, as a helpmate to a farming couple, the young woman learns to appreciate the difficulties of poor people and their straightforwardness, recognising the contrast to the minor problems and deviousness of her own class. Leaving aside the oversimplification, we can see that Brooke offers a solution to the woman problem in the integration of women into the work process so that they are an active part of human development. Yet, with the further development of the plot, Brooke indicates that an individual escape is no solution to a general problem.

Transition picks up the theme of women and society from an angle totally different from that of the previous novel. We are introduced to a highly intelligent Girton student who, after finishing her studies, plans to do research in Greek mythology. Instead, however, Honora is confronted with her father's decision not to live any longer on his income from the church, which means that she is forced to earn her own living by teaching—a fact she finds deeply humiliating since she had hoped to be able to ascend into the upper middle class. With Honora's reaction Brooke, though acknowledging the success of the women's movement in establishing the opportunity to study, points out the élitist consequences of bourgeois education. The character of this education becomes clear when the minister, who remembers the time of the Chartists, asks his daughter about them, and she has to plead ignorance except for the vague idea that they were 'demagogues'. Here father, however, stresses the justified demands of the Chartist movement which the Church had failed to support; he thus represents a group of Christians who towards the end of the century began to question the power of the official Church and sided with the working class.

With this constellation, two different class views are presented, involving the reader in the argument which is implicit in the statements of father and daughter. Brooke does not impose her position through the better argument of either character but through the practice of Honora's teaching career. In a London high school where because of her abilities she becomes headmistress after six months, she feels and is in fact isolated from the rest of the teachers because of her attitude towards this 'inferior' work. Only when she overcomes her prejudices with the help of her socialist colleague, Lucilla Dennison, does she begin to experience the pleasures of self-fulfilment through creative work and to appreciate the independence it offers her. Thus, after a conversation with her former Cambridge tutor, she realises her equality with him: 'I belong to myself now exactly as he belongs to himself! . . . I need not ask him, nor father, nor anyone.'[14]

The feminist theme is connected with the fight for socialism in the character of Lucilla, who 'never had pictured herself as the domestic companion of an unbroken and impossible happiness. In all her dreaming she went forward with a restless circle of fellow-workers, and waged warfare against a shameless world.[15] With the change of narration to Lucilla's perspective, the activities of the socialists are introduced. Brooke does not aim to show—as does Howell—the cause and process of people's conversion to socialism; she merely indicates it by presenting the socialists as coming from different social backgrounds (from self-educated journalist of lower-middle-class origin to civil servant and former Cambridge lecturer). She shows socialist leaders in their work with the masses and is able through language and atmosphere to capture their enthusiasm. Thus the speeches included in the novel are aimed not so much at converting characters in the novel (and by implication the reader), as at illustrating the commitment of the socialists to their cause and the satisfaction they gain from working for the good of the people. The identification with the working class becomes clear in the very conception of these characters, notably in Paul Sheridan, an International Labour Party (ILP) leader:

> Sheridan's conversation was apt to be dotted with figures; he would use them to meet vague clever-sounding generalities, introducing them side by side with quotations from the poets. . .
> In truth, the food for his imagination lay in the commonest things; he required no more than the every-day affairs of an every-day earth to set his heart a-working on its lifelong labour of divination. . .
> It was that to his divining eye the commonest things told the deepest earth histories. The rhythm of his poetry had in it the fall of hammers, the hum of wheels, the ceaseless tramp of the workers' feet, the rattle of traffic, and the rush of steam. As the genius of the historian out of broken pottery and scattered shreds revives the palpitating life of the long-dead city, so he out of figures would extract the passionate realities and tragedies of present existence.
> 'Your truest poetry is found in statistics', he would say.[16]

Besides characterisation, Brooke uses irony in order to illustrate the moral superiority of the socialist idea. In the election campaign the Conservative and Liberal candidates are called Mr Tootle and Mr Bootle respectively, thus ridiculing the similarity of their programmes. In contrast, Sheridan—the first candidate put forward by the Socialists—offers a clear alternative. And while Tootle/Bootle hire an ignorant hand to put up their posters (which he does by placing them always next to each other), Sheridan's election work is characterised by an efficiency that originates from conviction and tremendous support by party members and working-class people, mainly women, who in fact very often did the leg work.

Yet, while presenting the power of the socialist idea, Brooke also indicates differences within the movement that threatened its strength: the conflicts between reformists and revolutionists, which is no other than that between a socialist and an anarchist position. This conflict is located in Lucilla who has a deep commitment to the socialist cause but is increasingly worried about the growing reformism of the party Sheridan represents. Her doubts and inner conflicts isolate her from her former friends and comrades, causing her to suffer; yet, for her the separation seems inevitable since while she dreams of a communist future she is convinced that reforms contradict this aim rather than bring it about. The study of Lucilla, with her conflict between conviction in the cause and anxiety about strategy, shows Brooke's ability of drawing characters and making the tension of longing and being, of idealism and pragmatism visible. Though she seems to give both positions, the socialist and the anarchist, equal room in the novel,[17] the apparent neutrality is resolved by the plot: Lucilla gets fully involved with the anarchists only to realise that their leader sees in her merely a psycho-sexual prop; disappointment, awareness of her delusion and her isolation lead to her death. Thus, by combining the political argument with problems of gender—setting true comradeship against sexual humiliation—Brooke shows the moral superiority of socialism, notwithstanding its contemporary weaknesses. She argues for tolerance in the interest of unity and for the necessity of compromise in the struggle when she makes Lucilla say: 'My tremendous error was to dream that Truth is single.'[18]

What remains at the end, despite the heartache over personal losses, is the optimism of the socialist fight: Sheridan wins a seat for the Socialists; Honora, distanced from the cause throughout the novel, takes up Lucilla's place. It is this optimism, not just decoratively stated at the end but implied in the novel as a whole—by means of plot-construction, character-drawing and a passionate language full of metaphors—that makes the aesthetic quality of this narrative.

CLEMENTINA BLACK, *AN AGITATOR* (1894)

In her novel, *An Agitator*, Clementina Black combines problems of the socialist movement with questions of working-class leadership. Christopher Brand, of working-class origin and trained as an engineer, is introduced as a political activist who dedicates his life to the struggle of the working class. Being on his own (the premature death of his wife in childbed having been hastened by constant worries over his unemployment resulting from victimisation), he considers the working people of England his family, and Labour his party. He not only leads strikes and takes part in political debates, but also stands as a Labour candidate for Parliament. He becomes, however, the victim of an intrigue that loses him the newly-won seat and lands him in prison, which he eventually leaves with revived spirits and renewed conviction.

Yet, despite Brand's enthusiasm for the socialist cause and his uncompromising battling, he appears to be somewhat aloof from his class. Black offers an explanation for this distance in his biography: he is the illegitimate son of an aristocrat and a working-class woman. With this she also seems to indicate that Brand's abilities result from his 'aristocratic blood'. At the same time, she presents him with a deeply ingrained sense of class justice and makes him stand firmly with the working class on the occasion when his father suddenly appears and tempts him with the prospect of a professional or political career under his protection. We have then a contradiction between the political-ideological physiognomy of a working-class leader and the uneasy biologist 'explanation' of his abilities to formulate and present socialist theory. This contradiction suggests that Black was aware of a problem for which she did not have a sufficient theoretical understanding: the working class itself does not produce theory—a fact that Lenin was to make clear later. Being conscious of this—not least through her practical work with workers—[19] and yet determined to create a positive working-class leader, Black gets around the problem by offering the biologist 'explanation'. While this is clearly not satisfactory, giving the novel an aesthetic flaw, the important point is that Black is tackling a problem of great relevance for working-class literature. She stresses in the character of Brand that it is not only education that makes a working-class leader, but a combination of knowledge plus the experience of everyday exploitation and the political conviction resulting from both. Moreover, as she shows with Brand's development from self-imposed isolation to a sense of comradeship with other workers, it is not through capable individual leadership but through the joint fight with the workers that the struggle can be won. To make this point by way of aesthetic presentation is an important merit of the novel and gives it its optimistic quality.

In this apparently personal story of the development of a political agitator other problems of the working-class movement are inserted. Thus the description of the atmosphere during a strike—the well-organised distribution of money, the problems with blacklegs, the discussions among the workers about an enforced compromise—is a moving tableau and an introduction into the practice of class struggle. Part of this struggle was the growing necessity to fight for social improvements through Parliament and therefore to put up independent candidates in an election—a fact Black works out with political clarity asserting that the Liberal Party, traditionally 'representing' the workers, can never be a workers' party owing to its membership from among the property-owning class, and its politics. Also, the deviations and confusions within the socialist movement itself—an increasing problem in Britain during the 1890s—are ironically hinted at with the comment on the 'Russell Square Socialist Society':

> They are the middle-class wave of socialism . . . Socialism in the West End . . . is enthusiasm; in the East End it's revolt; in Bloomsbury it is business . . . The aim is to secure certain economic changes, one by one, without personal sacrifice. The methods are talking, lecturing, issuing pamphlets, joining Liberal and Radical Associations and blowing one another's trumpets . . .[20]

And with Mrs Pelham, the curate's wife, who supports the labour movement with commitment and intelligence yet cannot represent it in Parliament, Black raises the problem of the exclusion of women from public offices.

This enlargement of perspective functions as a sort of corrective to the concentration on an individual hero and points at the direction the socialist novel was to take with its further development. The novel is marked by the aesthetic weakness indicated above; yet, what I insist on is its importance in the historical context: picking up issues of the socialist struggle as a theme and presenting the movement in a positive light with a protagonist who retains his political faith despite the difficulties he faces, was a courageous effort by a woman who was surrounded by writers full of doubt and scepticism if not opposition and ridicule.

Common to all the novels briefly discussed here is their political radicalism. This radicalism is based, I would suggest, on the writer's experience of oppression as a woman and her politicisation during a time of the strengthening of the socialist movement which, in turn, led to a perception that her own problems were part of the problems of society as a whole and culminated, finally, in the conviction that a transformation of capitalism was necessary. Thus these middle-class women identified with the socialist movement because their own interests were ultimately intertwined with it—which is a very different situation from that of a male writer like Gissing who for a time felt drawn to the working class but never really identified himself with the aims of its vanguard. It is the writer's identification with the subject presented that accounts for partisanship in a novel—a quality of particular importance for the socialist novel.

The fact, however, that the socialist novels by women of that period were as outspoken as the feminist novels were frank, suggests that the radicalism of these women writers was not only politically caused but sociologically determined. While men had various opportunities to express their ideas—in positions of authority in the state apparatus, in the academic world, law and political organisations—women, practically excluded from official public life, felt that writing afforded them one possibility of taking part in discussions on issues important to them as women. Novels, that is, were used by women as a medium for the representation of opinions that could not otherwise be expressed since they were denied positions of influence. Moreover, since they felt misrepresented by patriarchal ideology, they used literature to inform and instruct, to offer an alternative ideological perspective. To put it more generally, the didactic quality found in early socialist and feminist novels (as well as in Black literature) is caused by the fact that this literature is forced to work in a literary discourse which excludes the experience and world view of the oppressed class/sex/race. It is under these conditions that literature assumes the function of instructing, which means that the signified is more essential than the signifier. Therefore, we find, also in the novels discussed here, not so much an elaborated presentation of a perceived view but the attempt—through construction of plot, presentation of character and the use of argument and debate—to inform the reader, clarify doubts and win her/his understanding of the subject matter.

NOTES

1. It is surely no coincidence that practically all of these women were politically active: Clementina Black was for thirty-five years a leading organiser of the women's trade-union movement; Margaret Harkness was an active member of the SDF; Constance Howell is known to have supported campaigns against sweated work, and Gertude Dix was part of the socialist movement in Bristol.
2. P. J. Keating, *The Working Classes in Victorian Fiction* (London, 1979), p.239.
3. Sarah Grand is best known for *The Heavenly Twins* (1893), Olive Schreiner for *The Story of an African Farm* (1884), Mona Caird for *The Daughters of Danaus* (1894) and George Egerton for her short stories collected as *Keynotes* (1893) and *Discords* (1894).
4. This fact is confirmed by Joseph Kestner in his informative study *Protest and Reform. The British Social Narrative by Women, 1827-1867* (London, 1985) where he says about the period under investigation: 'Female social novelists were more aggressive than male novelists like Disraeli or Kingsley in their specificity. Particularly in showing interactions among women of different classes these novelists surpassed their male counterparts' (p.18).
5. Gerda Lerner, *The Majority Finds Its Past: Placing Women in History* (Oxford, 1981), pp.170-1.
6. See Patricia Branca, 'A new perspective on women's work: a comparative typology', *Journal of Social History*, IX (1975), pp.129-53. Though men also worked as servants they tended to be hired by the upper class whereas women did service for the middle class who paid less for more and harder work.
7. The need of women's emancipation as a prerequisite for social development was pointed out by people as diverse as Fourier, Marx and John Stuart Mill, which demonstrates that the woman question is not bound to a single class position though its effective solution is connected with the abolition of capitalism.
8. 'On the Woman Question', *Westminster Review*, VI (1885), p.211.
9. The Women's Co-operative Guild formed in 1883 was the first proletarian women's organisation with economic and educational concerns as well as political aims (enfranchise-

ment). See Jean Gaffin and David Thoms, *Caring and Sharing. The Centenary History of the Co-operative Women's Guild* (Manchester, 1983).
10. Barbara L. Hutchins, *Women in Modern Industry* (London, 1915), p.199.
11. For the complex relationship between the two movements see the stimulating study by Meredith Tax, *The Rising of the Women. Feminist Solidarity and Class Conflict, 1880-1917* (New York, 1980).
12. Constance Howell, *A More Excellent Way* (London, 1888), p.90.
13. *ibid.*, p.214.
14. Emma Brooke, *Transition* (London, 1895), p.140.
15. *ibid.*, p.77.
16. *ibid.*, p.168.
17. The socialist and anarchist positions in the book are increasingly represented by Sheridan and Lucilla respectively, and their long argument at the end of the novel is perhaps the most powerful and moving part of the book, as it is both politically and personally final.
18. Brooke, *op. cit.*, p.308.
19. Detailed information about Clementina Black's extensive trade-union work can be found in Liselotte Glage, *Clementina Black: A Study in Social History and Literature* (Heidelberg, 1981).
20. Clementina Black, *An Agitator* (London, 1894), p.53.

· 3 ·

Tendencies in narrative fiction in the London-based socialist press of the 1880s and 1890s

JACK MITCHELL

The history of modern, revolutionary-socialist and working-class narrative fiction in Britain begins with William Morris and 'H. J. Bramsbury', the first being one of the most famous men of letters of his age, the other a man (?) whose real identity remains a mystery. I refer to four works, three by Morris and one by Bramsbury, all published in serial form in *Commonweal* and *Justice*, the central organs of the Socialist League and the Social Democratic Federation respectively. Morris's tales appeared in *Commonweal*, of course. They were: 'The Pilgrims of Hope' (April 1885 to June 1886), 'A Dream of John Ball' (November 1886 to January 1887), and 'News from Nowhere' (January to October 1890). Bramsbury's novel appeared in *Justice* between June 1888 and April 1889. Its title—'A Working Class Tragedy'.

Thanks partly to Morris's tremendous influence, British socialists of the period were intensely aware of the importance of art and literature in propaganda work. Morris taught them how important it was to woo the imagination, the emotions, the moral-aesthetic sense, as well as the mind, away from the corrupted channels and models through which the bourgeoisie exercised its in-depth control. Many of them saw, perhaps more clearly than we do, so much more immersed as we are in the desperate day-to-day struggle, the need to inspire, to provide the 'gleam'. They grasped the necessity of creating a body and tradition of militant socialist and working-class literature which would be independent of bourgeois hegemony. Not that they had a worked-out policy for the arts, or a theory. Morris's *theory*, which contained a tendency to view art as a florescence on healthy society rather than as an agent for helping to change society, did not always help them here. Sectarian though they were in many ways, some of them had moved beyond the tendency to be found in a good deal of Chartist criticism and fiction to reject the great tradition of bourgeois classical and critical realism as something alien to them. This was at least true of *Commonweal*, under Morris's guidance, from 1885 to 1889, where Dickens, Defoe and George Eliot, for instance, were recommended as great writers to learn from. Cobbett is criticised, but recommended for the poetry of his prose,[1] and, paradoxically, William Morris himself takes up the cudgels in defence of the truth of Zola's 'ugly realism' in the banned *Germinal*.[2]

Morris was not the only 'literary man' in the leading circles of the socialist movement. For such a small movement the proportion of this type of person was extremely high. By its very nature and the way it 'came to them' Socialism tended to attract people with an urge to express themselves in words. In the midst of a capitalism all too clearly entering upon its decadent imperialist stage, revolutionary socialism burst on them with the impact of an almost religious revelation. It stirred the imagination. Among the leading political workers who regularly contributed poetry or imaginative prose were, for instance, Tom Maguire, Edward Carpenter, Harry Quelch, Robert Blatchford, Bruce Glasier, James Connolly, R. B. Cunninghame Graham, Jim Connell.

Of course, in one sense this was symptomatic of an as yet undeveloped 'division of labour'. There were so few activists. Socialism at this stage was not a mass movement in any way comparable to Chartism, but a movement of a tiny minority. The Chartists had a far bigger reservoir to draw from. In criticising the severe limitations of socialist literature in the 1880s and 1890s we must keep in mind the narrowness of its base.

It was not just a matter of socialism attracting people of a literary bent. In their activities the socialist societies laid tremendous weight on the word. The literature produced by these politician-writers was seen as an integral part of their main, almost their only activity—propaganda. They had no conception of a modern revolutionary party of the working class with its roots in the daily struggle of the masses. The societies (if not always the individual members!) saw themselves almost exclusively in the role of socialist 'evangelists' preaching the Word, tearing the blinkers from the workers' eyes, revealing the true nature of capitalist exploitation, preparing them ideologically to know 'what to do' when the System collapsed more or less spontaneously under its own inner contradictions. So all their energies and talents were poured into the Word; and of course they became very good at it—at explaining exploitation. How often do we express wonder at Robert Tressell's genius for this in *The Ragged Trousered Philanthropists*. But Tressell's genius did not arise immaculate from the waves. It is the finest flowering of a talent developed by the socialists in the course of the twenty preceding years, Something that once again goes to show how, in the case of working-class literary culture, no crisp and holy frontier can be drawn between the 'non-artistic' and the 'artistic' literary (or verbal) modes.

Clearly this situation was, in certain ways, a favourable one for the cultivation of imaginative writing as one important and respected sector of the word-front. As we shall see, however, the total context also contained negative pressures which hampered and circumscribed the development and adequate functioning of the new literature, preventing a major breakthrough to realism. This was particularly damaging in prose.

Of course, in the early years especially, the literary activists tended to express themselves in lyrical verse more than in the narrative fictional forms. It took some time for the socialists reluctantly to realise that the collapse of capitalism was not necessarily imminent, that the here and now was not just a purgatory pure and simple, soon to be passed through leaving no trace, but an on-going contradictory process in which the foreshadowings of future life and struggle were already present—an object worthy of close scrutiny. But until this urge to scrutinise closely makes itself strongly felt there can be no firm foundation for the development of the realist narrative modes, which are *par excellence* the modes for getting to grips with the nitty-gritty of aesthetically unexplored terrain.

Morris was one of those who did at least realise that the revolution would be a long time a-coming, and that it was necessary to comb out the detested present for any glimmerings of Hope. Personally it went very much against the grain to do this, but with the courage and sense of responsibility so typical of the man, he set out to show the way.

This he attempted in his pioneering novel-in-verse 'The Pilgrims of Hope' (*Commonweal*, 1885-6).

Where might he find that gleam of hope for the future in his own time? The action shuttles between London and revolutionary Paris. A kind of socialist *Tale of Two Cities*. Feeling that the destiny of humanity is going to be forged in the modern city, the hero and his wife leave their country idyll to take up political work in London. At first the stupor of London deadens their hope, but the hero is 'born again' when he joins the communists. Forced down into the ranks of the proletariat, he works selflessly for the Cause despite losing the two things he treasures most—his pleasure in his work, and his wife's love, the latter to a well-off friend and comrade who supports them in time of need. All three go to Paris in 1871 to help in the defence of the Commune. There they are filled with the spirit of hope, for they have seen the future 'real, solid, and at hand'.[3] The hero's wife and friend are killed on the barricades. He is smuggled back to England, where he joins his young son in his native village, there to recuperate before plunging back into the struggle.

In the introduction ('The Message of the March Wind') Morris and his hero appear to be set on exchanging the outworn romance of the pastoral dream for a new, sober romance of the ugly urban fact and the revolutionary movement. But the story ultimately fails to fulfil this promise. Contemporary life as a whole is aesthetically distasteful to Morris and he is loath to look it steadily in the face *as an artist* in search of beauty. (This was a difficult thing to demand of *any* socialist artist at this point in time, that is before the *first stirrings* of the mass historic initiatives which brought movement into the 'fen of stagnant waters' at the end of the eighties.)

The narrative continuously veers away, after slight contact with the outer world, into the author–hero's subjectivity. Outer reality is only interesting in so far as fleeting figments of it provide 'signs' to nourish the narrator's real preoccupation—his hope. English life provides him with no such signals, except for the everlasting hope embodied in nature, the tradition-rich English countryside. Revolutionary Paris does provide them. But it is not so much the actual, embattled Commune that interests him, rather it is his inner *dream* of the commune, which the Commune helps to feed. This dream comes between us and actual reality. For Morris it is the true reality. Wherever it is a matter of telling us how the future will relate to the Commune his verse comes temporarily to life. The 'real, solid, and at hand' never does.

Also part of this is the way in which that conventional theme of the contemporary bourgeois novel, the love-triangle, comes to overlay and emasculate the main drive of the political action. Certainly, the love-triangle is treated in a new way, from the point of view of a truly communist ethos, but the manner in which it gets between Morris and what should be his real story shows, I think, firstly how his own marital problems sneaked into the story, and secondly, that he felt the thinness of his narrative and introduced the tragic 'love interest' to stiffen and anchor it.

With this tenuous aesthetic relationship to contemporary reality there could be no question of Morris laying the basis here for a *realist* narrative exploration of present life and struggle. But the only way to win a wider working-class audience was through realism (see Tressell). How wide an audience did Morris intend to reach? The very lack of concreteness was perhaps an advantage as regards one of the aims Morris seems to have been pursuing. The story assumes certain allegorical or metaphorical overtones. It can also be read as an 'individualised' version of the historical path followed by humanity from an (idealised) village community into the hell of urban capitalist exploitation and through to the first upsurge of modern revolt, with its striving towards the communist future. This is quite characteristic of the natural historicism and urge to wholeness which marked Morris's political vision. Seen from this angle the story is a 'disguised' version of a typical Socialist League lecture or tract on the historical development of society—but one composed for the amusement and edification of the more or less initiated. One of Morris's chief aims in writing was to warn and educate, encourage and inspire the small 'socialist band': the way will be fraught with setbacks; your generation might not see victory, but your lonely fight, modest though it appear, will be a living part of that true reality—the future. In this sense the Paris Commune becomes a heroic metaphor for the seemingly unheroic struggle of the socialists in Britain.

That Morris was not primarily aiming at a mass audience is clear from his choice of *verse* for this 'historical novel of the present'. Taking into account the general context discussed earlier, and also the whole complex problem of Morris's aesthetic relationship to his material, it was not unnatural that this first attempt at an extended narrative of the present from a revolutionary point of view should be in verse. On the one hand it indicates his underlying lyrical rather than epic, or objectivised, preoccupation. On the other hand it is a curiously shamefaced verse, for the most part, as if it felt it really ought to be prose. It moves in a stylistic limbo which corresponds to the vague setting the heroes move in. It has an evasive quality, helping to exalt material which Morris feels has, aesthetically, little to recommend it, and at the same time keeping this intransigent detail at arm's length.

He had done his best, but those seeking to 'conquer the present' would have to find their own more prosaic road. Morris was aware of his own unsuitedness for this job. He ends with the lines

And I cling to the love of the past and the love of the
   day to be,
And the present, it is but the building of the man to be
   strong in me.[4]

Four months after the conclusion of his first attempt to body forth his dream of the commune he was back in the columns of *Commonweal* with a new and more congenial strategy. Taking his cue from the last lines of 'The Pilgrims of Hope' he plunges into the past to find an image, this time in his own beloved England of the Middle Ages. Again he chooses a revolutionary situation—the Peasant Revolt of 1381.

In the prose tale 'A Dream of John Ball' the socialist narrator is transported back, in a dream, to an idealised Kentish village at the point of coming-together and upsurge of the peasants under the inspiring words of John Ball. The narrator experiences their *fellowship* (comradeship) and a victorious preliminary skirmish with the forces of the lords. In a long concluding conversation with John Ball he tells the latter how he and the peasants will be finally vindicated in 'the change beyond the change'.

In contrast to 'The Pilgrims of Hope' there is a wealth of concrete and loving detail here. Yet the image of society which emerges has the static quality of pageantry, almost of heraldry, where the brightness of the primary colours screens a tangle of historical illogicalities. Morris sought to achieve with his version of the Middle Ages what he could not achieve with the stuff of the alienated present—give real body to his vision of a fellowship in which the individual could flourish. But in order to do so he had to distort, to stylise. The result is 'beautiful' but lacking in intrinsic dynamism and so ultimately unconvincing. Indeed, the objective picture soon gives way to what it could not embody—a discussion of future perspectives. So once again it comes to a falling apart of the historically concrete and the real vision, the ideal. So Morris's Middle Ages 'fail' him too. Historical realism is not achieved.

These limitations are perhaps best put into perspective by considering Morris's apparent intentions in writing.

His aim was surely to indicate that fellowship, something containing real qualities of the commune, had once been at home in this England that now seemed the mockery of these things, to show that English men and women had sacrificed themselves to defend this fellowship and expand it into the envisioned commune of all humanity, increasing their own fellowship in the process of struggle. What once was, albeit in a partial form, would come again, perfected and universalised through the dialectic of historical struggle. Fellowship, the commune, was the people's birthright, of which they had been robbed, not the pipe-dream of a few freaks and enthusiasts.

Clearly these aims do not preclude a wider readership, but the whole nature and emphasis of the story indicate that Morris was again mainly writing with the small band of the socialist fellowship in view. Again his intention was to sustain and inspire, to educate, but also to impress upon them the historic responsibility they bore as the executors of those who had fought the good fight in the past, the vital, tenuous link between the past and the future. Given this primary intention and readership, the revolutionary-romantic, stylised pageant-vision could fulfil its function quite effectively. But only historical realism could have captured a wider audience.

The way in which the two heroes, John Ball and the narrator, function is further evidence of the somewhat inward-turning tendency of the whole structure. In a sense they are a retreat on the heroes of 'The Pilgrims of Hope'. They take no direct part in the actual fighting, but, in accordance with the role assigned to themselves by the socialist societies in a popular upsurge, give 'the ideological lead'. This is why John Ball and not, say, Wat Tyler, is the central figure. Ball plays the agitator's part at first hand, the narrator does so at one remove in that he gives the long historical perspective to Ball. The only real dynamism to be found in the story is contained in their *words*—in Ball's prophetic agitatory speech at the cross, and in the way the narrator leads Ball's mind and imagination into the distant future and the true realisation of their struggle.

The action-story is an induction leading into a disguised

version of a typical socialist excursion on the nature of capitalist exploitation, with a characteristic Morrisonian emphasis on its historical growth. Ball is a kind of 'alienating effect' here—the simple man whose naïveté serves as a sounding board for bringing out the social and historical paradoxes. Hence this conversation sets out not only to educate, but to educate the educators, providing an object lesson on how to relate to a simple audience.

Not that the socialist educator was expected to use the tortuous, at times almost incomprehensible pseudo-medieval no-language into which the style increasingly degenerates. Perhaps this was partly due to time pressure in meeting serialisation dead-lines (E. P. Thompson maintains that 'The Pilgrims of Hope' was written hastily in monthly instalments[5]), but basically, in the work under discussion as in its predecessor, the unsolved problem of style expresses firstly Morris's lack of real aesthetic-imaginative contact with the society he was portraying, and secondly the fact that he was primarily writing for a small circle of devotees. (Or does it indicate rather that he was not sure for whom he was, or ought to be, writing?)

Be that as it may, the limitations of Morris's attempts to get to artistic grips with actual, objective reality were clearly not only due to personal peculiarities but also to the isolation and sectarianism of the socialist sects, their 'contempt' for the present, for the day-to-day struggles of the masses to assert their humanity.

Morris's third serial in *Commonweal* did not follow immediately upon the second, but after an interval of three years. 'News from Nowhere' is by far the most considered of Morris's socialist narratives.

Now, in the free and uncluttered field of the far-off not-yet there can be no question of a falling apart of the historically concrete and the ideal. Here he can mould the 'historically concrete' to the exact specifications of his ideal. It is *his* historically concrete, his true reality realised, the product of his imagination in complete accordance with his ideal. Which does not mean with a dream, for his social ideal is 'scientific' in so far as it is a basically Marxist prognosis developed out of the revolutionary potential already pushing through the dirt of the present. All the 'signs' given him in the course of his rich life-experience, especially in the socialist and labour movements, come together here, transmuted, fused and filled out by the synthesising power of his poetic imagination into a living totality. There is no need here to turn his back on the facts of life in order to sing in praise of mere signs of hope, of the future. The systematised and completed pattern of signs *is* the future, the hope realised, reality. Nothing else now exists to confuse, mar and separate.

Many things motivated Morris to produce his definitive image of true reality when he did, in 1890. No doubt his failure to achieve concreteness and wholeness in the two preceding serials set in the present and the past also urged him into the future dimension. But it was part of a long-term strategy too. 'News from Nowhere' is the most complete and mature statement of all the main strands in his thinking. There was a third thing however. The way in which victory was won by the 'hopeless mass' of rank-and-file workers in the fight for the Dockers' Tanner in 1889 had, surely, more than a little to do with the novel's timing and its triumph over all the limitations in Morris, limitations both of a purely personal kind and those reflecting the weaknesses of the socialist sects of the day. The sudden historic initiative of the masses in 1888 to 1889, which Engels called 'one of the greatest and most fruitful facts of this *fin de siècle*',[6] had demonstrated that the reawakened giant could indeed mould a new world according to its own best image. Morris goes out ahead, so to speak, and shows them this new world. The spirit of the Great Dock Strike, the new type of human relations (of *culture*) which it indicated, must have given added conviction to Morris's emphasis on the transformation of *the way people live together*.

The host of improbabilities in 'News from Nowhere' emerges more clearly with the passing of time, but so does the living core. A. L. Morton writes that the great polemical theme of the book is that 'Man has the power to transform his environment and in doing so, to transform himself.'[7] This is what the revolt of the non-skilled showed above all—even the skilled artisans began at last to 'transform themselves' as a result. It is a universal theme embodied universally in the book and giving it a universal appeal. The narration is the product of 'scientific deduction' (from the present), the imagination, and a great love of humanity, all acting in unison. This appeal is universal also because it activates our thinking, our imagination and our emotions universally. Not only the working class of Morris's own day could recognise in 'News from Nowhere' all that was best, dynamic and forward-pointing in themselves. Succeeding generations, travelling towards the goal through all the contradictions and setbacks, recognise this core of *anticipatory realism* ever more clearly. The inspirational, activating intent, present in all Morris's political writing, but often narrowed in its appeal, reaches its final consummation here. In contrast to its two predecessors it possesses *the power to convert*.

One of the activating aspects of the work's realism is the way it encouraged, and encourages, people to look more closely at times present for the elusive signs of times to come. Thus it has helped to develop that positive, analytical curiosity about the present in all its ramifications which is a *sine qua non* of an artistic approach to contemporary life that is both socialist and realist. Anyone intimately acquainted with Tressell's *The Ragged Trousered Philanthropists* will agree that that great socialist realist novel of the here-and-now would not have been the same without 'News from Nowhere', the one socialist national classic that preceded it.

By the end of 1890 *Commonweal* had fallen hopelessly into the hands of the anarchists. But *Justice*, the rival journal run by the Social Democratic Federation, presumed to tread where the great man had preferred not to. In 1888 it began serialising a sustained narrative prose fiction called 'A Working Class Tragedy' by H. J. Bramsbury. The novel ran from June 1888 to April 1889. Its episodic, picaresque form points to its being written expressly for serialisation, possibly from one week to the next. This means it was probably composed during the rising wave of new mass militancy which led up to the Great Dock Strike in August, four months after the serial had finished.

It is the hunted-man-who-returns type of picaresque tale, set in the present. Frank Wilson, a skilled mechanic, is framed and hounded because of his militancy. He flees to London from the provincial town in the south of England which is his home. In London the terrible experience of fighting for work at the docks, plus conversations with a socialist workmate, make him a socialist. He returns to his native town, incognito, to be near the local squire's daughter with whom he has fallen in love after rescuing her from distress in London. His efforts to set up a co-operative farm on the estate under her auspices are wrecked when she marries the son of the factory owner who has persecuted the hero. The latter is killed when he throws himself in front of a poacher's bullet aimed at the husband of his beloved.

As a whole this novel gives a thin and rather summary impression. Too much happens too quickly. Almost the only place where it dwells on detail is in describing miserable living conditions. Here it can well stand comparison with good naturalism. Similarity to the naturalists is also there in the high number of inevitable tragic fates, ending in death. William Morris was loath to describe such conditions because he could not as an artist *see in its own terms* the hidden and thwarted vitality which was there behind the degradation. Socialist writers like Bramsbury had no such qualms, but in a sense they justify Morris in themselves failing to get beyond naturalism at such points.

Yet, in its basic tendency 'A Working Class Tragedy' is a militantly anti-naturalist work. Far from narrowing the social scene down to a mere slice of life, it drives towards a new quality of social totality. With one exception, every significant aspect of life and character is encompassed—a differentiated portrait gallery of working-class and ruling-class types, the rural and the urban scene, legal and economic persecution, the misery of work and of unemployment, etc. In this way the author sets out to complete the image of capitalist society as an interlocking *system* of oppression, an image started but left incomplete by the best of the bourgeois realists. Bramsbury demonstrates clearly that oppression is total and systematic because it is *class* determined. His method is the extensive (picaresque) mode of Fielding rather than the intensive mode of Dickens. (In Tressell there will be a final synthesis of the extensive and intensive dimension.)

Anti-naturalist, too, is the way the 'jungle law' operating in the labour market of the docks is shown as something *unnatural* and not in terms of social Darwinism.

The handling of the hero also runs directly counter to naturalism. Far from being a passive victim of circumstance he develops, through contact with socialist theory combined with what he learns from experience, from a traditional Radical into a class-conscious socialist. So instead of knuckling under to the death-trap in true naturalist style, he comes to grasp the only way in which it can be smashed. In this general trend of his development Frank Wilson is the prototype of a whole line of proletarian heroes in twentieth-century socialist literature. (Tressell's hero is fully 'made' when the action begins.)

The hunted-man picaresque mode was one already favoured by the Chartists writing novels for press serialisation.[8] 'A Working Class Tragedy' is in the tradition. So much can be made to happen in this kind of narrative. Among other things this is an advantage when one lacks an aesthetically intensive relationship to one's basic material. It is one sign that Bramsbury, like almost all the writers closely associated with the socialist sects, was not yet sufficiently moved by that curiosity about the feel and texture of the life described, which is so vital to the realist.

The picaresque hero-on-the-run is an isolated, flitting type who has no time to really cog in to life. In choosing this set-up the author seems to have rather wrongheadedly limited his opportunities for social typicalisation. In fact it is possible that this choice of hero to a certain extent reflects the isolation and 'distance' of the socialists themselves. Be that as it may, one must avoid too prescriptive an approach here. Having isolated his hero in this way the author turns this to negative advantage. For instance: it is quite true, and a real impoverishment of the book, that the *collective personality* of the organised working class, with all its rebelliousness and solidarity, remains unportrayed (the key missing component in Bramsbury's totality); it is equally true that the traditional-type plot of personal intrigue, which involves members of the opposing classes in personal relationships, creates an image quite out of keeping with the impersonal nature of class relations, especially in modern monopoly capitalism (contrast Tressell here). But the point is, Bramsbury shows that in this very isolation lies the real working-class tragedy: 'Frank cursed the mischance that had precluded him from taking an active part in the movement.'[9] It is this isolation that leads him into the fatal partnership with the landowner in the attempt to set up a co-operative farm, through which he goes down to tragic defeat, his great potential squandered.

Implicit, then, is the recognition that the only way to avoid tragedy is to integrate oneself into the collective movement of the working class.[10] And so, despite the fact that there is precious little sign of the coming revolt in the sections of the book set in the docks, Bramsbury indicates that the way forward lies in that direction only.

Was Bramsbury's aesthetic relationship to concrete working-class reality still relatively thin and one-sided because he was writing just too soon to experience the uplift of the New Unionism? Hard as it was to recognise the potentially revolutionising dynamism of the rank and file before 1888-9, a few writers did penetrate to it, notably the socialist poet Francis Adams in some of his *Songs of the Army of the Night* (first published in 1887).[11] But Adams was a 'loner'. His ties with the London leadership of the Social Democratic Federation were very tenuous, as was their theoretical influence on him. The London-based SDF was hardly less sectarian and isolated than the Socialist League, despite their policy of getting involved in (preferably) local elections and their admittance of a possible role for the trade unions, if only they would stop confusing the issue by fighting for 'palliatives' and get down to their proper job of overthrowing capitalism.

Despite the real anger at the suffering of working folk felt by most members, the élitist policy emanating from the leader Hyndman and his circle resulted in crippling ambiguities on all questions relating to the real life and struggle of the workers. Thus, there was a strong tendency to 'wash one's hands of them' as a set of incorrigible dolts who refused to see at once the patent logic of the socialist propaganda. *They* were the real enemy: 'It is not the active worker in the cause nor the tools at his disposal [which are to blame], it is, and can only be, the material upon which the propagandist has to work.'[12] It was a pity one could not abolish them and replace them with a more amenable version of the working class.

What was the answer? 'The worse the condition of the people, the quicker they must recognise the need for a change, and since the crisis must come, let us rejoice at anything which tends to hasten its coming'.[13] Absolute impoverishment of the masses, then, increasing misery, was seen as the only really dynamic element driving towards radical social transformation. This was the only interesting and encouraging aspect of working-class life. Strikes in defence of living standards were therefore rather frowned upon, although given half-hearted support once they had 'broken out'.

Clearly this set of attitudes was hardly conducive to an all-sided narrative exploration of working-class life! There was no point of departure here for meeting Engels's contemporary demand that *realism* must also show 'The rebellious reaction of the working class against the oppressive medium which surrounds them, their attempts—convulsive, half-conscious or conscious—at recovering their status as human beings'.[14] All things considered, the wonder is that Bramsbury's novel achieved as much breadth and life as it did.

How did the workers' determined attempt at 'recovering their status as human beings' in 1888-9 modify this position? As far as the London-based SDF nucleus was concerned, not at all. With the exception of Engels the above quotations are all from the nineties. When the strike wave failed to precipitate a revolutionary situation *Justice* lost interest. By 1898 the *Social Democrat* was proclaiming 'The end of the New Unionism'.[15]

Did this mean that the new stage in the development of the revolutionary historical personality of the working class found no reflection in advances towards realism in socialist literature, especially in the analytical prose genres? Yes, there were signs of a new, more complex and more confident approach to contemporary working-class life. This expressed itself indirectly in the poetry and in the prose parables of the Leeds-Irishman Tom Maguire, who was in the thick of the union struggle. His pieces were mainly published in provincial papers in the north (*Labour Leader, Labour Champion, Factory Times*).[16] Much more directly it appears in the lively novels of *Lancashire* working-class life by Charles Allen Clarke. Here at last is that inexhaustible curiosity about the lives of ordinary working-class men *and* women that leads straight into Tressell. But both these writers were active in the industrial north, far away from Hyndman and his doctrinaire sectarians.

Justice and, from 1897, also the *Social Democrat* certainly went on publishing pieces of imaginative prose with relative regularity, though there was never again (in our period) such a sustained and fruitful attempt as 'A Working Class Tragedy'. The following remarks are based on a close study of two sample periods taken from *Justice* (1895 and 1896) and the *Social Democrat* (1897 and 1898).

As one might expect from the narrowness of their approach, all the imaginative prose pieces published in these central socialist press organs were very short in the wind. Attempts at series rather than serials were now the rule. There were series of an essayistic type, for instance by the above-quoted H. W. Hobart who wrote on various aspects and 'illusions' of daily working-class life and character such as 'Home', 'Work', 'Drink', 'Borrowing', 'Bank Holiday', 'Leisure', etc.[17] Hobart was only one of those who specialised in scoffing at what he calls the B.W. (British Workman). In tune with the 'increasing misery' theory John Tamlyn tells the latter 'You'll have to be lowered. You'll have to come down!!!'[18] One can understand how an average worker might think *Justice* was more against him than the *Daily Telegraph*. Of course, there was something here that leads into Tressell's satire on the 'ragged trousered philanthropists', but in the Hobart school it is unrelieved by Tressell's ability to present the 'habits and customs' of the working class as something contradictory, containing creative potential in an estranged form. Hobart reaches the depths of crass insensitivity around May Day 1895 when he jeers at the workers' traditional bank holiday behaviour and leisure activities— 'Leisure! The average British workman is as big a fool with his leisure as with everything else he has.'[19] This was around the same time as Allen Clarke was revelling in the vitality and inventiveness of the northern workers in their traditional holiday and leisure pursuits.[20]

Another type of series run by *Justice* at this time was short stories appearing under a common general heading indicating the direction to be taken. A series of this kind, written by 'Devilshoof' (Harry Quelch?), was published in 1895 and 1896, under the ominous title 'Creatures of Circumstance'. Pieces here included were 'The Agitator', 'The Self-Made Man', 'Orphans', 'A Gaol Bird', 'A Blackleg', etc.[21] Most of the titles indicate in themselves the 'increasing misery' tenor of the stories. In 1895 another series of a broadly similar nature was started (they ran partially parallel) called 'Types of the Day'. These were the work of 'Eugh Jay'. Despite their general depressive tendency they exhibit a real curiosity about circumstantial detail.[22] There is a hint of Tressell here.

In the sample years studied 'Eugh Jay's' paired stories 'Joe Buggins Learns the Fife' and 'Buggins Senior Joins the SDF'[23] are far and away the best of all the short stories. They are set in Birmingham (almost without exception the other stories printed are set in London).

Buggins senior, a gruff old cove who hasn't paid too much attention to his wild and motherless 'lad' Joe, comes home to a fiendish din. It's the 'lad' and some cronies playing the fife of all things. What's got into them? Joe mollifies and moves his Old 'Un with a competent rendering of the *Marseillaise* (old B. has joined the Socialists a short time before). The latter is less pleased however, when he hears the lads have joined the band of the Labour Church, a politically suspect organisation to the sectarian Buggins senior. An inconclusive argument ensues, but young Joe knows one thing—it'll be him and not his dad that'll be playing the fife in the united Labour Day procession.

The second story goes back to Pa Buggins's joining the SDF, and the roles are reversed. Having joined, he is so full of the milk of human kindness he decides to take an unprecedented step—he invites the incredulous Joe to a pie shop for a feed. Joe thinks he's sickening for something and asks what's up.

> 'I'm blowed if I know exactly, but I think it must be because I joined the Socialists to-day.
> 'I joined the Socialists! repeated Joe. 'You! Well, strike, that takes the cake. Here, old 'un, you'd better join the Socialists every day', etc.[24]

This is diametrically opposed both to the naturalist and the 'Hobart' spirit. There is complete aesthetic confidence in one's material here. We are shown ordinary working people, old and young, rising above their sordid environment in their daily lives and pastimes, capable of creative enjoyment. Because these stories achieve the status of art they are fine propaganda for joining the socialist movement. It is subtly put forward as a step which humanises, which brings out the best in you, which heightens your appreciation of the bodily and spiritual joys of living, which socialises you and brings people closer together.

There is a *realist's* interest here in the characters and their speech for their own sake. They are shown in their contradictoriness and development. At the same time the stories remain openly didactic. In fact drawing the moral becomes part of the fun. The author works confidently in the grand discursive manner of the all-knowing and manipulating creator. There is something of the Sterne of *Tristram Shandy* here in these modest stories (an 'Irish' element that did *not* find a place in Tressell). He enters into discussions of his own story with an assumed critical reader—a disarming distancing effect enabling him to 'sell' his moral while appearing to make fun of moralisers in a story within the story. (The author has interrupted his narrative just before Joe gets his feed in order to draw a moral-political lesson.)

'Is Joe ever going to get any dinner' [impatient reader]
'Certainly.'
But your impatience puts me in mind of a story told by old Batty the circus man. Hush, no profanity. I must tell you this. He had commissioned a recognised writer to write him a Christmas pantomime. The author put his whole soul into it, the fairy queen gave vent to moral sentiments of an austere intensity that would have qualified her for holding a leading position in the maw worm brigade of the London County Council. The comic man dealt with all the topics of the day with a stupendous ignorance and self-satisfied assurance that marked him out as fit, if not to be Prime Minister, at any rate to hold a high position in the Cabinet.
The pretty conceits of the heroine would (in the opinion of the author) have done credit to the Poet Laureate . . .
The effect was hardly satisfactory. Old Batty's face wore a bored nonchalant look; the bored air becoming heavier and heavier as the reader proceeded. Until at last, in the midst of one of the fairy queen's highest flights of virtue, he broke coarsely in with, 'Cut all that cackle and come to the horses.' And thou, thou unregenerate savage, would have me in the words of thy villain's slang, 'To cut all moral reflection and come to the grubbing stakes.'[25]

This is sophisticated sword-play in many directions at once! But perhaps a qualifying note to the Buggins stories is necessary. The basic process around which they are built is the *one* act recognised by the SDF as a valid one for a working man—joining their organisation.

The *Social Democrat*, started in 1897, also featured short stories—one in each monthly issue in its first years. Initially about half of these were definitely written by Harry Quelch, long-time editor of *Justice*. They never bear his name, but one can establish authorship through comparison with texts collected in a volume published in tribute to Quelch (*Literary Remains*).[26] Quelch was a self-educated worker who became one of the most respected leaders of the SDF. He was not without literary talent. He had a good ear for working-class speech and those pieces where he uses a character-narrator (such as 'your-average-working-man' or a policeman)[27] to distance, relativise or add conviction to the scenes and attitudes portrayed, still retain a certain vigour. However, on the whole, his plots, conflicts and approach are quite characteristic of the type of story favoured by the London-based socialist press of the nineties. (There is circumstantial evidence that several of the unsigned or pseudonymous pieces in both the *Social Democrat* and *Justice* which cannot be traced back to *Literary Remains* are also by Quelch.)

All the stories in the *Social Democrat* seem to be set in London, though the degree of specification is so slight that usually one simply assumes this. The atmosphere is dark and claustrophobic. As with the stories in *Justice* one gets the impression that the author is intent on discouraging the workers from taking militant action, showing it as leading only to disaster and tragedy. This is a period when, although the employers were on the counter-attack, the new spirit was spreading and beginning to affect even the traditional skilled sections. The 'new' men and women of the new movement badly needed all the support, constructive criticism and inspiration they could get. The stories in *Justice* and the *Social Democrat*, including Quelch's, failed to provide this new spirit with a means of realist self-contemplation.

There is no portrayal of mass initiatives in organisation (which could have provided the much-needed narrative backbone for sustained work). The only form in which the collective personality of the workers appears is as an object of mockery (*Justice* is the worse offender here). Instead we are given individual 'fates'—people driven into isolation, defeat and death by the machinations of individual capitalists (there is no sign of the growing dominance of 'faceless' monopoly). These capitalists are often old-type self-made men who were initially the friends and mates of the hounded worker. But the latter is equally thrust down by lack of solidarity and betrayal on the part of his workmates who turn on him after the defeat of strikes, strikes which they themselves had 'irresponsibly' instigated, which they had then asked him to lead, and which he had reluctantly led, out of a sense of solidarity. Women often feature as the worst offenders against gratitude and class loyalty. In a story like 'Companions in Misfortune' (three parts)[28] the line is that if you 'give a woman her head' the forces of official society will gang up with her and her 'legal rights' (!) to wring the man dry. This is so near the misogynist outpourings of Belfort Bax which mar the contemporary columns of the *Social Democrat* that one suspects he may actually have written this story (it is unsigned). Rank-and-file militancy of the kind that started the new unionism is depicted as a source of *dis*integration, the implication being that the workers should keep their heads down in face of the employers' counter-offensive. What this boils down to is a vulgarised naturalism in which the worker and his family are totally 'determined' by their alienated environment. In the few cases where the worker triumphs over circumstances it is through his becoming, by dint of ability, a capitalist himself (a socialist capitalist of course),[29] or through the support of his employer.[30]

Certainly, in these propaganda stories there is also something important that runs sharply counter to contemporary bourgeois English naturalism of the Gissing type— the attempt to show that the root of the misery lies not in man's inherent nature but in the inhuman system of capitalist exploitation. But even here the real enemy, as indicated above, is not kept firmly in the sights, and social typicality is so crudely and narrowly understood that the writers are continuously obliged to fall back on melodramatic 'extreme situations'. All this means that the actual fund of plots and situations is so circumscribed that cumulatively one gets the impression of merely reading variations on three or four basic stories. This makes the process of trying to establish possible authorship on the basis of analogy extremely problematic.

They were ineffective mass propaganda. But were they really aimed at a broad working-class readership? Both journals give a markedly inward-turning impression as a whole. The stories seem aimed mainly at bolstering up the Hyndman leadership's view of the working class and of 'significant' social tendencies. They are a mirror in which the SDF contemplates with satisfaction its own isolation from the wellsprings of proletarian life and culture, its frustration at the 'thanklessness' of the workers, the view that since the workers will not listen to them the only thing that will bring matters to a head is the 'iron law' of increasing misery. The typical story is, in this sense, a piece of self-justification, a comforter, a piece of wish-fulfilment. Increasing misery is the theme of themes.

Of course there is another side to all this. Many of these tales contain elements which later find a place in the realist synthesis of *The Ragged Trousered Philanthropists*—such as the satire on the delusions of the workers, the lonely, often thankless fight of the isolated socialist, the actual descending spiral of social misery under maturing imperialism, even the use of melodramatic episodes, etc. Tressell emerges partly out of this background.

Then again, there are also occasional stories—in which the working class does not figure—which are worth reading in themselves. There is, for instance, Dan Baxter's excellent little fable 'The New-Shilling' in *Justice*.[31] The story is related by a newly-minted shilling, aware of its own beauty, believing it will be used as a brooch, and flabbergasted to find itself used instead as a mere counter to keep the rich rich and the poor poor. Socialist writers tended to be good at parables and fables: these kept the unruly stuff of actual living at arm's length while profiting from the relatively whole and systematic grasp of the workings of capitalist production relations, which the socialists possessed.

On the whole, however, anyone seeking inspiration, critical analysis and sheer literary enjoyment in the columns of *Justice* or the *Social Democrat* would find it first and foremost in the precise analytical prose of Theodore Rothstein in his exemplary political and historical articles,[32] or in the Whitmanesque sweep and passion of R. B. Cunninghame Graham in one of his anti-colonial essays.[33]

Tendencies in narrative fiction 71

As far as imaginative prose from within the SDF was concerned, the situation at the turn of the century looked anything but promising. Yet five years later, Robert Tressell, a member of the SDF in the south-east of England, began work on our great socialist classic. In my essay in the predecessor to the present volume I tried to suggest some of the strategic developments that made this 'jump' possible.[34]

NOTES

1. *Commonweal*, 16 June 1888.
2. *Commonweal*, 25 August 1888.
3. 'The Pilgrims of Hope', in *Three Works by William Morris* (London and Berlin, 1968), p.168.
4. *ibid.*, p.178.
5. E. P. Thompson, *William Morris. Romantic to Revolutionary* (London, 1955), p.777.
6. *Marx and Engels on Britain* (Moscow, 1953), p.32.
7. In the *Morning Star*, 19 September 1968.
8. See Thomas Martin Wheeler, 'Sunshine and Shadow', *Northern Star* (1849-1850), and Ernest Jones, 'De Brassier; the history of a democratic movement', *Notes to the People* (1851-2).
9. 'A Working Class Tragedy', *Justice*, 2 February 1889.
10. The same theme is central to James Plunkett's *Strumpet City* (London, 1969).
11. See for instance 'In Trafalgar Square' and 'England in Egypt'.
12. H. W. Hobart, *Justice*, 7 September 1895.
13. William Sowdon, *Justice*, 25 May 1895.
14. Engels in his letter to Margaret Harkness ('John Law'), beginning of April 1888, in Marx-Engels, *Selected Correspondence* (Moscow, n.d.), p.479.
15. *Social Democrat*, March 1898.
16. Some of the best of these are collected in *Tom Maguire: a Remembrance* (Manchester, 1895).
17. *Justice*, 2 February, 9 February, 2 March, 9 March, 20 April, and 18 May 1895.
18. J. Tamlyn, *Justice*, 23 March 1895.

19. *Justice*, 18 May 1895.
20. See especially his *Lancashire Lasses and Lads*, published in 1906 (Manchester) but actually written ten years earlier. On Clarke see also chapter 8 by Paul Salveson.
21. *Justice*, 20 July, 3 August, 31 August, 30 November 1895; 11 April 1896.
22. See for instance 'The commercial hack', *Justice*, 23 November 1895.
23. *Justice*, 8 June, 6 July and 13 July 1895.
24. *Justice*, 13 July 1895.
25. ibid.
26. *Literary Remains* (London, 1914).
27. See 'Only—he was a socialist' and 'The dynamiter', *Social Democrat*, February and April 1897 respectively.
28. *Social Democrat*, September, October, November 1898.
29. See 'The rent of ability', *Social Democrat*, August 1898.
30. See 'The dynamiter', *Social Democrat*, April 1897.
31. *Justice*, 23 March 1895.
32. See for instance his 'Why is socialism in England at a discount?', *Social Democrat*, March and April 1898.
33. See 'Bloody niggers', *Social Democrat*, April 1897.
34. Jack Mitchell, 'Early harvest: three anti-capitalist novels published in 1914', in *The Socialist Novel in Britain. Towards the Recovery of a Tradition*, ed H. Gustav Klaus (Brighton, 1982).

· 4 ·

The strike novel in the 1890s

H. GUSTAV KLAUS

The strike fiction of the 1840s and 1850s has, under the rubric of 'industrial' or 'social (-problem)' novel, often been studied. Even a number of lesser works from the middle of the century, such as Camilla Toulmin's 'A Story of the Factories' or Fanny Mayne's *Jane Rutherford*, have recently found a sympathetic historian.[1] Scant attention has been paid, by contrast, to the strike novels of the end of the nineteenth century, just as the social fiction of this period has been generally neglected, except for an interest in the slum or Cockney novelists.[2]

One reason for this critical silence, and a major difference to the situation in early and mid-Victorian times, is no doubt the abstention of the leading novelists of the day from an engagement with the industrial scene in general and the strike issue in particular. Gissing was exceptional in his consistent grappling, in the 1880s, with the condition of the working class, but his proletarians are for the most part the casual poor of an industrially backward London, and he abandoned the treatment of working-class themes at precisely the moment when these downtrodden masses showed signs of awakening. Had he continued his imaginative investigation of London labour, or looked at the quite different working class of his native Yorkshire, Luke Ackroyd in *Thyrza* (1887) and John Hewett in *The Nether World* (1889) might have taken a different line of development, or found more confident and dignified successors. But this remains a matter for speculation.

Beyond mere conjecture there is meanwhile evidence of

various fictional representations of the theme of industrial conflict, and these narratives can claim at least as much interest as the works of Harriet Martineau or Charlotte Tonna who pioneered the treatment of the strike in English fiction in the early 1830s.[3] For some of the novels discussed below adopt, almost for the first time, an unequivocally working-class perspective in that they are written from a standpoint which is neither above nor outside that of the strikers portrayed. Given the archaic, almost pre-industrial character of the London economy, it is no surprise that the more militant and, at the same time, more rewarding of these novels should come from the industrial north rather than the metropolis.

Yet London led the way in other respects. It was here that the 'new unionism' of the low-paid and unskilled workers, who had hitherto been considered as unorganisable, celebrated its first triumphs, and from here the tide swept over to other parts of the country rousing the entire labour movement. In quick succession the matchgirls, the gas-workers and the dockers of the East End won major concessions from their employers, either through strikes or through the threat of action, aided in each case by prominent members of the new socialist groupings, which had likewise first taken root in London.

No labour struggle of these turbulent years captured the public mind so absorbingly as the great Dock Strike in the summer of 1889. That the waterside workers, who were generally regarded as synonymous with the helpless and demoralised 'residuum', should have the courage to challenge, hold out against and finally claim a sweeping victory over their bosses—all in a spirit of perfect order and discipline—was greeted enthusiastically not only by the labour movement but by large sections of the middle classes. Naturally the bourgeoisie had different motives for seeing the strike as a positive achievement. As two contemporary commentators put it: 'The effect of the organisation of dock labour—as of all classes of labour—will be to squeeze out the residium. The loafer, the cadger, the failure in the industrial race . . . will be no gainers by the change.'[4] Trade-union organisation is valued here as a more effective instrument for the exertion of social control.

This sigh of relief from the middle classes is also audible in a novel by Emma Leslie, *The Seed She Sowed: A Tale of the Great Dock Strike* (1891), particularly when contrasted with one of her earlier works. In *How the Strike Began: A Story for Girls* (1888) a young girl in the domestic service of a cotton master is shown to be unwittingly contributing to the outbreak of a strike through her loose tongue. If Leslie's primary aim is to warn her juvenile readers of becoming a 'village gossip', she also seizes the opportunity to instil in them a distrust of strikes as a suitable means of solving industrial conflict. For though she is careful to share out the blame for what appears less a clash of antagonistic interests than a breakdown of mutual understanding on both sides, it would be difficult for an unguarded reader to resist the conclusion that strike action can only bring mischief.

Like the earlier work, *The Seed She Sowed* is written with a specific audience and an overtly didactic purpose in mind. Again we find a young working-class girl at the centre of the story. But there are also important differences. First, the cast and topography are now entirely working-class, whereas the former tale shifted not only between the factory owner's mansion and the working-class home but correspondingly revealed a narrator anxious to balance her sympathies between Capital and Labour. Second, Leslie fully endorses the demand for 'the full round orb of the docker's tanner',[5] whereas in *How the Strike Began* she expected the dye-factory workers to share their employer's losses in times of bad trade by consenting to wage reductions.

Three socially graded working-class families are depicted in *The Seed She Sowed*. Among these the Chaplins represent the once respectable section of the proletariat, which has become, under the conditions prevailing on the waterfront, increasingly derelict and depressed. Mr Chaplin is of visibly poor constitution and hence seldom picked out any more for a job. His wife, therefore, has to make up for the irregular income of the main breadwinner by taking on all kinds of domestic work. The fate of the

Chaplins illustrates the plight of the London dockers. In 1889 one of them was quoted as saying: 'Only a dock rat, that's what I've been called ever since I lost my place, and became a docker.'⁶ Chaplin's words reiterate this loss of self-respect: 'Treat a man like a dog and you'll only get dog's work out of him.'⁷ His growing bitterness in face of the casual nature of the work, the hideous system of the 'call-on', the short duration of an engagement and the starvation pay are all related with considerable sympathy. Were it not for the good influence of Winnie, their alert and unselfish daughter, the family would be doomed.

A step below the Chaplins, and fast approaching the status of *lumpenproletariat*, are Mr Brown and his daughter Annie: the father given to drink and generally of a vulgar and disorderly character; the girl good-natured but hot-tempered. On one occasion, when refused a respite from the demands for the rent, she flings a glass of beer at the landlord, for which she is promptly arrested and imprisoned.

At the upper end of the social scale we have the landlord's family. Rutter, once an ordinary docker himself, has, since his appointment as a foreman and subsequent rise to wealth, become the most hated man in the neighbourhood because of his intransigence over the rent.

Winnie's exemplary deed consists in presenting Annie, after the latter's release from prison, with a chance to start a new life in the country. This act soon bears fruit: Annie finds work in a rural pickle factory; and the prospect opening up to his daughter even reforms Brown, who now turns into a model strike leader, sober, disciplined and moderate. To crown it all, Annie repays the Chaplins by informing them of a vacant carpenter's post in her factory so that the worn-out docker can return to his former trade.

This conclusion echoes the contemporary discussions about the resettlement of the urban poor in rural areas. Though the docker's 'tanner' had been won, Leslie sees no future for the demoralised underemployed in the city. As a general remedy for chronic poverty, her proposal is about as helpful as the emigration schemes to the colonies earlier in the century—indeed there was talk of 'labour colonies' in

Britain in the 1880s.[8] But it provides Leslie with a fictional resolution, as emigration had furnished her mid-century predecessors with an escape route for their embattled characters.[9] Both devices amount to an implicit critique, not fully acknowledged in its consequences, of the inadequacies of the existing social order.

Leslie's immediate concern was, of course, to convey her simple-hearted philosophy that a beneficent attitude produces the most fruitful results. She demonstrates this on a personal level and expresses the hope that somehow the principle will also work in the social and economic sphere. But the trouble is that the two planes of action remain unconnected. The docks never enter her picture directly, and the whole Winnie–Annie plot with its happy end for the Chaplins is in fact conceivable independently of the strike issue. In other words, the Dock Strike only provides the background for the story, but is not its central theme.

One remarkable aspect of *The Seed She Sowed* is the lack of expiation for the death of Rutter, who has been found drowned in the dock. Though it is not stated explicitly that he met a violent death, there are strong hints of such a possibility. The mid-century novelists would not have missed the chance to track down the culprit and bring him to repent, while laying the blame at the door of the 'combinations' or outside agitators. It speaks volumes for the author's sympathetic treatment of the strikers that she does not follow this track. She still preaches the familiar virtues of moderation, endurance and self-denial, but instead of disarming and discrediting the strikers they are used to reassure and morally strengthen their wives and daughters:

> In this way women like Mrs. Chaplin and weak girls like Winnie saved London from riot and bloodshed, and gained for themselves a name of imperishable honour, setting the whole world an example of patient endurance and the divine might of doing the duty that lay nearest to them.[10]

It is a vast claim but entirely consistent with the domestic focus of the tale.

Leslie's change of mind in such a short span of time is only explicable against the background of the upsurge of the 'new unionism' and its initially favourable reception by a significant part of middle-class opinion. Our next novel registers, among other things, the particular impact made on this public by Cardinal Manning's decisive intervention in the Dock Strike.

William Oakhurst's *The Universal Strike of 1899* (1891) draws its inspiration not only from the most dramatic labour conflict of the period, but also from the founding of the Second International in 1889. It considers the effects of a strike launched on a worldwide scale by the 'International Working Men's Society'.[11] Projected into the near future, it combines the narrative situation of a Utopia with the descriptive style of a reportage, but does not finally commit itself to either of these forms.

An intrusive narrator, who purports to be writing in 1909, is looking back at the stupendous seven days that shook the world in 1899. What fascinates and disturbs him (and the author alike) is the potential power wielded by the Paris-based 'Board' of the International. After secret deliberations this body issues the call for a simultaneous strike of the workers of all industrialised nations. The action immediately succeeds in paralysing Britain's economy, while provoking alarm and near-panic accompanied by occasional outbreaks of violence among the population. The anarchy prevailing on the first day is, however, checked by the establishment of a force of volunteers, recruited mainly from the middle class, who patrol the Clubland of the metropolis. These 'lovers of order' recall the 'Friends of Order' in William Morris's general strike and civil war chapter from *News from Nowhere*, of which there is more than one echo in *The Universal Strike of 1899*, and foreshadow the real historical Organisation for the Maintenance of Supplies in the General Strike of 1926. Incoming reports from Germany, France and Italy suggest similar, if more violent confrontations between the two sides; Russia is cut off.

The scenes of lawlessness and mob violence described here no longer reflect, of course, the atmosphere of the Dock Strike but reenact the traumatic experience of propertied London during the Trafalgar Square Riot of February 1886:

> London was an abomination of desolation, and there I was in the midst of it, cut off from all I cared about—without one atom of feeling in common with those around me, the noise of whose howling was occasionally varied by that of broken glass and the laughter that followed.[12]

That the disorderly elements 'around me', who have invaded the West End, include the strikers as well as 'the dregs of crime' corresponds to the undifferentiated view of the London proletariat prevalent among middle-class observers in the mid-1880s. In these years, as Gareth Stedman Jones has noted, 'propertied London came to regard the residuum as virtually co-extensive with the workforce in casualised industries, and the East End as an almost unalloyed centre of degeneration'.[13] Only as a result of the orderly and peaceful spectacle provided by the daily processions of the striking dockers in the City of London did more perceptive observers draw a line between the respectable working class and the casual poor.

Oakhurst, who writes in the aftermath of the strike, generally adheres to the latter view; the threat to civilisation has shifted in his novel, as will be seen, from the barbarians of the East End to a different degenerate race. But when the author relives the horror of real or imagined exposure to the 'scum' his tone becomes shrill with alarm and vindictiveness. His narrator cannot conceal the 'fiendish delight' he felt after he 'knocked one [aggressor] over at once with my stick and gave the other a merciless thrashing with my fists'.[14] The vicious sadism articulated in such sentences is the complement of the deep-seated fears noted above.

The 'universal' strike then takes an unexpected turn as hungry and freezing crowds implore their leaders to call it off. But for Richard King, the 'General Secretary of the

British Section of the International Working Men's Society', it is a matter of honour to stick to the decision of the Central 'Board'. Hurrying from one meeting to another, exhorting the men to stay firm, he eventually suffers a breakdown, and his death from exhaustion is accelerated by a noble refusal to eat more than the starving rank and file. Dying he quotes Browning's 'Pisgah-Sights':

> Over the ball of it,
>   Peering and prying,
> How I see all of it,
>   Life there outlying!
>
> Roughness and smoothness,
>   Shine and defilement,
> Grace and uncouthness:
>   One reconcilement—[15]

The idealised portrait of the working-class leader is another instance of the altered approach of middle-class novelists at the end of the century to the theme of industrial conflict. Once a ruthless demagogue or impostor, he now appears as the embodiment of integrity and self-abnegation. Similarly with the unions: if there is still something dangerous about them, it is their unfortunate international links, which are blamed for the unnecessary prolongation of the strike. What is still upheld, however, as the Browning quotation demonstrates, is the ideal of class reconciliation. And it remains to a clergyman, the 'Canon of St. Paul's Cathedral', to end the deadlock and bring about a peaceful settlement of the dispute in a truly Christian spirit.

The concern for national security is given added weight in a chapter which has no real bearing on the course of the strike but is clearly added as a warning. The day after the return to work the Russian fleet is suddenly sighted in the mouth of the Thames. The Tsar, it emerges, having quickly dealt with his subservient subjects, is now trying to profit from the situation. Recognising, however, a nation no longer defenceless, the warships swiftly clap on all sail and retreat. Had the strike entered its second week, as originally planned, 'the calamity that might have befallen Europe—and the world—surpasses imagination'.[16] This clever construction not only validates the Canon's intervention but at the same time serves to throw doubt on one of the foremost principles of the International, namely that 'Men must regard themselves as workers first, as Frenchman, Germans, Italians, English, after.'[17]

So obsessed is Oakhurst with his fears of the International that he overlooks, or chooses to ignore, the wild improbability at the heart of his narrative: how can one plan a strike of this dimension in secrecy and yet expect millions across the world to follow it? But the conspiratorial tactics imputed to the International are very much part of the author's alarmist attitude.

To the very end his view of the labour movement remains deeply ambivalent. On the one hand, he insists that a general strike is a terrible expedient which had better be buried for ever. On the other hand, 'I am inclined to think that life has been made appreciably easier by that awful week of 1899.'[18] Among the remarkable results of the strike he lists: a decline of abject poverty, a check to millionaires and monopolies, greatly improved industrial relations (watched over by arbitration boards with an equal representation of capital and labour) and, on the moral side, a lesson of mutual forbearance.

The two works discussed so far, though obviously inspired by the trade-union explosion of the late 1880s are not based on first-hand experience of an actual strike. For a much more faithful representation of an industrial conflict we have to wait until the appearance of Allen Clarke's *The Knobstick: A Story of Love and Labour* (1893). The title of this work immediately conveys two of its essential characteristics: a rootedness in a regional class culture, and a thoroughgoing identification with the labour movement. 'Knobstick' was a Lancashire term for what was elsewhere called a blackleg. Only someone writing from within the community portrayed in this novel could have used such a term as a matter of course. Charles Allen Clarke (1863-1935) was born into a large family of cotton-mill workers, and though he himself left the mill at the age of fourteen to become first a pupil teacher, then a journalist, editor and writer, he never lost touch with his background.[19]

The distinguishing mark of Clarke's style is his effective use of local traditions and habits, and an effortless handling of the Lancashire dialect, often coupled with a down-to-earth and at times subversive brand of humour. Take this dialogue from the chapter 'A Lancashire Funeral':

> 'It's a bloomin cowd day', said the driver of the hearse, blowing his hands and holding them close to his rough red nose.
> 'It's a sneezer', returned the driver of the nearest mourning coach, 'it's nearly as cowd as a hepitaph. Is this affair a teetotal funeral?'
> 'I hopes not', said the hearse man, 'for if it is we'st be frozen into coffins.'
> 'Ay', rejoined the other, 'it's time enoof to be teetotal when yo're a corpse. But for 't forestall bein a corpse afore yore time, keep takkin summit warm. Warmth is life, and cowd is deeth. I wish they'd bring summat t' sup—a nice hot glass of whiskey.'
> 'Ay, it's time they were shapin. I feel as if I'd geet a hiceberg on my stomach, and a snow-storm dancin in my bowels.'[20]

Earthly wisdom also hampers the progress of the Methodist preacher Twillman. When, after ranting in one of the foulest districts in the town and despairing at the scant response, he closes a fervent tirade with the words 'Oh, where will you spend eternity, my friends?', a half-drunken voice answers him: 'We corn't spend it in a worse place than this' (p.91).

Add the 'Lancashire Wedding' to the 'Lancashire Funeral', the figure of the tramp to that of the street preacher, the early morning round of the 'knocker-up' to the presence of the Irish, the dire poverty in the slums to the Whitsun seaside excursion, and a mosaic of Lancashire working-class life in the late nineteenth century takes shape, peopled not by downtrodden masses but by a living and multi-faceted community. To the spinners and engineers, who were among Clarke's first readers, these were all familiar sights and occurrences. But in presenting these things in a new light or humorous guise, Clarke not only retained the interest of his readers but offered them fresh insights into their lives. This was possible because he 'never pandered to some lowest common denominator or insulted people's intelligence'.[21]

A case in point is his demonstration of how the strikers are doubly tricked by the Municipality of Spindleton. The damage caused during an anti-blackleg riot has to be paid

> 'out of the rates, so I hear,' said Belton, 'and that's what galls the men. They've to pay for the keep of these extra police and soldiers, and pay for the damage done to property out of their own pockets. That is wormwood to them; to have police and soldiers brought here to keep them down and protect their foes, the knobsticks, and then pay for it all out of their own pockets; that's where the rub comes in' (p.172)

In essence this argument prefigures the mordant attack on the Forty Thieves of the Mugsborough Council in *The Ragged Trousered Philanthropists*. But Clarke anticipates Tressell, with whom he shares his Irish origins, in more ways than one. Other common features include the satirical naming of the capitalists, the irony heaped on the representative of organised religion and the exemption of the socialist from idiomatic speech. Belton is, of course, a Londoner, but he does not speak Cockney either. Rather, as in a host of working-class novels to follow, his greater (self-) erudition and political awareness are seen to necessitate the use of Standard English as well as a solemn outlook. Both traits mark him off from Banks, the local trade-union leader.

As engineers, Belton and Banks are involved in their union's effort to redress a wage cut imposed during a trade depression. The resulting strike is the culminating point of the novel, which now gains substance from lively scenes of picket lines, demonstrations, assaults on blacklegs, clashes with police and the perversion of the law in the hands of the town magistrates. A real achievement is the centrally placed chapter 'The Great Strike Riot', which relates the 'welcome' reserved by the population for the knobsticks.

Though Clarke occasionally still uses the word 'mob' here, he effectively breaks with the abstract notion of a soulless rabble driven by criminal instincts, in depicting a body of real men, women and children engaged in a desperate common effort, to hold up the blackleg convoy. Throughout the assault on the bus and the counter-attack of the police, the adopted point of view is that of the pickets and their supporters.

An incident during the savage police charge, in which a child receives a fatal truncheon blow on the forehead, is also structurally important in that it links up with an earlier scene. When Belton had first arrived in Spindleton as a destitute tramp with a motherless child on his arms, he had been helped and cheered up on the wayside by a group of labourers. Now the roles are reversed: Belton carries the dying child into the wretched hovel of the Irish labourer, the father having been arrested after dragging the bludgeoning policeman off his horse. In this and other ways, as Mary Ashraf has shown, the idea of practical working-class solidarity is woven into the text.[22]

A weakness in the treatment of the strike, however, is the failure to lay bare its origins and illuminate the motivations of the men behind it. As it is, the strike comes almost out of the blue, casually introduced through a remark of Banks's at home: 'We're goin to strike, Jane' (p.71). When the idea is first mooted, Belton and Banks appear even set against it, though the reasons for their caution are not clear either. Nor is the progress or outcome of the strike, which is shown to have lasted for several months, set forth in any detail.

Another problem is the author's growing preoccupation with the intricacies of the plot, so that what had started as a social drama eventually gravitates towards melodrama and romance (as the subtitle suggests). Clarke had obviously intended to connect the two strands through the figure of the knobstick, Rugden, who is at the same time the seducer of Belton's wife. But the two interlocking love triangles command too much attention in themselves, and the only interesting side-aspect here is that the author associates depravity with brutal male chauvinism. This is true not only of a miscreant such as Rugden but also of his fellow knobsticks, who, when hearing the story of how he treated Belton's wife, 'burst into loud laughter. Not one touch of sympathy for the woman. They regarded the whole tragedy as a screaming farce' (p.187).

The thoroughly negative portrayal of the strike-breakers is no doubt a reflection of the bitterness and anger aroused by their recruitment *en masse* from outside the town. But Clarke takes care to let his two most advanced-thinking characters assume a more understanding position: 'They may have left starvin wives and childer awhum, an may be decent enough, but poverty makes dastards of many good souls', remarks Banks. And Belton adds: 'As long as I shall live I shall always be on the side of the unfortunate, be they knobsticks or strikers. Both are to be pitied, and it's our accursed social system that's at the bottom of all the mischief, and that sets man against man' (pp.151-2).

Only an active Socialist could tackle this difficult subject so confidently and intelligently in the nineties, avoiding both the hysterical fear of 'mob' violence still rampant in *The Universal Strike of 1899* and the pitfalls of a fatalistic naturalism in the depiction of a poverty-stricken community. Clarke had become a member of the SDF in 1887, during the strike in his home town of Bolton that provided him with the material for *The Knobstick*. Probably still in the year of the book's publication he joined the newly-founded ILP, and in 1900 the two parties were to nominate him as joint candidate for the general election.

On the other hand, Clarke's socialism did not prevent him from occasionally wading deep into sentimentality and mysticism. The love-scenes of *The Knobstick* are difficult to stomach today. And an even greater impediment to a modern reception of the novel are the mystical bonds, based on a belief in spiritualism, that he establishes towards the end between some of the characters. His great *forte* remained the humorous sketch, and it is no coincidence that he is better remembered for the countless dialect pieces that he published under the pseudonym of Teddy Ashton. Yet when all is said and done *The Knobstick* remains a turning point in the history of English strike fiction, and a contribution to working-class and socialist literature that no critical reassessment of the period can afford to overlook.

Like Clarke, W. E. Tirebuck (1854-1900) was attracted by the ethical socialism of the early ILP. He was, in fact, one of the contributors to the symposium *The New Party*, published in 1894 with essays by Robert Blatchford, Keir Hardie, Grant Allen and others. In his statement, 'On the verge of change', Tirebuck asserts the dignity and social value of work:

> Life depends upon Labour. That law alone elevates all necessary labour, however rough, however hard, above degradation. If it is no degradation to eat bread, it is no degradation to prepare the ground, and sow the seed, and reap the harvest . . . If it is no degradation to walk through clean streets, it is no degradation to brush them.[23]

From an emphasis on the primal necessity of labour Tirebuck goes on to proclaim the 'irrevocable inter-dependence of one kind of labour upon another'. By implication there is then no basic difference of value between manual and mental work. None of these propositions is exactly new, but in the face of constant denials of them, both theoretically and practically, Tirebuck felt that these simple truths needed hammering home through a joint effort of 'the priest, the politician, the poet, the scientist, and the artist'.[24]

Miss Grace of All Souls' (1895) is the poet's contribution to this end. It is on the basis of love and a mutual recognition of the principle that 'all necessary labour is co-equal'[25] that Grace Waide, a vicar's daughter, and Sam Ockleshaw, a miners' leader, enter a marriage of perfect understanding at the end of the novel. And their relationship is unlikely to end in the deadlock reached by the Morels in Lawrence's *Sons and Lovers*. Grace has proved during the 'Coal War' that she has freed herself from the shackles of a bourgeois upbringing. She has taken an unequivocal stand on the miners' side, alleviating their hardship wherever she could and pleading their case before her unimpressed father and the mine-owners themselves, only to meet flat refusal and mild ridicule. 'Sentiment isn't business' (p.232), old Mr Brookster, the local coal magnate, reminds her as he gloats over the prospect of outwitting his competitors by means of this, to him not entirely unwelcome, industrial conflict. His son Harry, an MP, meanwhile exhibits an even uglier face of capitalism when told of some disturbances in the neighbourhood: 'I'm not afraid of the beastly fellows. By Jove, but they shall suffer for this. They'll be taught to—howl. They mean riots, do they? Dawbairn can soon get a few redcoats down; that will gallop them in their senses' (p.226).

In turning a cold shoulder to the approaches of Harry Brookster and marrying beneath her station, Grace wins the respect of the working people and baffles her own class. Not even the one other middle-class person who has sympathised with the miners can make sense of this choice. Mr Rew, her father's successor in the vicarage of All Souls, exemplifies the gap between compassionate feeling and practised social equality that Grace has closed. More doubts are cast on the future role of the newly appointed vicar when one bears in mind that in his early days Grace's father, the Reverend Egerton Waide, had also been 'on the side of the workers, the doers, the poor, the oppressed' (p.56), before he degenerated into a hypocrite and lackey of the ruling class, publicly preaching moderation to the miners, while inwardly fearing for his coal shares.

The picture of the industrial bourgeoisie and its auxiliary forces—a distorting press, a corrupt church, an oppressive military—is essential to Tirebuck's argument accounting as it does for Grace's final desertion of her class. But the chief interest of the novel lies in its contrasting re-creation of a mining community in time of strife.

It is with a view of a miner's home that *Miss Grace* opens (and closes). We see the inmates of the cottage, a three-generation family of miners, but we perceive them immediately as part of their neighbourhood as we catch a glimpse of Brookster's Yard, the miners' row, through the open cottage door. And through the window, illuminated only for the fragment of a second by a flash of lightning, we see something else: the pit where Sam Ockleshaw is on night shift; and, in another instant, Beckerton Old Hall, the Brooksters' Estate. From the outset we are thus made aware of the two dominating influences in the life of a mining community, stretching right to the collier's hearth: the relations of ownership and dependency, further underlined by the name of the miners' row and some scathing remarks of Ned Ockleshaw about the man who 'what they call "owns" coal' (p.3); and the pit itself with its harsh and dangerous work, epitomised in the final scene of the first chapter when the injured Sam is carried home under the eyes of the neighbours.

Tirebuck's presentation of the mining village combines typicality with graphic detail. 'Beckerton was another version of Barnsley; Barnsley another version of St. Helen's and Wigan. St. Helen's and Wigan had counterparts in the Wrexhams and Molds of North Wales; and North Wales had fighting counterparts in Gloucester and Warwick' (p.195). All these colliery districts belong to the Miners' Federation and are thus hit by the sixteen-week lock-out of 1893, which originated in the mine-owners' attempt to reduce the rates of wages by 25 per cent. Beckerton could be anywhere, but through the use of a specific dialect and the incorporation into the plot of the Featherstone incident, in which troops opened fire on the strikers, it is clearly located in Yorkshire.

The characterisation of the miners displays a similar combination of the representative and the individualised. For Grandfather Dan Ockleshaw, who has lived a quiet life governed by religious feelings and modest wishes, the present grim determination of the miners not to give in to the coal-owners' demand (later reduced in reality, though not in the novel, to 15 per cent) is presumptuous. 'There'll be mesters for men an' minds for muscles till doomsday!' (p.154) is his firm belief. Dan's attitude is contrasted with the militant spirit of his son Ned, whose fits of rage against ignominious social inequalities constantly lead him into trouble and eventually cost him his life. The limitations of this unerring, but also unreflecting class consciousness are indicated by Ned's habit of seeing the whole conflict in personal terms, as a private feud between a clearly identifiable capitalist (Brookster) and an equally tangible group of workmen like himself. Finally, there is the youngest Ockleshaw, Sam, a working-class intellectual (whose early diet has included Cobbett's *Grammar*) with a sensitive nature and unfailing patience, fully dedicated to the cause of the miners and yet endowed, like Belton in *The Knobstick*, with a dim vision of socialism beyond the immediate struggle:

> 'I'm not after money *as* money, or we would be no better than those who in my opinion sin agen us, for it; but money means food, furniture, clothes; and these mean comfort; and comfort means better conditions of body and mind; and body and mind means morals. I've thought, and thought, and *thought*— and always come back to that.' (p.165)

The attitudes of these three men can be taken to represent the historical march of the miners from subordination via militancy to socialism, but they also point to the divisions still existing within the contemporary mining population, temporarily forged together in a struggle for a great principle, a guaranteed living wage irrespective of profits.

These differences of outlook notwithstanding, we find, again as in Clarke,[26] several examples of unceremonious neighbourly help and active solidarity, suggestive of widely shared class values: when a miner is killed in a flooded pit and his wife as a consequence suffers a breakdown, the Ockleshaws look after their four children; when food parcels arrive in Brookster's Yard, Ned wastes no time in sharing his ration with his famished fellow-colliers. Traces of this class solidarity even survive in ex-miners such as Dick Ockleshaw, Sam's brother, now a soldier in the troops to be deployed in the coalfields, who prefers to go into hiding and to serve a month's hard labour for it rather than turn 'agen my owd mates' (p.284).[27]

Standing midway between Zola's *Germinal* (1885) and Lawrence's earliest short stories on mining life (1911), *Miss Grace* contains the first closely observed and sympathetic view of a mining community in English fiction.²⁸ And this community, active and resourceful, suffering and yet stubbornly resisting, is the real protagonist of the novel, its collective hero. Not only the immorality of her own class but also the living humanity embodied by this community are at the root of Grace's conversion to the working-class cause.

One central aspect of the life of a mining community is not confronted squarely by Tirebuck: the work process underground. That this omission does not result from an unconscious neglect of the point of production is obvious from the author's programmatic statement quoted above, from the hazardous presence of the mine in the background of the story, and from a passage which shows the pit-bank girls at work. But Tirebuck had no first-hand knowledge of the various stages of coal-getting and made no pretence of covering up this lacuna.

For Zola, the minutely detailed descriptions of the pit, which appears at the same time as a voracious monster (le 'Voreux'), of the physical exertion involved in extracting and transporting the coal below ground, and of the human relations bred in this 'bestial' atmosphere, formed a major part of his project. In Tirebuck, or Lawrence, this 'underworld', though not its various consequences, is simply absent.²⁹

An account of the working conditions underground can, however, be found in another novel dealing with the lockout of 1893—Alfred H. Fletcher's *Lost in the Mine. A Tale of the Great Coal Strike* (1895). The author uses one of the two devices that will reappear time and again in twentieth-century mining fiction: the initiation into work of an outsider, a non-miner (as in Zola), through whose unaccustomed eyes we penetrate the obscurity of the mine:³⁰

> Lights twinkled in every direction. Corves full of various kinds of coal came swinging along tiny sets of rails to the cage, where they were rapidly lifted aloft. There was a whizzing sensation in the air, and a giddiness in his brain as he stood uneasily upon his legs . . . The gloom was intense, and Jack

had great difficulty in following his guide. The ground seemed to oscillate under his feet, and to be as unstable as the surface of the sea during a stiff breeze. His confusion was 'worse confounded' because of the strangeness of his surroundings and the difficulty he experienced with his organs of vision.[31]

There can be little doubt that Fletcher, who appears to have been a Sheffield journalist, had observed pit-work and pit-villages from close quarters. His description of Mudtown, though it bears some fleeting resemblances to Dickens's uniform view of an industrial agglomeration in *Hard Times*, emphatically points to the 'many differences' among the miners and their families 'on close acquaintance' (p.52).

But despite close observation the narration always retains a sense of distance from its subject. It is not only that the (middle-class) reader is addressed in contorted, if well-meant explanations of the hazards of pit work. The external representation of the world of the miners is also strengthened through the weaving of the social and political content of the story into a curious tapestry of popular fictional forms ranging from mystery and melodrama to romance. Jack Harland, the new collier, is none other than the actual mine-owner, a gentleman compelled to take cover because he is unjustly suspected of having assassinated his father—an act in reality perpetrated by the mine-manager, who is also a Harland. With such a long-winded opening in the higher sphere of the gentry, it takes the author some sixty pages to arrive at the aforementioned description of the colliery town, and to descend at last into the depths of the mine.

In relating the origins and early progress of the strike Fletcher assumes at first a strictly neutral tone. He says of both sides in the industrial arena that 'the weapons with which they decided to fight were eminently fair and eminently British' (p.89). But then he introduces a presumably un-British element, a subversive organisation deceptively christened The Guild of Progress. Commanded by the immensely talented and idealistic, but also hopelessly fanatical, even 'Satanic', Dan Darrell, another gentleman-turned-miner in search of a new identity (after the killing of his wife's lover), the Guild's ultimate aim is the overthrow of the existing social order. In one of several impassioned speeches Darrell addresses his followers thus:

> 'Awaken from your lethargy, men of Yorkshire! You are strong in number, and think that because of this your growl will suffice to subdue your tyrants instead of your deadly bite. Passive resistance leads to enslavement. 'Tis active rebellion, the outcome of indignation, which points the way to freedom . . .
>
> You may have to endure hardship, bodily pain, imprisonment, but fight on. Stab the coward Capital with the sword of the oppressed, and hew your way to victory over the corpse of a dishonoured past.' (p. 167)

If there ever was a sizeable body of revolutionaries at work attempting to turn the lock-out into a full-scale confrontation with state power,[32] it is doubtful that they would have been spurred on, in 1893, by this kind of Shelleyan rhetoric. But verisimilitude is not one of Fletcher's concerns. Aesthetic and structural considerations remain firmly subordinated in his novel to a 'demonstration' that whatever scenes of violence there were during the stoppage were the deeds of an initially marginal, but, as the situation deteriorated, increasingly dangerous band of political desperadoes. Hence the Guild is even blamed for having provoked the real historical Featherstone incident in which two men were killed and sixteen wounded when troops opened fire—an interpretation not only at odds with the true course of events,[33] but also diametrically opposed to Tirebuck's treatment of them.

Quite plainly then, where Clarke and Tirebuck had depicted a community in united action against employers, blacklegs and troops, Fletcher separates out the more intransigent of the strikers. He whitewashes the main body of the miners and their union only to discredit the pursuit of more far-reaching goals. There is, indeed, a systematic confusion of working-class militancy with sabotage, of the struggle for a political takeover with the 'madness for power' (p. 220).[34] On a political level, this strategy continues the assessment made of the Dock Strike by the social explorers; only instead of 'the loafer, the cadger, the failure in the industrial race',[35] whom they were anxious to see squeezed out, it is now the 'extremist' (p.219), the 'Anarchist' (p.220), the 'agitator' (p.232), whose hold on the working class must be checked and eliminated.

Consequently, in *Lost in the Mine* the insurrectionary force has to be wiped out before 'the country breathed again more freely' (p.233). Darrell is killed by a bullet arriving mysteriously out of the dark, and in another echo of *Hard Times*, he is described as saying, as he dies: 'This is all—a mistake. But it is my Destiny!' (p.232), his last wish being that he be buried in a disused mine shaft. The novel's title can thus be taken to refer, if unintentionally, not only to the younger Harland's temporary submergence among the miners, but also to the disappearance from the industrial battlefield of the Anarchist.

Once this obstacle to an undivided sympathy for the miner's cause has been removed, Fletcher can record with deeply-felt compassion the distress of the starving, turnip-fed, typhoid-ridden mining families, whose morale nevertheless remains unbroken. Of course, the principal pole of identification for the reader remains the incognito figure of Jack Harland, whose constitution breaks first under the strain of deprivation and suffering. Yet in his unflagging support for the strike Jack is no exception to the rest of the miners. As one determined collier says: 'Aw doan't deny', . . . 'that sum on us will bite t'dust and goa under, but t'great army o' t' workmen will march on to victory' (p.242). As if he felt he had gone too far in his sympathetic treatment of the main body of the strikers, and in singling out two members of the upper middle class as villains of the story, Fletcher apologised, in his Preface, for the negative portrayal of the mine-manager, while predictably making no such amends for the blackening of the representative of the Guild of Progress.[36]

This survey of strike fiction during the first half of the 1890s has charted the differing responses of middle-class and working-class novelists to the union upsurge of the late

1880s[37] and the counter-offensive led by the employers around 1893. Perhaps the most significant aspect of the middle-class response is not—despite continued fears—the acceptance of trade unions and the strike weapon, or the shift from denunciation to idealisation in the portrayal of the (moderate) working-class leader, but the unwillingness of the major practitioners of the novel to engage with industrial conflict at all. Class collision was, if at all, located elsewhere. When contrasted with the fictional interventions of Dickens, Gaskell and Eliot earlier in the century, this abstention appears as one more symptom of the novel's often-observed loss of public centrality towards the close of the century. In this respect Leslie, Oakhurst and Fletcher clearly fought a rearguard battle. And as often happens with insignificant descendants, their works, instead of inspiring others, quickly passed into oblivion, and are unlikely ever to be read again. This is not the case with Clarke and Tirebuck, whose novels were reprinted during the period covered by this book,[38] and who found a number of immediate followers. Chief amongst these are the writers of the 'Lancashire school', Arthur Laycock and Fred Plant, but also Ethel Carnie, who was not part of Allen Clarke's circle.[39]

Thus it is in the 1890s that the treatment of the strike is finally wrenched from the hands of middle-class novelists, whose domain it had been since early Victorian times, and given a distinct socialist slant. Strikes and lock-outs, while remaining 'exceptional moments' of working-class life, would henceforth be depicted not only as occasions of distress and tragedy (and no longer as acts of destruction and self-destruction), but also as ways of crystallising class consciousness and testing the values of humanity and solidarity, and thereby furthering the working-class cause. As such the strike issue has entered twentieth-century socialist fiction as a recurring theme and a central concern.

NOTES

1. Jospeh Kestner, *Protest and Reform. The British Social Narrative by Women, 1827-1867* (London, 1985), pp.114-16, 177-82. For a more sceptical view of Fanny Mayne's novel see my *The Literature of Labour. Two Hundred Years of Working-Class Writing* (Brighton, 1985), pp.85-6.
2. A critical account of this area of writing can be found in P. J. Keating's *The Working Classes in Victorian Fiction* (London, 1971); see also his collection of *Working-Class Stories of the 1890s* (London, 1971).
3. Charlotte Elizabeth Tonna, *Combination (1832); Harriet Martineau, A Manchester Strike* (1832). For a discussion of both authors see Ivanka Kovačević, *Fact into Fiction. English Literature and the Industrial Scene* (Leicester, 1975), pp.211-23, 303-12. This book contains a complete reprint of *A Manchester Strike*. See also Catherine Gallagher, *The Industrial Reformation of English Fiction. Social Discourse and Narrative Form 1832-1867* (Chicago, 1985), pp.43-51, 55-61.
4. H. Llewellyn Smith and Vaughan Nash, *The Story of the Dockers' Strike* (London, n.d. [1889]), pp.164-5.
5. Coined by the union organiser John Burns, this was the ringing slogan of the struggle.
6. John Lovell, 'The new unionism and the Dock Strike of 1889' in David Rubinstein (ed.), *People for the People* (London, 1973), pp.154-5.
7. Emma Leslie, *The Seed She Sowed. A Tale of the Great Dock Strike* (London, 1891), p.19.
8. Cf. Gareth Stedman Jones, *Outcast London. A Study in the Relationship Between Classes in Victorian Society* (Harmondsworth, 1976; first pub. 1971), pp.302-8.
9. Mid-century industrial novels which use the emigration device include Frances Trollope, *Michael Armstrong, the Factory Boy* (1840); Elizabeth Gaskell, *Mary Barton* (1848); Charles Kingsley, *Alton Locke* (1850); and Fanny Mayne, *Jane Rutherford* (1854).
10. Leslie, *op. cit.*, p.137.
11. The misnaming of the International and its organs are among the minor confusions of this work.
12. William Oakhurst, *The Universal Strike of 1899* (London, 1891), p.34.
13. Stedman Jones, *op. cit.*, p.319.
14. Oakhurst, *op. cit.*, p.34.

15. *ibid.*, p.57. The quote is from Robert Browning's 'Pisgah-Sights I', which is included in his *Pacchiarotto* (1876). See *The Poetical Works of Robert Browning*, vol. XIV (London, 1889), p.49.

    For the popularity of the poem or at least its theme among Socialists of the day, see the following remark by Hugh Holmes Gore from the *Labour Prophet* of May 1895: 'We . . . sang them Pisgah-songs, we drew vivid pictures of the Promised Land, and enjoined them to hurry up and journey thither.' Quoted from Stephen Yeo, 'A new life: the religion of socialism in Britain 1883-1896', *History Workshop*, 4 (1977), p.45.
16. Oakhurst, *op. cit.*, p.34.
17. *ibid.*, p.6. The phrase is contained in a 'private and confidential' Manifesto. Note the contradiction in terms!
18. *ibid.*, p.86.
19. For further information about Clarke see chapter 8 by Paul Salveson.
20. C. Allen Clarke, *The Knobstick. A Story of Love and Labour* (Manchester, n.d. [1893]), pp.77-8. Subsequent page numbers given in the text are to this edition.
21. Paul Salveson, Preface to *Teddy Ashton's Lancashire Scrapbook* (Farnworth, 1985), p.1.
22. P. M. Ashraf, *Introduction to Working-Class Literature in Great Britain*, 2 vols, Part II: Prose (Berlin, 1979), p.156. This contains a full discussion of the novel.
23. William Tirebuck, 'On the verge of change' in Andrew Reid (ed.), *The New Party* (London, 1894), p.366.
24. *ibid.*, p.367.
25. William Edwards Tirebuck, *Miss Grace of All Souls'* (London, 1895), p.266. Subsequent page numbers given in the text are to this edition.
26. Another feature reminiscent of Clarke, emphasising the continuity and change of the labour movement, is the figure of 'a very old Chartist, with his long full grey hair, pass[ing] through dreamy resurrections of social strife.' *ibid.*, p.148.

    In all likelihood the two authors had knowledge of one another's work. Both were north of England authors, Clarke associated with Bolton and Blackpool, Tirebuck with Liverpool, though he spent his later years in Scotland and Wales. Clarke reprinted at least one of Tirebuck's short stories, 'Joe Clayton's Last Clogs', in his *Northern Weekly*, 1 February

1902.
27. This sub-strand of the plot may look contrived. But an incident during the Silesian weavers' uprising of 1844, which is the subject of Gerhart Hauptmann's famous naturalist play of the nineties, *The Weavers* (written 1892, first performed 1894), shows that Tirebuck's fiction is only catching up with real history. One of the soldiers deployed in Silesia was reported as having identified his own brother among the weavers killed, and as subsequently having thrown away his gun in despair; cf. *Kölnische Zeitung*, 18 June 1844, quoted from Hans Schwab-Felisch (ed.), Gerhart Hauptmann, *Die Weber. Dichtung und Wirklichkeit* (Frankfurt, 1974), pp.119-20.
28. Keating credits Tirebuck for having produced 'the most important industrial novel to be published in England since *Hard Times* almost exactly forty years earlier, and the most successful portrayal of industrial working-class life since *Mary Barton*'; *The Working Classes in Victorian Fiction*, p.235. For a reading of Tirebuck's novel, which differs from Keating's but also from my own, see chapter 7 by Ingrid von Rosenberg.
29. The term 'underworld' does not appear in Tirebuck but in H. G. Wells's tale *The Time Machine* from the same year (1895), where it refers to the subterranean work installations and habitations of the Morlocks, those repugnant spider- and monkey-like creatures that eat the refined upper-world species and threaten the Time Traveller, too.

Although this has to my knowledge never been established by Wells criticism, it is more than likely that the treatment of the Morlocks owes something to the action taken by the miners in the late summer of 1893. According to Wells's first biographer Geoffrey West, the fourth version of *The Time Machine*, which had a long and complex genesis, was written towards the end of 1893 (and published from March to June 1894 in the *National Observer*). The miners' lock-out lasted from July to November 1893.

Still according to West, this fourth version is 'the first recognisable casting of the familiar story. Certain incidents—such as . . . the descent to the underworld of the Morlocks (already thus named, though the Elois are still anonymous) are given practically as in the book,' Geoffrey West, *H. G. Wells* (London, 1930), Appendix, p.292.

So although the underworld appears to have existed

already in the second version, of which no draft has survived, it was only resumed and given its recognisable shape contemporaneously with, or in the immediate aftermath of, the lock-out. Certainly no social thinker of the time could have remained indifferent to this, the largest industrial dispute the country had ever seen.

Wells's beastly image of the underground toilers was not forgotten by the first British miner novelist. James C. Welsh's first novel was entitled *The Underworld* (1920), his second *The Morlocks* (1924). For a discussion of these works see H. Gustav Klaus, 'James C. Welsh. Major miner novelist', *Scottish Literary Journal*, XIII, 2 (1986), pp.54-75.

30. The other path, first chosen by James C. Welsh in 1920 (see preceding note), is the beginning of the working life of a boy, an empathetic description of the first day down the pit.
31. Alfred H. Fletcher, *Lost in the Mine. A Tale of the Great Coal Strike* (London, n.d. [1895]), p.60. Subsequent page numbers in the text are to this edition.
32. There is no historical evidence for this.
33. Cf. R. Page Arnot, *The Miners* (London, 1949), pp.236-41.
34. For an analysis of this confusion, see chapter 6 by Graham Holderness.
35. See note 4.
36. Fletcher was also the author of another strike novel, *The Clevelands of the Peak. A Derbyshire Romance* (Manchester, n.d. [1897]), which deals with union 'outrages' in the 1860s in the brickmakers' trade.
37. Clementina Black's *An Agitator* (1894) also opens with a view (of the last stage) of a strike, by wire-workers, another group of unskilled, low-paid and difficult-to-organise workers. However, its focus is on the subsequent political career of the strike leader, himself an engineer and the agitator of the title. For a discussion of this novel see chapter 2 by Brunhild de la Motte.
38. *The Knobstick*, repr. 1906; *Miss Grace of All Souls'*, repr. 1912. Oakhurst's work was admittedly also reprinted in 1911.
39. See the discussion of Laycock's *The Young Gaffer* (1898) and Plant's *The Conductor's Sweetheart* (1900-1) in chapter 8 by Paul Salveson; and of Carnie's *Miss Nobody* (1913) in chapter 11 by Edmund and Ruth Frow.

· 5 ·

Struggles of the past: brushing history against the grain

J. M. RIGNALL

Historicism, Walter Benjamin maintained, involves empathy with the victors in the struggles of history.[1] The historical novel, on the other hand, has, from *Waverley* onwards, commonly exploited the romantic potential of the lost cause. Yet the Jacobite rebellions that Scott focuses on, with their colourful trappings of highland clans, aristocratic intrigues and exiled royalty, allow a fictional treatment that is in the end quite compatible with an historicist perspective. The defeated Jacobites are given their romantic due of heroism and nobility while, at the same time, Scotland's future is shown to belong quite properly to the Union with England, the constitutional Hanoverian monarchy and the values of bourgeois society. The victors are shown to have history on their side and their success, however painful its price, is seen as necessary, inevitable and, on balance, welcome. It is this endorsement of the winning side that is markedly absent from the historical novels of the late nineteenth and early twentieth century that I shall discuss here: William Hale White ('Mark Rutherford'), *The Revolution in Tanner's Lane* (1887); E. L. Voynich, *The Gadfly* (1897); D. F. E. Sykes and Geo. Henry Walker, *Ben o' Bill's, the Luddite: A Yorkshire Tale* (1898); and James Haslam, *The Handloom Weaver's Daughter* (1904). Taking as their subject less romantic acts of rebellion against economic and political power than did Scott, they re-create history from the perspective of the dispossessed and defeated. Even if that defeat may be seen as only one lost battle in a continuing struggle, it is not written off as the necessary and inevitable price of progress. In different ways all these novels adapt the conventions of historical fiction to perform what Benjamin saw as the proper task of a materialist historiography, 'to brush history against the grain'.[2]

Formally and ideologically these are very disparate works and they cannot conveniently be marshalled into a coherent alternative tradition of historical fiction with a clear set of common characteristics and a shared socialist outlook. Indeed, of these authors only Haslam was definitely a socialist.[3] However, in presenting history from the perspective of the oppressed they all deal openly and explicitly with violence, both of oppression and insurrection, and confront the problems that it poses. In so doing they lay themselves open to the problematic nature of history, often at the expense of that formal unity which better-known novels aspire to and which one kind of critical orthodoxy likes to honour as organic. It is on the different ways in which these works maintain this openness and manipulate or resist conventional forms of closure that I shall concentrate here.

Ben o' Bill's, the Luddite is a first-person account of the Luddite activity in Yorkshire in 1812 which culminated in the unsuccessful attack on Rawfolds mill and the murder of the mill-owner Horsfall a few days later. The authors, two local historians, claim that their work is 'mostly true' and varies in no significant respect 'from the story as it was gleaned from the lips and in part from the papers of the narrator',[4] a survivor of the Luddite rising, one Benjamin Bamforth, the Ben o' Bill's of the title. Nevertheless, the work reads like a lively novel, creating a world and peopling it with characters, and, as E. P. Thompson has suggested, it succeeds better as an 'imaginative reconstruction of the way of life, folk wisdom, and dialect of the Luddite community' than as factual history.[5] As Thompson also points out, the authors follow closely the account of events given by their fellow historian and contemporary Frank Peel in *The Risings of the Luddites* (1880), and, given that Peel's work precedes theirs by several years, seem to have leant heavily upon it. However, the fact that Peel makes no mention of a Benjamin Bamforth may not be conclusive evidence of invention but it does indicate how, by centring their activities on this entirely decent and sympathetic young man, Sykes and Walker have done more than merely reproduce Peel's history in a different form. If they lean on his account they none the less significantly change the emphasis. Seeking to present a sympathetic understanding of the Luddites' actions and motives and to counter the commonly held view that they were 'a set of idle, dissolute knaves and cut-throats the country was well rid of' (p.1), the authors can be seen to be working against the grain of Peel's more critical history and also, of course, of Charlotte Brontë's middle-class view of Luddism in *Shirley*.

The apology for the Luddites involves setting them in the context of a whole community and a way of life, and rooting the violent insurrection in the collective experience of that community and the personal characters and relationships of its members. George Mellor, the leader of the attack on Rawfolds mill and one of the three men who were eventually hanged for the murder of Horsfall, is presented as a cousin of the narrator and given the human countenance that Peel's history denies him. Where Peel describes him in the language of melodrama—'his black heart full of impotent rage'; 'his dark, flinty heart'[6]—*Ben o' Bill's* views him through the affectionate but not uncritical eyes of his cousin as 'a right proper man . . . six feet by the stick and with shoulders well back and strong, firm hands that gripped you to make you tingle' and who 'had a temper if you like, but never bore malice' (p.54). Even when he commits the murder of Horsfall, a deed which the horrified narrator cannot condone, he is shown to be acting not out of villainy but from a combination of outrage at social conditions and personal animosity. The novel includes a scene, not mentioned by Peel, which establishes a motive for the murder in these terms. A hot-headed, compassionate man, Mellor is moved to violent anger by the sight of a starving cropper's wife by the side of the road clutching a dead baby to her breast; and that anger focuses on

Horsfall who happens to ride past. Confronting the mill-owner with what Mellor sees as the direct, tragic result of his introduction of new machinery—' "Look at thi work William Horsfall; look at thi work an' be glad" ' (p.168)—he receives a cut across the face with a horse-whip in return. Horsfall rides away swearing ' "Yo's none heard th' last of this" ' while Mellor leaves the scene with a similarly strong resolve: ' "But, as the Lord's above me, that blow shall cost William Horsfall dear" ' (p.169). The incident, melodramatic in outline but saved from staginess by being recounted in Mellor's own earthy vernacular, provides grounds for the murder that are at once intensely personal and, at the same time, social and historical.

Despite the melodramatic quality of this scene, *Ben o' Bill's* does not reproduce stereotypes of class conflict. Horsfall, 'brusque, and a little petulant, but not unkindly of heart' (p.39), is a masterful man but not a tyrannical exploiter; and he is shown to be as much part of the community as those he employs and on friendly terms with the narrator's family. What is achieved by his murder, which 'revolted the general mind' (p.271), is not a strengthening of support for the Luddite cause but rather a rending of the community which destroys the popular basis of Luddism. The murder is, of course, only the last link in a chain of violence that can be traced back to the war with France and the Napoleonic blockade which has destroyed the continental market for the weaving industry, but the novel does not offer that wider pattern of historical causality as a moral justification of the murder. This is not a work of historical or metaphysical determinism. When a coin is tossed by the Luddites to determine whether Horsfall's mill or Cartwright's Rawfolds mill should be attacked first—an incident that is also recorded by Peel—Mellor, knowing that his cousin the narrator is well disposed towards Horsfall, surreptitiously turns the coin in his hand so that Cartwright's is chosen:

> 'But I knew tha wanted tails, so I turned it i' my palm when I stooped o'er th' fire.'
> And yet men talk about fate. (p.46)

It is neither fate nor historical necessity that determines the course of history in this work, but the actions and decisions of individuals in determinate conditions. And if Mellor is not excused, neither is Horsfall, for the narrator, having described the desperate state of the local economy in 1812 and the starvation visible in the pinched and haggard faces of the famished Huddersfield workmen, concludes that the mill-owners could and should have acted differently:

> Now I cannot for my part think such a time was fitting for bringing in machinery. I know full well that water power and steam power and improved machinery have been of untold good to the poor; but those who were to reap the first profit should to my thinking have bided their time. But Mr. Cartwright, of Rawfolds, Mr. Horsfall, of Ottiwells' and some others, seemed callous to the sufferings around them. (p.75)

The Luddite violence and the specific actions and conditions that provoked it are thus not presented as inevitable, but they do bring about a fundamental change, rending the pattern of life of a whole community. That traditional pattern is affectionately re-created early in the novel in the Christmas scene at which George Mellor first appears, announcing his arrival out of the darkness and the snow with a strong baritone rendering of 'Christians Awake'. The contrast between this first appearance 'with a great red muffler round his neck and his coat all flaked with snow . . . now stamping his feet and now kicking them against the door-post' (p.53), and his last is striking and poignant. As the narrator stands before the scaffold in York his eyes fail him:

> There was a haze before my sight. I did not see the bolt withdrawn; only as through a mist see the quivering, swaying form. A long drawn sign, that ended in a sob like one deep breath from a thousand hearts, proclaimed the end, and Mr. Webster and I made our way from that tragic scene. (p.320)

In the shift from vivid, sensuous detail to distanced, hazy outline there is registered not only the tragic loss of an individual life, but also, vigorously if crudely emphasised by that 'one deep breadth from a thousand hearts', the passing of a vital culture.

In its treatment of an unsuccessful historical rebellion *Ben o' Bill's* follows in some respects the conventions established by Scott, corresponding quite closely to the classical form of the historical novel as Lukács defines it with reference to the Waverley novels.[7] The narrator is cast in the mould of the neutral Waverley hero, caught up in a violent struggle but not wholeheartedly committed to either side in the conflict. In contrast to the passionately radical Mellor he is a moderate, unpolitical figure with modest expectations of what life has to offer: 'to make fair goods, to sell them at a fair price, to live in peace with my neighbours, and in time to marry, such was the sum of my ambition' (p.69). Sceptical from the outset of any attempt to fight against the law of the land, he finds himself torn between compassion for the starving weavers and his law-abiding inclinations: although 'filled with an intense sorrow for the suffering I know to be rife around us . . . I shrank from violence of any kind and from the conflict with the law, of which I had a wholesome dread' (p.79). His participation in the frame-breaking is thus reluctant and ridden with anxiety, and his equivocal stance could be said to allow Sykes and Walker to give an inside account of the Luddite rising while maintaining a respectable distance from the violence involved. However, this is not in effect a timid concession to respectability and the ruling class, but, rather, a graphic means of defending the Luddites against charges of criminality, of showing how they were, like the narrator, decent law-abiding men driven to desperate measures by desperate conditions.

Ben Bamforth's contempt for the military pretensions of some of the Luddites—their practice of drilling with arms 'seemed to me to be poor fooling, then and always' (p.96)—does not prevent him from honouring his promise to Mellor by joining the attack on Rawfolds mill, serving as one of the hammer-men who try to beat down the doors. His subsequent fate follows very much the pattern of Scott's typical neutral hero. Wounded in the attack, he is carried off unconscious and remains passively dependent on family and friends to hide him from discovery by the forces of the law. Like Scott's Waverley he requires some authorially directed good fortune, which includes the good offices of magistrates and aristocrats, to prevent him from sharing the fate of many of his colleagues. George Mellor goes to his historical end on the gallows while Ben Bamforth, again like Waverley, is allowed the happy ending of marriage and a secure future. The novel comes close, indeed, to presenting a complacently conventional conclusion which consigns historical suffering to the safely distant past and dispenses morally appropriate rewards and punishments. The Luddite traitor Benjamin Walker, who informs on Mellor and others out of a combination of greed, cowardice, and jealousy over a girl, makes his last appearance immediately before the narrator's marriage, reduced now, having squandered his reward, to begging for a crust of bread. But even though in Ben Bamforth's final attitude to the informer charity gets the better of anger, the last paragraph of the novel strikes a note not of reconciliation but of resolute rejection—rejection of the criminal reputation commonly assigned to the Luddites: 'But don't tell me the Luds were a bad lot—misguided, short-sighted, ignorant, if you like, but rogues, and idle, dissolute n'er-do-weels—No! and still no!' (p.339). That emphatic final negation marks the novel's resistance to conventional closure and its refusal to acquiesce in the victors' verdict on the victims of history.

Sykes' and Walker's use of a narrator who is a relatively uncommitted but percipient participant in the struggle roots the story in the life and language of the community and creates a consistent tone and perspective. James Haslam's *The Handloom Weaver's Daughter* is a more uneven work in which a loftily generalising authorial commentary and an action that tends towards the melodramatic are never entirely integrated. However, Haslam certainly knew the world about which he was writing. The son of a handloom weaver himself, he later became a journalist after starting as a factory-worker, and he drew on his childhood memories as well as the testimony of old handloom weavers for his novel about 'the tragedy involved in the struggle of the last of these cellar-workers against the development of steam machinery and the spread of the factory system'.[8] Although this tragedy is cast in the form of melodrama, and personal engagement too often manifests itself as a sentimental evocation of the pre-industrial past, Haslam does hold to a clear and uncompromising understanding of history to offset the formal clumsiness of what seems to have been his only attempt at a novel.[9]

Set in the late 1860s and early 1870s the story is that of Titus Bonney, one of the last of the handloom weavers of the old school, and his daughter Nancy; and it traces the course of their ruin by a self-made mill-owner William Bailey and his son Albert. The expansion of Bailey senior's business puts Titus out of work and drives him from his home, which is razed to the ground to make room for Bailey's new powerloom mill and spinning factory. At the same time Nancy is seduced, abducted and then abandoned, pregnant and destitute, by the evil Albert. This conflict of classes is temporarily mitigated by the activity of the enlightened younger son Willie Bailey, whose reading of Ruskin 'had imbued his mind with a love for idealism in industry' (p.116). But his scheme for organising and supporting the remaining handloom weavers fails and, in the violence that erupts at the end of the novel, he is shot by Titus and his accomplices who mistake him for his brother. Titus, now demented, proceeds to burn down Bailey's new mill and dies himself in the fire. Nancy has to emigrate to America to work as an operative in a new spinning mill. The other principal working-class character, Nancy's one-time fiancé the mechanic John Blake, suffers less dramatically but is similarly a victim of social and historical forces. Having invented a device for improving the operation of a spinning mill, he is cheated out of the patent by his employer Bailey and the local mayor, sacked and forced in the end to take work in India. He returns none the wealthier to witness the degradation of Nancy and continue a life of honest labour without social advancement.

In bare outline this is crude enough, and in some of its

details its fails to rise above the lowest level of cliché. Albert Bailey, 'pressing his voluptuous lips to the chastely chiselled mouth of the trembling maiden' (p.90), is never more than the stock villain of melodrama. And the evocation of life before the industrial fall slips too often into a sentimental version of pastoral: once, we are told, the weavers

> flourished everywhere in the neighbourhood like the delicious wild flowers they so dearly loved. But as the weavers had been crushed by the advancing wheel of time, the flowers also had been maimed and broken by the jerry-builder; where once the daisy and the cowslip reared their modest, fragrant heads side by side, badly-paved and sombre-looking streets had been formed. (p.4)

Nevertheless, despite such banalities, the simple polarities of melodrama and sentimental hyperbole do play a positive part in creating a distinctive vision of history. They articulate a stark conception of the irreconcilable nature of the contending forces. Haslam refuses to entertain the possibility of that reconciliation of classes, and of the old and the new, that is consistently urged by, for instance, the great industrial novels of the middle of the nineteenth century. When Nancy believes herself to be on the brink of marriage to Albert Bailey she projects a role for her marriage that might have been devised by Disraeli or Gaskell, or, in terms of historical development, by Scott;

> Then she fell to dreaming. It seemed to her present state of mind as if by her prospective marriage with Albert Bailey the representatives of the two great industrial periods were being joined together—the old and the new. (p.76)

But as soon as it is advanced this version of history is rejected:

> Had she been in a more philosophic mood, as was sometimes her wont, she would have asked herself if it were possible for the old and the new order of things to become as one consistent whole. (p.76)

The clear implication is that it is not, that the union of the old order and the new is merely the wishful dream of innocence. The intensification of the melodramatic mode towards the end of the novel serves to drive home this uncompromising lesson. The death of the Ruskinite reformer and Titus's suicidal attack on the new mill symbolically spell out the impossibility of peacefully resolving the class conflict inherent in the advance of industrial capitalism. The 'ever-grinding wheel of progress' (p.11) demands the destruction of the old by the new; and that destruction is seen as a violation of a state of nature, of an original organic unity. It is for this reason that the relationship of the pre-industrial handloom weavers to their work is nostalgically defined in terms of a harmony with nature. In the handloom cellar of the Bonneys' cottage Nancy 'could always see the flowers, the flight of birds, and the fall of the rain or snow outside, which made her feel more in touch with nature, and helped to retain her passion for the earth' (p.67). By contrast, the factory-workers 'breathed poison in the mill and poison in the bedroom. They were compelled through shortness of money to load their stomachs with unwholesome food and their minds with spurious notions' (p.35). In this context the melodramatic violence of the ending can be seen as an intensified rendering of the violence being done to a whole harmonious way of life.

This stark and uncompromising historical vision may owe something to Marxist thought,[10] but *The Handloom Weaver's Daughter* is clearly not the work of a revolutionary socialist. Like *Ben o' Bill's* it distances itself firmly from the use of violence as a political weapon. Whatever moral or emotional justification there may be for the arson that Titus commits, it is in no way excused, but labelled as 'criminal destruction' (p.279). When the handloom weavers are driven to revolt they are shown as descending to the level of animals:

> The handloom weavers' pride and independence began to assert themselves guardlessly. All human sympathy seemed to have been lost in the increased excitations of their animal

feelings. Their minds seemed only moved by the spirit of revenge, by desperation. They appeared not as reasoning men and women. They seemed to display that savage instinct only, which must have mainly characterised human beings before they had evolved to an intellectual beginning. (p.247)

The abhorrence expressed here would not be out of place in any middle-class novel of the nineteenth century. But, unlike such works, Haslam's novel does not end with reconciliation and a consoling conclusion. Its radicalism lies not in any advocacy of revolution but in its open-ended vision of history as a continuing struggle:

> The criminal destruction of the extensive spinning mill was the last impressive act of the defeated handloom weavers in the great Industrial Revolution. The conflict has still been waged in other ways, by other industrial forces, and was never, perhaps, more fierce than it is today. (p.279)

There is no certainty of progress towards socialism expressed here, but neither is there resignation or despair. And if there is at least one concession to conventional closure in the marriage of the surviving John Blake, the final sentence of the novel deploys a nice irony against any interpretation of this as a definitive resolution of the conflicts presented in the novel: John Blake and Lily Braithwaite 'married at the little chapel of Lupton Yard, where they continued to live, strive, and bear children in the approved fashion of a respectable working-class family' (p.280). The ironic 'approved' identifies this respectable existence as all that a working-class family is permitted, not all that it might properly aspire to. The defeat of the weavers has put no one definitively in their place.

The Revolution in Tanner's Lane is the only one of the novels discussed here that has already received considerable critical attention, and my reading of it will be necessarily selective, seeking to establish Hale White's view of popular political action and its relation to the historical process rather than examining in any detail his account of the decline of dissenting religion. The 'revolution' of the title is, of course, ironic, since nothing like a revolution occurs in the novel, least of all in Tanner's Lane; and irony is the mode in which radical political action is presented in the novel. From the great, comically satirical, opening scene of Louis the Eighteenth arriving in London to meet the Prince Regent amidst popular patriotic rejoicing, the novel looks sceptically at the collective intelligence and capacity of the people:

> There was a great crowd in the street when he came out of the hotel, and immense applause; the mob crying out, 'God bless your Majesty!' as if they owed him all they had, and even their lives. It was very touching, people thought at the time, and so it was. Is there anything more touching than the waste of human loyalty and love? As we read the history of the Highlands or a story of Jacobite loyalty such as that of Cooper's Admiral Bluewater, dear to boys, we sadden that destiny should decree that in a world in which piety is not too plentiful it should run so pitifully to waste, and that men and women should weep hot tears and break their hearts over bran-stuffing and wax.[11]

The mention of Jacobite loyalty and the history of the Highlands provokes a comparison between this ironic view of popular monarchism and that to be found in so many historical novels and romances from Scott onwards. The kind of loyalty that Scott celebrates even while exposing its anachronism is seen here as merely pitiful waste, and this signals at the outset how Hale White is going to work against the grain of conventional historical fiction. Yet this disenchanted view of the people is scarcely compatible with a radical alternative to Scott's conservatism, and, indeed, Hale White alternates disconcertingly between contempt for an oppressive autocratic regime and disdain for popular attempts to challenge it:

> What is so lamentable in the history of those times is the undisciplined wildness and feebleness of the attempts made by the people to better themselves. Nothing is more saddening than the spectacle of a huge mass of humanity goaded, writhing, starving, and yet so ignorant that it cannot choose

capable leaders, cannot obey them if perchance it gets them, and does not even know how to name its wrongs. (p.159)

In this perspective it is not the people, but the leaders whom they fail to heed, who become the principal objects of sympathy; and the novel's account of the march of the Blanketeers centres on the actions and fates of Major Maitland, Caillaud, and Zachariah Coleman. It might seem that the popular movement only proves worthy of respect in the persons of a few enlightened and atypical individuals. But it is noticeable that, in honouring the latter, Hale White slips unobtrusively from the individual back to the general again:

> To work hard for those who will thank us, to head a majority against oppressors, is a brave thing; but far more honour is due to the Maitlands, Caillauds, Colemans, and others of that stamp who strove for thirty years from the outbreak of the French revolution onwards not merely to rend the chains of the prisoners, but had to achieve the more difficult task of convincing them that they would be happier if they were free. These heroes are forgotten, or nearly so. Who remembers the poor creatures who met in the early mornings on the Lancashire moors or were shot by the yeomanry? They sleep in graves over which stands no tombstone, or probably their bodies have been carted away to make room for a railway which has been driven through their resting place.
> (pp.110-11)

The named individuals are elided into the nameless masses, the heroic leaders become 'the poor creatures', indistinguishable from those whom they lead, and all of them forgotten victims of history.

The contradictions in the novel's attitude to the Blanketeers and working-class political action in general have been seen as the characteristic waverings of a well-disposed liberal of the 1880s. In the best critical account of Hale White's fiction to date John Lucas argues that, in creating the persona of Mark Rutherford, Hale White has deliberately presented a narrator who exhibits the classical dilemma of the liberal conscience, and that the novel is in part concerned to expose the limitations of such a figure and his point of view.[12] Leaving aside the difficulty of establishing the grounds for taking Mark Rutherford as the object of Hale White's irony, for seeing the contradictions as deliberately posed rather than honestly entertained by the author himself, this reading has the defect of making sense of the novel's inconsistencies solely in terms of the narrator's limitations. Lucas is right to view the march of the Blanketeers as an historical crisis that is difficult to make sense of, but to argue that it produces crises and contradictions only in a liberal attempt to account for it is to define the difficulty too narrowly. What Hale White seems to show is that it resists recuperation in terms of conventional history altogether. The Blanketeers are shown to be peculiarly difficult to get clearly into focus; they are at once touchingly naïve in their faith in the good will of government and the Prince Regent; unjustly suspicious of their leader; misled by their literal-minded belief in the word of the Bible and their own imagined role as outnumbered Israelites; ignorantly determined to proceed with the march despite all the arguments against it; altogether absurd and foolish, and yet 'less ridiculous than those who hung and sabred them, less ridiculous than the Crimean war and numberless dignified events in human history, the united achievements of the sovereigns and ministries of Europe' (p.184). Their contradictions and weaknesses make them impossible subjects for the kind of conventional historian who narrates 'the dignified events in human history'; but such offical historians, with their bland assumptions of what is important, are themselves absurdly deluded. However foolish the Blanketeers, those 'silly God-fearing souls', may be, they are in the end right, it is implied, to believe that 'their Master's time was not their time . . . and that when it pleased Him they would triumph' (p.186). The ultimate success that would make sense of their defeat is not available to the narrator, or to any person, and can only be conjectured:

> It was not yet God's time in 1817, but God's time was helped forward, as it generally is, by this anticipation of it. It is a

commonplace that a premature outbreak puts back the hands of the clock and is a blunder. Nine times out of ten this is untrue, and a revolt instantaneously quenched in blood is not merely the precursor, but the direct progenitor of success.
(pp.186-7)

In writing the alternative history of the oppressed and defeated Hale White cannot produce a coherent teleological narrative that bestows meaning on events in the light of their positive conclusion, for, in consigning the success of which the Blanketeers are the progenitor to a millennial future known only to God, he indicates that the ending which would resolve contradiction and redeem inadequacy is one that cannot yet be written. Thus the kind of organic unity which he so admired in Scott[13] is one that he has deliberately to eschew since it has no part in his project. Seen from the point of view of the defeated, history must inevitably be incoherent, tailing off into darkness and oblivion.

The prospect of being consigned to oblivion, together with the doubts thus raised about the meaningfulness of their actions, is one that the characters in the novel consciously face up to. When Zachariah visits Caillaud in the condemned cell the latter reflects on the fact that his own life and the march of the Blanketeers are certain to be forgotten:

'To be hung like a forger of bank-notes—not even to be shot—and then to be forgotten. Forgotten utterly! This does not happen to be one of those revolutions which men remember.'

'No! men will not remember,' said Pauline, with an elevation of voice and manner almost oratorical. 'Men will not remember, but there is a memory in the world which forgets nothing.' (p.226)

Pauline's answer appears to be endorsed, however tentatively, by the novel. The notion of a memory in the world which forgets nothing is more than a secular and sentimental substitute for God; it is a way of asserting that actions may have significant consequences despite the insignificance or obliteration of the individuals who perform them. In rescuing from oblivion 'the poor creatures who met in the early mornings on the Lancashire moors or were shot by the yeomanry' (p.110) the novel affirms the existence of a memory which forgets nothing. And in the second half of the work there is one incident which echoes Caillaud's own violent action—keeping his memory alive by example, as it were—and demonstrates quite literally the ability of individuals to leave their mark. When the young Pauline, Zachariah's daughter, has the unwelcome attentions of Thomas Broad forced upon her, she turns on him both verbally and physically:

> 'I will be silent,' she cried—what a relief it was to him to hear her say that!—'but I will mark you,' and before he could comprehend what she was doing she had seized a little pair of scissors which lay near her, had caught his wrist, and had scored a deep cross on the back of the hand. The blood burst out, and she threw him a handkerchief. (p.291)

This melodramatic action, a violent reaction to violence like Caillaud's shooting of the soldier who killed Major Maitland, stands out vividly in the prosaic account of domestic and provincial life which comprises the second half of the novel. And unlike the election-night riot, which repeats the popular uprising of the Blanketeers as tawdry farce, it cannot be seen as another ironic illustration of the way the forces of the first part of the novel have dwindled into mocking shadows. Decline there may be in the radical energy of the dissenting tradition, but some continuity remains in the figures of individuals. The younger Pauline retains the fiery spirit of her mother and grandfather, and in this scene she makes a mark whose long-term effects cannot be foreseen. The scar left on Thomas Broad's hand later causes his disgrace in Cowfold, frustrates his father's arbitrary and unjust exercise of power as the minister in Tanner's Lane, and most probably precipitates the latter's fatal illness. None of these consequences is exactly momentous, but Pauline's action leads at least to the thwarting of a petty tyrant and the defeat of injustice in the diminished sphere of Cowfold. What benefit she may derive from it, however, is never established for she herself is lost to sight. The laconic final sentences of the novel despatch her and her father into oblivion: 'What became of Zachariah and Pauline? At present I do not know' (p.388). They sink back, at least temporarily, into unrecorded history and the novel remains open-ended, but in a way that does not represent a capitulation to hopelessness. The individuals themselves may not be remembered but their lives have left a mark, and in that respect 'there is a memory in the world which forgets nothing' (p.226).

E. L. Voynich's flamboyant historical romance *The Gadfly* is as far removed from the sober restraint of Hale White's novel as her early life was from his quiet routine as an official in the Admiralty. Born in 1864 the youngest daughter of George Boole, professor of mathematics at Queen's College, Cork, she studied music in Berlin, was captivated by the idea of Russian revolution, became friends with the Russian revolutionary Stepniak in exile in London, lived and travelled in Russia in the late 1880s, and worked for the Russian revolutionary movement, travelling for instance to Lvov to help arrange the passage of illegal publications into Russia through the Galician frontier.[14] It was through her association with Stepniak that she met her husband Wilfred Voynich, a Lithuanian who escaped to London in 1890 from political imprisonment in Siberia. *The Gadfly*, her first novel, published in 1897, was an immediate success, particularly in Russia where it has continued to be a bestseller to the present day.[15] Drawing on her knowledge of European revolutionaries it deals not with popular insurrections of the English nineteenth century but with the Italian struggle for independence from the Austrian empire in the 1830s and 1840s. Where the other novels are provincial, this is exotic; where they aspire to realism, this is an unashamed romance.

The terms of its popular appeal lie doubtless in its qualities as a romantic adventure story. It is dramatic, fast-moving, far-fetched, always poised on the brink of outright absurdity, and yet undeniably compelling. At the beginning of the novel Arthur Burton, the youngest son of an English merchant in Leghorn, is a student in the theological seminary in Pisa and idealistically involved in the underground Young Italy movement. Since both his parents are dead and his step-brothers unsympathetic, his one close relationship is with his father-confessor, canon Montanelli. When Montanelli leaves Pisa on his appointment as a bishop, Arthur accepts the new head of the seminary, father Cardi, as his confessor and reveals to him in confession the details of his political involvement. Shortly afterwards he is arrested along with other student revolutionaries. After refusing to betray his associates he is eventually released through the intercession of Montanelli. Cardi, it emerges, has betrayed the secrets of the confessional to the authorities; but, through a combination of misunderstanding and official rumour, Arthur is believed at first to have been the traitor. At the same time he learns from his family that he is in fact the illegitimate son of Montanelli, who once had an affair with his mother. This double revelation shatters his faith in Christianity, and, making it look as though he has drowned himself in the harbour at Leghorn, he stows away on a ship to South America. Thirteen years later, half-crippled by his experiences in South America and unrecognisable to his former associates, he reappears in Italy as the notorious radical and anti-clerical pamphleteer Felice Rivarez, the gadfly of the title. Neurotically scarred and physically debilitated by his humiliating time in South America he nevertheless enters energetically into the activities of the revolutionary underground, until on a final mission he is arrested in the very town where his father is now a cardinal. Montanelli has the power to save the prisoner whom at first he does not recognise. But when Arthur reveals his identity he insists that Montanelli choose between him and Christ, that he will only accept assistance from his father if the latter renounces Christianity, joins the revolutionaries, and publicly acknowledges him as his son. Unable to abjure his faith, Montanelli is forced to leave Arthur to his fate, a bloody and bungled execution by an unwilling firing-squad. Torn apart by grief and pain the cardinal finally goes mad.

History is here cast in the form of a Freudian family romance. The passionate resentment felt by the gadfly towards his unfortunate father cannot be understood in terms of reason and logic. Conrad, who roundly disliked *The Gadfly*, made the point with amusing irony: 'Look at the logic: He found his mutton-chop very tough *therefore* he arose and cursed his aunt.'[16] The tirade that Arthur directs at Montanelli in their final meeting certainly goes beyond justice or reason:

> 'You say you love me,—your love has cost me dear enough! Do you think I can blot out everything, and turn back into Arthur at a few soft words— I, that have been dish-washer in filthy half-caste brothels and stable-boy to Creole farmers that were worse brutes than their own cattle? I, that have been zany in cap and bells for a strolling variety show—drudge and Jack-of-all-trades to the matadors in the bull-fighting ring: I, that have been slave to every black beast who cared to set his foot on my neck; I, that have been starved and spat upon and trampled under foot; I, that have begged for mouldy scraps and been refused because the dogs had the first right? Oh, what is the use of all this! How can I *tell* you what you have brought on me? And now—you love me! How much do you love me? Enough to give up your God for me?'[17]

The margin of emotional excess in this demand for an absolute, unconditional love points to an unresolved Oedipal conflict that is rooted in the unconscious; and this unconscious is both personal and political. The oppressive power of the father that is charged here with causing the social degradation of Arthur is not adequately represented by the humane and sensitive Montanelli; and, in any case, the exile in South America is in the first place self-chosen. But the indictment attains socially symbolic proportions, passing through the biological father to implicate the institution of the Catholic Church and, through the treacherous father-confessor Cardi, the imperial régime itself. The political law of the father has banished Arthur to the lowest level of human society, lower even than the 'Creole farmers' and 'black beasts', the brutalised victims of European imperial exploitation. It is a whole social and political order that is under attack, and the revolutionary hero has to be seen as an Oedipal rebel in the widest sense, who suffers in his person the pain and humiliation of the socially and politically oppressed.

It is, then, through the socially symbolic ramifications of the Freudian family romance that the violent and often melodramatic emotions in the novel are brought into relation with historical reality. Melodrama and romance provide a means of articulating the violent nature of the struggle for political emancipation. There are, however, problems involved in this treatment of history in terms of an unresolved Oedipal conflict, since the charge of personal feeling that it generates is so powerful that it constantly threatens to overwhelm the wider social and political implications. In particular the individual suffering and attendant pathos of the revolutionary as hero of romance are so dominant that the cause for which he fights, and the people whose champion he ostensibly is, are effectively marginalised. Whilst soliciting unqualified compassion for the victimised gadfly himself, the novel is, indeed, curiously ambiguous in its treatment of the collective victims of oppression, those coolies, negroes and half-castes of whom Arthur speaks with such bitter hostility.[18] And in the scene where Montanelli goes mad while conducting a service in his cathedral, it is the people rather than the church itself that he turns on, accusing them of having robbed him of his son: 'You have killed him! You have killed him! And I suffered it, because I would not let you die' (p.249). In his demented, guilt-ridden outburst he acts out the passion of God the father, whilst Arthur is elided into the crucified Christ, whose sacrifice has been undertaken for an undeserving and ungrateful people;

> 'The price of your banquet is paid for you; come, then, and gorge yourselves, cannibals, bloodsuckers—carrion beasts that feed on the dead! See where the blood streams down from the altar, foaming and hot from my darling's heart—the blood that was shed for you!' (p.250)

The logic and language of this tirade may be those of a crazed mind, but it illustrates the way in which the personal pathos of this Oedipal drama is created at the expense of sympathy for the generality of human beings.

If it remains problematic in this respect, the novel does achieve a form of radical openness in its conclusion. As Arnold Kettle has pointed out, where everything seems to be set for 'either a happy ending or a morally comforting one', Voynich refuses to satisfy the expectations she has raised.'[19] In his prison cell Arthur confronts Montanelli with a stark choice and insists on his commitment to violent revolutionary action: 'I am not a man; I am a knife. If you let me live, you sanction knives' (p.231). No possibility of compromise is offered in either the personal or the political struggle; and although *The Gadfly* reaches an emotional closure with death, grief and madness, the wider conflict that it has brought dramatically to life remains resolutely unresolved. The fiction registers the unfulfilled, but also undimmed, revolutionary aspirations of Voynich's own time; and this novel, like the other three, shows how history, seen from the perspective of its victims, is never a closed chapter.

NOTES

1. Walter Benjamin, *Illuminations*, translated by Harry Zohn (London, 1973), p.258.
2. *ibid.*, p.259.
3. See for example his ILP Penny Pamphlet, *Cotton and Competition: Striking Facts and Figures* (London, 1909).
4. D. F. E. Sykes and Geo. Henry Walker, *Ben o' Bill's, the Luddite: A Yorkshire Tale* (London and Huddersfield, n.d.) p.i. Further references to this edition are given in parentheses. Although the title page carries no date, the British Library catalogue records 1898.
5. Introduction to the fourth edition of Frank Peel, *The Risings of the Luddites* (London, 1968), p.x.
6. Peel, *Luddites*, pp.93, 95.

7. Georg Lukács, *The Historical Novel*, translated by Hannah and Stanley Mitchell (Harmondsworth, 1969), pp.29-69.
8. James Haslam, *The Handloom Weaver's Daughter* (London, 1904), p.vii. Further references to this edition are given in parentheses.
9. See P. M. Ashraf, *Introduction to Working-class Literature in Great Britain*, Part II: Prose (Berlin, 1979), p.130, who gives a brief sketch of Haslam's career.
10. As Ashraf claims, *op. cit.*, p.131.
11. Mark Rutherford, *The Revolution in Tanner's Lane* (London, 1971), p.7. Further references to this edition are given in parentheses. The novel was first published in 1887.
12. John Lucas, 'William Hale White and the problems of deliverance', in his *The Literature of Change* (Hassocks, 1977), pp.57-118.
13. W. Hale White, *Last Pages from a Journal* (London, 1915), p.274.
14. See Anne Fremantle, 'The Russian best seller: *The Gadfly*', *History Today*, XXV (1975), pp.629-37.
15. Fremantle, *op. cit.*, cites sales of 5 million copies in over 100 editions in 22 languages of the USSR.
16. Letter of 11 October 1897. *The Collected Letters of Joseph Conrad: Volume I; 1861-1897*, Frederick R. Karl and Laurence Davies (London, 1983), p.395.
17. E. L. Voynich, *The Gadfly* (St Albans, 1973), pp.228-9. Further references to this Mayflower paperback edition are given in parentheses. The novel was first published in 1897.
18. The political ambiguity of the gadfly's stance was more than matched by that of his probable historical model, Sigmund Rosenblum, who had an affair with Voynich in 1895 and in later life became a passionate anti-Bolshevist. As the British spy Sidney Reilly he was executed in the USSR in 1925 while his fictional counterpart lived on as a hero to the Soviet reading public. See Fremantle, *op. cit.*
19. Arnold Kettle, 'E. L. Voynich: a forgotten English novelist', *Essays in Criticism*, VII (1957), pp.163-74 (p.171). Another, more recent, sympathetic study of Voynich is James G. Kennedy, 'Voynich, Bennett, and Tressell: two alternatives for realism in the transition age', *English Literature in Transition 1880-1970*, XIII (1970), pp.254-86.

· 6 ·

Anarchism and fiction

GRAHAM HOLDERNESS

It would be misleading to speak, at least in relation to British culture, of a fiction of anarchism in the same sense that there is a fiction of socialism.[1] The various traditions of socialist and communist philosophy and political practice that penetrated British society within the period in question reflected and helped to constitute a broad socialist movement incorporating mass working-class experience and exerting powerful political influence over the tendencies of historical development. Although socialist fiction inevitably operated in a cultural terrain peripheral to the dominant ideology, its practitioners were able to found a genre capable of producing, at a later stage, in the writings of Tressell and Grassic Gibbon and Lewis Jones, novels of such artistic power and political impact that they could hardly be ignored by bourgeois culture: texts which called forth from literary criticism strategies of negotiation designed to isolate them from the historical movement as 'classics' of artistic achievement.

Anarchism, as theoretical philosophy and as political practice, has never been within British society more than a fringe activity, based on tiny libertarian groups and isolated individual intellectuals: 'a chorus of voices', in George Woodcock's memorable phrase 'crying in the wilderness'.[2] Anarchism in Britain never gained the kind of mass following that could make it an important social force in, for example, Republican Spain:[3] although instances to the contrary can be found, the labour movement in Britain has exhibited little more sympathy towards anarchism than the established order itself. It is perhaps surprising that there is a fiction of anarchism at all: yet it is possible to discover in British fiction both an engagement with anarchism in the work of 'major' writers like Henry James and Joseph Conrad, and a body of fictional writing, small but significant, expressing some degree of commitment to anarchist ideas. Furthermore, as I will attempt to demonstrate, for particular social and cultural reasons anarchism exerted over the minds of certain writers an influence disproportionate to its historical role in the development of British society.

To some degree the fiction exhibits a serious interest in and engagement with the salient points of anarchist philosophy: the outright rejection not only of capitalist society, but of all social systems *per se*; the opposing of collectivist forms of socialism as dogmatic and contrary to the true nature of freedom; the belief in the natural goodness and perfectibility of man; the emphasis on the freedom and sovereignty of the individual; and the vision of a libertarian society of voluntary co-operation and mutual assistance. On the other hand there is a much wider and stronger reflection in fiction of the forms of political violence espoused by some anarchist groups and individuals: the employment in their war against society of weapons of terrorism and assassination. At some time and in some place the entire vocabulary of political dissent— socialist, communist, radical, left—has been demonised by conservative and reactionary interests: but no political term has been so comprehensively and systematically smeared as anarchism. The deliberate equation anarchy = chaos deflects the force of all arguments against government, and turns the anarchist's own title back on him with a charge of wanton destructiveness. In British culture anarchy has always meant what it meant to Matthew Arnold: barbarism, the negation of culture and civilisation. The almost automatic association, in the later nineteenth century, by the press and by other writers as well as by politicians, of anarchism with political violence, individual assassination and terrorist operations, was drawn from a general European experience: but the equation was, in British conditions, to say the least, misleading. All the terrorist attacks which shocked, outraged and frightened London in the 1880s and 1890s were the work of Fenian nationalists: as George Woodcock observes, 'the only victim of anarchist violence in England was a Frenchman named Marcel Bourdin, who in 1894 accidentally blew himself up in Greenwich Park with a home-made bomb . . .'[4]

The Victorian establishment—monarchy, government, church, press etc.—had a vested interest in maximising the association of radical politics with destructive violence, and in blurring the distinctions between gradualist constitutional socialism, the revolutionary collectivism of the marxist parties and the libertarianism of the anarchists. Much writing of the period addresses anarchism within an ideological structure derived from the 'social-problem' novels of the 1840s: and systematically confuses working-class militancy, trade-union organisations, political demonstrations, secret societies, sabotage, terrorism, assassination and pointless destructiveness.[5] The identification of anarchism with terrorism also led several writers to confuse anarchism with the Russian nihilists, who certainly employed terrorism but with the very un-anarchistic objective of establishing constitutional government.[6] I have restricted my attention here to novels which represent some form of serious engagement with the historical phenomenon of anarchism: even though in some cases (especially that of Henry James) the contours of history are hard to discern through the obfuscating ideological texture of the fiction. I have begun with a non-British novel, Zola's *Germinal* (1885), since that remarkable text seems to have established parameters within which other fictional explorers of anarchism were content to operate.

THE NOVEL OF ANARCHISM

Emile Zola (1840-1902)

Zola's treatment of anarchism is, as we might expect, much

more historically specific and politically informed than the corresponding visions of Conrad and James. Where many writers, including James, could or would not distinguish between socialism and anarchism, Zola carefully differentiates marxist and more evolutionary forms of socialism from the anarchists, referring explicitly to the 1872 Marx/Bakunin split in the International. Zola's anarchist Souvarine is defined specifically in terms of his hostility to properly socialist ideas:

> 'Your friend Karl Marx is still at the stage of wanting to leave things to natural evolution. No politics, no conspiracies, isn't that the idea? . . . Don't talk to me about evolution! Raise fires in the four corners of cities, mow people down, wipe everything out, and when nothing whatever is left of this rotten world perhaps a better will spring up.'[7]

A dissident scion of the Russian nobility, Souvarine has served a terrorist apprenticeship with the Nihilists or Social-Revolutionaries, fleeing to France after an unsuccessful attempt on the life of the Tsar. Among the miners of France he lives a modest existence, emulating a spartan simplicity of proletarian lifestyle; he echoes (with a rather un-anarchistic emphasis on hegemony) the destructive rhetoric of his master, Bakunin: ' "He is the only one who can deal the knock-out blow . . . the International under his command is bound to wipe out the old world" ' (p.236); and in true anarchist fashion he refuses to construct or act upon any systematic vision of future social development: ' "Any reasoning about the future is criminal, for it prevents pure destruction and holds up the march of the revolution" ' (p.237).[8]

On the other hand Zola's novel shares with other less politically conscious works some of the cruder and more popular conventions employed in the fictionalising of anarchism. Souvarine exemplifies a type of dual personality often used by portrayers of anarchists to link, in a contradictory fictional archetype, the apparently baffling combinations of idealism and violence, philosophical intellectualism and destructive determination, a quasi-religious faith in the good of humanity with a willingness to destroy those institutions by which humanity lives.⁹ Souvarine combines physical weakness with an 'insanely intrepid' heroism, effeminacy of appearance with incredible tenacity of will: 'On the fair, girlish face of Souvarine . . . appeared an expression of silent scorn, the crushing scorn of the man prepared to sacrifice his own life in obscurity without even the glory of a martyr's crown' (p.234).¹⁰ The narrative constantly foregrounds Souvarine's pet rabbit, 'Poland', to symbolise a tenderness for the cause of liberty utterly at odds with the apocalyptic severity of his revolutionary faith.

In some ways Souvarine represents a type akin to the 'Professor' in Conrad's *The Secret Agent*: the strange phenomenon of an individual devoted to a social cause, yet ostensibly independent of all effective social relationships. Having witnessed his lover and fellow-conspirator hanged in Moscow, Souvarine embraces and achieves a complete autonomy of the will, devoid of reciprocal obligations and affectional bonds: 'He did not want any ties, whether of women or friends, and then he was free to do what he liked with his own blood and the blood of others' (pp.142-3). The image of the anarchist as a fanatical devotee to some chiliastic religion is a popular one, and can indeed be found reflected in the Bakunin/Nechayev pamphlet *Revolutionary Chatechism* (1866): 'The revolutionary is a man under vow. He ought to occupy himself with one exclusive interest, with one thought and one passion: the Revolution . . . he has only one aim, one science: destruction.'¹¹ 'I have no weakness left in my heart' vows Souvarine; 'Nothing at all: no family, no wife, no friends, nothing to make my hand falter on the day when I have to take other people's lives or give my own' (p.430).

There is little trace in Souvarine of any special philosophy of anarchism—nothing of mutuality, co-operation, freedom of association, workers' control—his anarchism is a purely *individual* belief, a personal religion of destruction, fabricated by the simple expedient of hiving-off Bakunin's apocalyptic rhetoric from his constructive vision of a libertarian society.

Souvarine's climactic act of sabotage, carefully planned and executed, is to destroy the mine, 'Le Voreux', by damaging the lining of the main shaft sufficiently to permit inundation by the floodwaters of the 'underground sea'. By juxtaposing narrative perspectives—that of the fanatical saboteur and that of the miners (including the central characters Etienne and Catherine) who become trapped in the flooded pit, Zola foregrounds and insists emphatically on the inescapable interdependence of people and institutions: the terrorist who (quite correctly, in Zola's view) sees certain social institutions as oppressive and obstructive of human freedom and progress, must in order to strike at them by violence somehow suppress his sympathy for those whose lives are inevitably bound up with the 'target' of his destructive energy. Souvarine is portrayed in this connection as a callous murderer: he watches the miners file towards the doomed pit, 'counting them as a butcher might count animals going into a slaughter-house' (p.437).

Zola's description of the act of sabotage itself is far more ambiguous in its implications:

> Then he worked like one possessed. The breath of the invisible elated him, and the black horror of this rain-swept cavern filled him with a frenzy of destruction. He attacked the lining at random, hitting wherever he could, using his brace and bit or his saw as though his one idea were to rip everything open there and then on top of him. He put into the task the sort of ferocity with which he might have driven a knife into the flesh of some living being whom he loathed. He would kill this foul beast in the end, this pit with the ever-open jaws that had swallowed down so much human flesh. (p.434)

The atmosphere of terror and fascination combines a horror at Souvarine's determined destructiveness with an intense admiration for his heroic self-disregard. Such aesthetic disjunctures of tone arise from deep emotional contradictions in the text's ideological structure: at one level of the novel's discourse, which might be described as a 'fabulous' or 'mythic' dimension, Souvarine appears as an epic hero, a dragonslayer confronting the 'foul beast' in its lair and destroying it in single combat. The mine itself has been transformed into such a mythological monster only by the operations of the author's imagination: quite contrary to his own theory of naturalism, Zola has converted 'Le Voreux' from a piece of productive machinery into a monstrous and fabulous devourer of human flesh. The intense moral hatred of the pit, and the fanatical will to see it demolished, emanate from the author's contradictory ideology, and are constructed by the particular metaphoric texture of the narrative. The bourgeois novelist thus finds himself in a strange kinship with the anarchistic terrorist: each represents the faculty of daring imagination capable of conceiving of an economic institution as an autonomous force hostile and alien to human aspirations, threatening and devouring, challenging the heroic individual to a murderous final combat. The extravagant surrealism and imaginative finality of the writer's vision correspond therefore to the totalising purity of the anarchist's social philosophy.

The closing vision of the novel is attributed, in narrative terms, to the departing Etienne, who has never been shown to share Souvarine's anarchist faith: but in Etienne's meditations, the mythic conception of 'Le Voreux' is extrapolated to a general vision of a society under threat, and the anarchist's destruction of the mine becomes a model for a general apocalyptic transformation of society:

> One morning, confident in their solidarity, millions of workers against a few thousand idlers, they would take over power and be the masters. Ah, then indeed truth and justice would awake! Then that crouching, sated god, that monstrous idol hidden away in his secret tabernacle, gorged with the flesh of poor creatures who never even saw him, would instantly perish. (p.498)

The novel closes with the imagery implicit in its title, of natural regeneration and springtime growth. The visionary revelation of social transformation is effected not spontaneously by natural evolution, but by the spontaneous revolutionary activity of the working class. Metaphors of fertility, birth, germination, are combined with a language of destructive vengeance in a juxtaposition fundamental to the language of anarchism. Here, for example, is Shelley, giving poetic form to Godwin's anarchist philosophy:

> The earth's great age begins anew
> The golden years return,
> The earth doth like a snake renew
> Her winter weeds outworn:
> Heaven smiles, and faiths and empires gleam
>   Like wrecks in a dissolving dream.[12]

Here Bakunin:

> Let us therefore trust the eternal spirit which destroys and annihilates only because it is the unfathomable and eternal source of all life. The passion for destruction is a creative passion, too![13]

And here is Zola:

> Life was springing from her fertile womb, buds were bursting into leaf and the fields were quickening with fresh green grass . . . Men were springing up, a black avenging host was slowly germinating in the furrows, thrusting upwards for the harvests of future ages. And very soon, their germination would crack the earth asunder. (pp.489-9)

Joseph Conrad (1857-1924)

> The subject of *The Secret Agent*—I mean the tale—came to me in the shape of a few words uttered by a friend in a casual conversation about anarchists or rather anarchist activities . . . I remember remarking on the criminal futility of the whole thing, doctrine, action, mentality; and on the contemptible aspect of the half-crazy pose as of a brazen cheat exploiting the poignant miseries and passionate credulities of a mankind always so tragically eager for self-destruction. That was what made for me its philosophical pretences so unpardonable. Presently . . . we recalled the already old story of the attempt to blow up Greenwich Observatory; a bloodstained inanity of so fatuous a kind that it was impos-

sible to fathom its origin by any reasonable or even unreasonable process of thought . . . that outrage could not be laid hold of mentally in any sort of way, so that one remained faced by the fact of a man blown to bits for nothing even remotely resembling an idea, anarchistic or other. As to the outer wall of the Observatory, it did not show so much as the faintest crack.[14]

The point of view expressed here about anarchism and its links with terrorist activities is substantially that of the contemporary government and of the conservative press: simple, crude, unenlightened and containing all the elements of popular prejudice. Conrad takes terrorism as the prerogative of the anarchist: though in fact all the bombings in the metropolis in the last decade of the nineteenth century had Fenian nationalist origins. The argument that anarchism could have no philosophical or ideological basis is a crude elision of a powerful and highly intellectual body of political thought. The identification of anarchism and terror seems to echo the outraged prejudices of a society challenged by the widespread radical movements of the period, and anxious to pin as much blame as possible on a political group already demonised into a mythological nightmare: as an intellectual position, it seems an unlikely basis for the ideological substratum of a 'great' novel. Even the central anecdote of the discussion, the death of Marcel Bourdin in 1884, shows Conrad's own 'reasonable process of thought' comfortably aligned with the headlines of contemporary newspapers like *The Times* (which simply voiced what was probably a deliberate fiction of the government). The whole notion of a plot to blow up Greenwich Observatory was fabricated without any circumstantial or substantiating evidence: Bourdin was either delivering or hiding the explosive, and had no designs at all on the First Meridian. The 'Author's Note' speaks of another element in the tale's development:

> the vision of an enormous town presented itself, of a monstrous town more populous than some continents and in its man-made might as if indifferent to heaven's frowns and smiles; a cruel devourer of the world's light. There was room

> enough there to place any story, depth enough for any passion, variety enough there for any setting, darkness enough to bury five millions of lives.
>   Slowly the dawning conviction of Mrs. Verloc's maternal passion grew up to a flame between me and that background, tingeing it with its secret ardour, and receiving from it in exchange some of its own sombre colouring.

We seem then to be confronted with a novel which is more about personal relationships and their social context—especially perhaps the institution of marriage, which is at once a personal connection and a social institution—than it is about anarchism. Verloc's profession of secret agent, and the bomb-blast itself, seem more like symbols of the duplicity and violence immanent in bourgeois marriage, of the domestic lives of those trapped and lonely people who inhabit that monstrous city, 'great devourer of the world's light'. How then do the private and public dimensions of the novel intersect? What is the nature of its political and social vision?

We can begin, as Conrad does, with Verloc. What exactly is Verloc's *secret*?

> The door of the shop was the only means of entrance to the house in which Mr Verloc carried on his business of a seller of shady wares, exercised his vocation of a protector of society, and cultivated his domestic virtues. (pp.14-15)

The emphasis on domestic virtues is ironic but not misleading; Mr Verloc *is* in fact a protector of society—a police informer and the confidant of a reactionary foreign government which is concerned to 'protect society' in the form of defending the prominent political figures and crowned heads who were in practice anarchist targets. *Secrecy* seems necessary to preserve the general social fabric as well as particular social institutions (such as the Verloc marriage): for the larger unit, the social macrocosm, embassy intrigues, *agents provacateurs*, the secrecy and professional rivalry of the police; for the smaller, the domestic microcosm, the silence of Verloc about the true sources of his income, and the acceptance by Winnie of a barren, hollow, conventional marriage.

The plot to bomb Greenwich Observatory, which ends in Stevie's death, is hatched and organised by Mr Vladimir, official of the Tsarist state, working through his paid informer: it is a rigged terrorist atrocity, an act of calculated provocation. The plot owes its *insanity* entirely to Mr Vladimir's bizarre conception of what a truly frightening terrorist attack should be: 'an act of destructive ferocity so absurd as to be incomprehensible'. Verloc perceives it very clearly as an insane project: the man who knows the anarchists seems to be of the opinion that this is simply not the sort of thing they would dream of doing. None of the novel's revolutionaries, indeed, seems remotely capable of such an act: Conrad presents them as utterly impotent and innocuous individuals, all apparently incapable of hurting a fly.

The exception is the Professor, who is potentially a serious threat to society. A peculiar mixture of physical inadequacy and enormous egoism, he measures his own value by the 'force of will' necessary to make himself into a walking bomb. Though he seems perhaps to menace himself more than anyone else, he has some of the qualities of the historical anarchist: Conrad gives him at least integrity and consistency; his explosive potentialities render him, in line with the anarchist policy of 'propaganda by deed', a 'true propagandist'; and his professed intention—'to destroy public faith in legality'—would be a motive recognisable to an anarchist terrorist.[15]

The professor's opposite number is Inspector Heat, the police officer investigating the Greenwich Park explosion. Conrad spins around Heat the same web of irony that surrounds his other characters: he is presented as foolish and concerned only with his own reputation, his own status in his department. He also, like everyone else in the novel, has his secrets, which lead him to misunderstand or deliberately distort the evidence before him (see pp. 104-5). It is difficult to understand, given this degree of irony, Barbara Arnett Melchiori's suggestion that Conrad 'sides with Chief Inspector Heat'.[16] It is a combination of secret personal interests, rather than the amazing intelligence of the British police so stunning to Mr Vladimir, that leads to the disclosure of the truth. The end-product of the investigation is, finally, nothing: Mr Vladimir is blackballed from an 'extremely exclusive club', and the police plan to prosecute the hireling Verloc as a foreign spy. Nothing much will change, either in the world of anarchism, in that of the public services, or in terms of the pernicious vitality of that 'monstrous town' within whose secret shadows all these events take place.

Conrad's comprehensive vision of a corrupt society, involving the institutions of marriage and private property, police and parliament, city and state, comes strikingly close to the vision of the anarchist. Yet any philosophical acknowledgement of such a relationship is implicitly denied, since even Conrad's marxists and anarchists are not permitted any genuine theory or political belief. Revolutionary philosophy in *The Secret Agent* is reduced to ineffectual vanity or mere destructiveness: all ideologies are dismissed or negated. Once the whole philosophical side of marxist and anarchist politics has been sheared away, the writer is forced into a position where the only kind of imaginative commitment he can make is to the Professor's dream of total annihilation. What can be done with a world like this, once it has been created; a world devoid of internal possibilities for redemption or improvement? There is only one final solution: destruction. The only people who can dream of destroying a world are the anarchist and the artist: the novelist who can unmake the world he has made at will. As this novel ends, the Professor's dream is realised: the whole murky, shadowy, corrupt and secretive world of the novel disappears: into the blank whiteness of the unprinted page—'a whitewashed wall with no writing on it'.

It is not for nothing that Conrad once professed himself a kind of anarchist:

> Mankind is an evil animal. His wickedness must be controlled. Society exists to organise that wickedness. Therefore society is criminal. That's why I agree with the extreme

anarchist: 'I want *total destruction*. That's good; above all, it's clear'.[17]

THE ROMANCE OF ANARCHISM

Henry James (1843-1916)

W. H. Tilley demonstrated plausibly that Henry James drew his plot for *The Princess Casamassima* (1886) from an unsuccessful attempt on the part of two conspirators, Rupsch and Küchler, acting under the orders of an anarchist leader named Reinsdorf, to assassinate the German emperor William I at Niederwald on 28 September 1883.[18] The detail that seems to have attracted James to the story was the fact that at their trial one of the would-be assassins, the twenty-one-year-old Rupsch, claimed to have deliberately frustrated the attempt out of some misgiving or change of heart. From these circumstances—extensively reported in the British magazines and newspapers of late 1884—James derived his story of a young radical whose political commitment compels him to swear to a great European anarchist a mysterious oath to undertake at some future time some unspecified act of terrorism. With the oath Hyacinth Robinson's revolutionary zeal begins to wither, and the novel ends with his frustrating by suicide his own appointed task of assassination.[19]

The historical origin does not in practice confer on James's novel any very obvious specificity of historical presentation: James's interest in the story is so far from any particularity of political definition that I have categorised *The Princess Casamassima* as a romance rather than a novel of anarchism. The heart of the plot is a conventional 'moral-problem' dilemma: Hyacinth finds himself compelled to choose between a growing love of 'life' (represented by his increasing fascination with the slumming radical aristocrat-by-marriage, Princess Christina, and by brief trips to Paris and Venice); and the 'duty' which devolves to him by virtue of his revolutionary allegiance. In the 'Preface' James characterises Hyacinth as 'some individual sensitive nature of fine mind, some small obscure intelligent creature'[20] whose social deprivation fills him with jealousy of 'all the ease of life of which he tastes so little'. That intelligible envy is figured (in James's metaphor) as a kind of rabid dog which infects the subject with socialism: 'bitter, under this exasperation, with an aggressive, vindictive, destructive social faith' (p.18). The plot is made to turn on a 'change-of-heart' crisis: 'the deep dilemma of the disillusioned and repentant conspirator', whose 'militant socialism' becomes 'out of all tune with his passion, at any cost, for life itself, the life, whatever it be, that surrounds him' (p.18). The ideological innocence, the naïve transparency of the novel's underlying ideas is quite alarming when one considers James's 'status' in the literary hierarchy: political radicalism springs from envy and is incompatible with a love of life; 'love' and 'life' itself are conceived as inseparably bound up with aristocratic affiliation and with bourgeois culture.

The allusions to socialism and anarchism are positively Gothic in their elusive and spectral mysteriousness: though so acutely 'sensitive' to fine discriminations of social nuance and emotional subtlety, James was as little concerned as *The Times* to make any serious political distinction between socialism, communism, anarchism and terrorist violence. The 'militant socialism' of the novel appears in the curiously unrecognisable form of a vast international underground conspiracy dedicated in some unspecified way to the destruction of civilisation as Henry James knew it. Paul Muniment describes it:

> 'there's an immense underworld peopled with a thousand forms of revolutionary passion and devotion. The manner in which it's organised astonished me . . . In silence, in darkness, but under the feet of each one of us, the revolution lives and works. It's a wonderful, immeasurable trap, on the lid of which society performs its antics. When once the machinery is complete there'll be a great rehearsal.' (pp.290-1)

The defensive convolutions of James's 'Preface' stand as a sufficient acknowledgement of the fact that this immense subterranean conspiracy corresponds to nothing other than the author's social paranoia:

> My vision of the aspects I more or less fortunately rendered was, exactly, my knowledge. If I made my appearances live, what was this but the utmost one could do with them? Let me at the same time not deny that, in answer to probable ironic relections on the full licence for sketchiness and vagueness and dimness taken indeed by my picture, I had to bethink myself in advance of a defence of my 'artistic position'. Shouldn't I find it in the happy contention that the value I wished most to render and the effect I wished most to produce were precisely those of our not knowing, of society's not knowing, but only guessing and suspecting and trying to ignore, what 'goes on' irreconcilably, subversively, beneath the vast smug surface?
> (p.22)

Hyacinth's mysterious vow of commitment derives directly from the political novels and romances of the 1840s (for example *Mary Barton* and *Sybil*) in which trade unions enjoin on their members, by arcane rituals and threats of violent reprisal, terrible oaths of obligation. The emotional reverberations of moral panic surrounding this motif can only derive from a deep-seated ideological terror of dissent: a profound anxiety at the very thought of ritualised commitment to something other than the established order—'He had taken a vow of blind obedience, the vow as of the Jesuit fathers to the head of their order' (p.294).

James's approach to the subject differs most strikingly from Zola's and Conrad's, not in his lack of interest in political and historical actuality, but in his relative incapacity to participate in the operations of the destructive imagination, or to recognise that link between artist and anarchist so evident in the other two writers. A passage of *The Princess Casamassima* may seem to echo exactly both *Germinal* and *The Secret Agent:*

> he seemed to see, immensely magnified, the monstrosity of the great ulcers and sores of London—the sick, eternal misery crying out in the darkness in vain, confronted with granaries and treasure-houses and palaces of delight where shameless

satiety kept guard. In such a mood as this he felt there was no need to consider, to reason: the facts themselves were as imperative as the cry of the drowning . . . the day had come for a forcible rectification of horrible iniquities. (p.254)

Yet the narrative tone here is in fact ironic: the fanatic's apocalyptic vision of outcast London is offered as in itself a betrayal of the 'reason' and 'consideration' which should, presumably, be applied to the understanding of social problems and the manner of their solution. Denied any access to the aesthetic power of the libertarian imagination, James's concluding artistic gesture is to occlude the social dimension and contain the destructive energies of anarchism within the melodramatic perimeters of individual self-sacrifice: 'Mr Robinson has shot himself through the heart!' (p.537).

E. Douglas Fawcett (1866-19?)

E. Douglas Fawcett's *Hartmann the Anarchist: or the Doom of the Great City* (1893), a futuristic romance in the manner of Jules Verne and H. G. Wells, offers (perhaps with the greater transparency of popular fiction) a more overt disclosure of the contradictions at the heart of contemporary artistic responses to anarchism. Narrative devices and manipulations of plot secure for the reader a voyeuristic fantasy of anarchist violence, while the narrator is privileged to remain consistently aloof from anarchist activities, and free to erect a barrier of moral diatribe between his own bourgeois consciousness and the revolutionary terrorism he witnesses and becomes involved in.

From the narrative perspective of an old man reminiscing in a quiet German retreat, Arthur Stanley offers a detached retrospective of events supposed to have occurred in 1920. His avowed narrative purpose is empirical documentation: 'to weigh each event impartially in the balance';[21] yet his story is one of reluctant participation in an unsuccessful European revolution engineered by a combination of anarchist terrorism and violent insurrection—he is drawn unintentionally into the political action, and wastes no opportunity of reassuring the reader of the probity of his motives.

As in *Germinal* anarchism is defined politically in opposition to evolutionary socialism: the narrator is a 'labour advocate and socialist', and prospective parliamentary candidate for Stepney. His Socialism is explicitly defined as moderate and gradualist: 'I myself, though a socialist, was averse to barricades. "Not revolution, but evolution" was the watchword of my section' (p.5). Socialism is defined as the peaceful 'nationalisation of land and capital, of the means of production and distribution' (p.5). The spectre of independent political action by the working class is depicted in all the lurid colours of the Victorian reformist novel:

> How were the details of this vast change to be grappled with amid the throes of revolution? How deliberate with streets slippery with blood, the vilest passions unchained, stores, factories and workshops wrecked . . . what man or convention could beat out a workable constitution in the turmoil?
> (pp.5-6)

The narrator Arthur Stanley's social-democratic ideology is challenged by his friend Burnett,

> a man of the most advanced revolutionary opinions, in fact an apostle of what is generally known as anarchical communism. No law, no force, reference of all social energies to voluntary associations of individuals, were his substitutes for the all-regulating executive of the socialist. He made no secret of his intentions: he meant to wage war in every effective mode, violent or otherwise, against the existing social system. (p.8)

Stanley characterises the anarchists, by comparison with the broad popular basis of the labour movement, as a 'handful of people, politically speaking of no account' (p.10); Burnett, in rejecting the possibility of a peaceful transition to socialism, invokes in a 'dark hint' an alternative source of political power, which might become available to such a dedicated minority group:

I detest both society as it is and society as you hope it will be. Today the capitalist wolves and a slavish multitude; tomorrow a corrupt officialism and the same slavish multitude, only with new masters. But about our numbers, my friend, you think that we must be politically impotent because we are relatively few . . . But suppose, suppose, I say, our people had some incalculable force . . . (p.11)

That force is in fact already available in the hands of the anarchist Hartmann, the Captain Nemo of the story, who proposes to use it to destroy capitalist civilisation and establish a system of 'supervised anarchy'. It is in fact a flying machine, barbarically christened the *Attila*, with which the anarchists are able to attack London from the air. By drawing into fictional relationship anarchist terrorism and the popular fantasy of the miraculous invention, Fawcett was able to link in contradictory unity the intense excitements and anxieties created by terrorist attacks, with the ambivalent hopes and fears provoked by technological advance. Even the inviolable morality of the narrator is captivated by the excitements of the flying machine, which combine aesthetic pleasures with a realisation of power—'when to these purely artistic joys are added those of power, when the roar of wondering cities rises upwards, and you lean over the bulwarks serenely conscious of superiority, you must be described as realising here on earth one of the paradises of dreamland' (p.138). Equally strong is his moral outrage of compassion at the vulnerability of the city and its people as that 'power' is exercised destructively on London:

As we rode over the heart of the city—that sanctum of capital, where the Bank of England, many other banks of scarcely less brilliant fame, the Royal Exchange, Stock Exchange, where credit companies, insurance offices, and discount houses innumerable lie herded—the bombs fell in a tempest, shattering fabric after fabric, and uprooting their very foundations. There was a constant roar of explosions, and the loss of life must have been something terrible. (p.151)

Terrorist attacks on London during the 1880s and 1890s

created an intense awareness of the vulnerability of a city to clandestine assault. Fawcett's fantasy extrapolates that anxiety to a futuristic fear of aerial bombardment, as Hartmann's craft unloads explosive bombs, boiling oil and blazing petrol on to the buildings and crowds below. The effect, for us, is sharply ironic: the fantasy of an illegal, dissident force wielding such weapons clashes against the known and familiar violence of constitutional governments—incendiary bombs on Hamburg and Dresden, nuclear explosions over Hiroshima and Nagasaki, napalm billowing over the forests of Cambodia and North Vietnam.

The dominant image of the novel, effectively foregrounded in a frontispiece illustration, is the fall of the Houses of Parliament under the assault of Hartmann's bombs. Inevitably writers who touched this topic were concerned to stress the inseparable nature of the state and its citizens, of institutions and the people whose lives are interrelated with them. There can be no such thing as a violent physical attack on an institution (which many writers could have understood or even condoned) which is not also an 'outrage' directed against innocent people. Where Zola focused on the identity of the mine and its workforce, so Souvarine could not destroy the one without damaging the other; Fawcett focuses on the interdependence of Parliament and people, as Westminster falls, 'bruising into jelly a legion of buried wretches' (p.15).

Hartmann's plot fails, and in the established context of anarchist atrocity the narrator heartily endorses the brutal repression—such as summary execution of suspected anarchists—entailed in a re-establishing of 'order'. The most curious feature of the book lies, not in its disclosure of contradictory responses, but in its absent conclusion. Hartmann's global ambition was to deal what Souvarine called the 'knock-out blow' to world capitalism.

> His aim was to pierce the ventricle of the heart of civilisation, that heart which pumps the blood of capital everywhere, through the arteries of Russia, of Australia, of India . . . 'Paralyse this heart,' he has said, 'and you paralyse credit and

the mechanism of finance almost universally.' (p.148)

But this objective recording of Hartmann's fanatical aspiration is completed by a striking conclusion: 'The result already known to history proves that he was right' (p.148). By means of some unspecified and undescribed social transition, the anarchist ideals and terrorist violence of Hartmann have in practice succeeded in destroying capitalism and clearing a path for the development of a socialist state. The narrator's final relapse into civilised domestic life and individual creativity (he retires from politics to take up the secluded domestic pleasures of marriage and 'literary studies') takes place on the basis of a quiet revolution effected in the aftermath of Hartmann's war. An eloquent silence thus articulates in the novel the desirability of that which is most feared.

ANARCHIST NOVELS

Olivia Rossetti (1873-19?)

'Isabel Meredith', pseudonymous authoress of *A Girl among the Anarchists,* (1903) was in fact Olivia Rossetti, daughter of William Michael of the pre-Raphaelite circle. With her sister Helen she began in 1895 to publish *The Torch: a Revolutionary Journal of Anarchist Communism*, a short-lived but impressive production, which published work by European anarchists such as Louise Michel, Malatesta and Zhukovsky, and managed to include writing by Zola himself. This youthful involvement with the cultural propaganda of anarchism is addressed retrospectively in the prose work in question.

A Girl among the Anarchists does not employ the classic novel form, though it is certainly a work of fiction: it gives the appearance of a fictionalised memoir or semi-documentary *Bildungsroman*. In an interesting preface, Morley Roberts suggests that it is in fact an autobiographical 'testament of youth':

> There is nothing whatever in *A Girl among the Anarchists* which is invented, the whole thing is an experience told very simply, but I think convincingly. Nevertheless as such a human document must seem incredible to the ordinary reader, I have no little pleasure in saying that I know what she has written to be true . . . I knew 'Kosinski' and still have an admiration for 'Nekrovitch'.[22]

Considered as such the novel is a useful historical document, an informed eye-witness account of the intellectual and political circle gathered around Kropotkin during his long residence in England from 1886, and of its links with the anarchist movement in Europe. None the less, despite these documentary pretensions, the work possesses a particular artistic form which in turn is the articulation of its ideological engagement with anarchist philosophy and political practice.

The book's design enacts a trajectory of disillusionment, as the narrator–heroine throws herself with enthusiasm into the anarchist movement and is ultimately expelled on a curve of chastened disenchantment. Its 'deep structure' could therefore be said to align with that of *The Princess Casamassima;* but the effective differences are substantial and instructive. Rossetti's narrative describes and enacts an actual engagement with anarchist ideas, which are articulated and debated in the text with clarity and understanding; and testifies to the actuality of radical political commitment on the cultural fringes of the labour movement during the 1890s. 'Isabel's' ultimate decision to turn her back on anarchism, though articulated, like Hyacinth Robinson's, as a decision in favour of 'life', is remote from the Jamesian revulsion against his own crude popular identification of anarchism with violence. It is not an abhorrence of terrorism that induces Isabel to leave the movement, but a confirmed dissatisfaction with anarchism as an effective political force, and with the anarchist philosophy as a satisfactory guide to individual living (pp.271 ff.).

The familiar paradox of idealism and violence is broached immediately in Roberts's 'Preface':

> Curiously enough I have found most Anarchists of the mildest dispositions . . . For it must be understood that the 'red wing' of the Anarachists is a very small section of the body of philosophers known as Anarchists. There is no doubt that those of the dynamite section are practically insane. (p.vi)

Where the 'Preface' is defensively apologetic (though quite clear about the repression of anarchism as a pretext for illegitimate state violence) the text turns on a rather different version of that paradox: where Roberts reproduces the conventional antithesis between innocuous idealism and pernicious violence, Rossetti constantly poses anarchist idealism, as morally heroic and politically powerful, against the various kinds of selfishness, weakness, laziness and sordid calculation which are seen as drawing people to the fringes of an anarchist group. Isabel is initially attracted to the anarchist position for its lofty idealism, which seems to shame the mundanity and petty materialism of Social Democracy:

> Quite a new side of the problem—that of its moral bearings and abstract rights as opposed to the merely material right to daily bread which had first appealed to my sense of justice and humanity—now opened before me. The right to complete liberty of action, the conviction that morality is relative and personal and can never be imposed from without, that men are not responsible, or only very partially so, for their surroundings, by which their actions are determined, and that consequently no man has the right to judge his fellow; such and similar doctrines which I heard frequently upheld, impressed me deeply. I was morally convinced of their truth, and consequently more than half an anarchist. (p.17)

This structural opposition often relegates 'politics' to the realm of the trivial and sordid: while true anarchism is admired both for its moral purity and for the decisive political will expressed in acts of terrorism. The Greenwich Park explosion of 1892 which stands at the centre of *The Secret Agent* is woven into the action of *A Girl among the Anarchists*. But where the 'supremely intelligent' Conrad followed *The Times* in suspecting and condemning some insane project of destruction, Rossetti offers an interestingly different version: the dead anarchist is seen as a victim of his brother's treachery, and the brother subjected to an intense moral condemnation for the cowardice of denying any terrorist intention (pp.50-2). Isabel assists in procuring the escape of one 'Jean Matthieu', 'suspected of complicity in the Paris bomb explosions' (p.160).[23] Later in the novel an attempt is made to explain the psychological condition of the anarchist terrorist, by the case of Emile Henry, who was historically responsible for the bombing of the Café Terminus at the Gare St Lazare in 1894. The fanaticism of the terrorist is related to the fanaticism of the 'secular saint':

> Among the Anarchists, who may be said to represent the intellectual rather than the material side of the Socialist movement—there were many fanatics. This fanaticism showed itself in different ways—sometimes in the most admirable self-abnegation, in the sacrifice of wealth, position, and happiness; frequently in abnormal actions of other kinds, and most noticeably in deeds of violence.
> ... Emile Henry, the dynamitard of the Café Terminus, belonged to the number of what I may call the theoretical dynamitard. His terrible acts were the outcome of long and earnest thought; they were born of his mental analysis of the social canker. He committed them not in moments of passion, but with all the *sang froid* of a man governed by reason. His defence when on trial was a masterpiece of logical deduction.
> (p.188)

The culminating action of the novel appears to be a fictionalisation of more than one incident in the history of Spanish anarchist terrorism: including the failed attempt on the life of Martínez Campos, Captain-General of Barcelona, in 1893, and the shooting of Antonio Canovas by an Italian anarchist Michele Angiolilli, in reprisal for the widespread repression and appalling tortures that followed the Barcelona bombing of June 1886. In the novel the Italian anarchist 'Giannoli' makes an unsuccessful attempt on the life of the Spanish Prime Minister in Madrid. The narrative presents this action not as a providentially deflected atrocity, but as an unfortunately unsuccesful attempt to secure justice:

> This then was the deed he had been contemplating! . . . he would be garotted; I only hoped that he might not be tortured first. I gave a hasty glance at the other details given by the paper. A column was dedicated to the virtues of the prime-minister. He was . . . represented as the man who had saved Spain from ruin and disaster by his firm repression of the revolutionary parties: by which euphonious phrase the papers referred to the massacres of strikers which had taken place at Barcelona and Valladolid, and the wholesale arrest and imprisonment of Anarchists and Socialists in connection with a recent anti-clerical movement which had convulsed the Peninsula. (p.291)

Olivia Rossetti's proximity to the *avant-garde* cultural circle which had its firm connections, through figures like William Morris, with the revolutionary socialist movement, render her interests in anarchism to some extent aesthetic-bohemian in nature; and her romantic adulation for political idealism and moral perfection is capable of projecting the very category of politics into the untouchable sordidness of a mean and petty present. Her intellectual grasp of political ideas enables her however to recognise, in an insight inaccessible to Conrad or James, that anarchist philosophy could be seen to embody enduring and imperative values, and that anarchist politics should be evaluated in the context of the legitimised violence and repression of the imperialist nation-states.

Frank Harris (1855-1931)

Frank Harris's *The Bomb* (1908) is distinguished by its consistent endorsement not only of anarchist philosophy and ideals, but even of acts of revolutionary terrorism—specifically the bomb which killed a number of policemen in Chicago in 1886. A workers' demonstration was fired on by police and several men killed. The following day, as the police moved in to break up a protest meeting, a bomb was thrown from a side-alley and casualties fell. A round-up of anarchists followed, and eight local leaders, including August Spies and Albert Parsons, editors respectively of two of Chicago's five anarchist papers, were put on trial. The process was clearly a show trial, since no attempt was made to prove complicity in the bombing: the prosecution sought only to prove that the accused were anarchists and revolutionaries. A subsequent enquiry found that none of the accused had any part in the bombing: but four had already been executed.

The Bomb is thus a historical novel, weaving a fictional framework around documented facts, and presenting a vivid and open dramatisation of the anarchist point of view. The central incident of the bomb-throwing is used both to portray a legitimate resistance to intolerable economic, social and political conditions, particularly the aggressive brutality of the police, mobilised to break up peaceful demonstrations; and to disclose the machinery of injustice provoked into action to secure the judicial murder of Chicago labour leaders.

The true Chicago bomb-thrower was never discovered, and Harris's fiction supplies that absence by attributing the deed to his narrator–hero, Rudolph Schnaubelt. An expatriate German 'freethinker and republican', Schnaubelt arrives in the United States with lofty egalitarian ideals and a meritocratic confidence in the likelihood of personal success. But the experience of prolonged unemployment breeds bitter and vindictive thoughts:

> The humiliations filled me with rage, and this rage and fear fermented in me into bitterness which bred all-hating thoughts. When I saw rich men entering a restaurant, or driving in Central Park, I grew murderous . . . One conclusion settled itself in me; there was something rotten in a society which left good brains and willing hands without work.[24]

Harris describes effectively the misery of unemployment, with its burden of shame, humiliation and personal guilt. Among the workers Schnaubelt finds comradeship and the solidarity of 'human sympathy'; and gradually his feelings set in anger against the rich: 'It is only the poor who help the poor. I have been down in the depths, and have brought back scarcely anything more certain than that. One does not learn much in hell except hate . . .' (p.27). Finding work at last, he enters the physically intolerable conditions of working on the foundations of the Brooklyn Bridge (pp.31-8); and from that baptism of fire emerges in full political consciousness to join the ranks of a 'proletariat ready for revolt'. Against that growing force Chicago arraigns its notoriously brutal police force: 'for the first time in America orderly meetings on vacant lots are dispersed with force, and thoughts are met with police bludgeons' (p.85).

As in *Hartmann the Anarchist*, the power of the organised working class is not deemed sufficient to resist the aggression of an incited state: and the force required is found in an anarchist saint, Louis Lingg. To Schnaubelt he is a saviour, a Redeemer: 'the greatest man that ever lived, I think . . . He had vitality enough in him to bring the dead to life, passion enough for a hundred men . . . he is the spring of all my growth' (pp.8-9). Lingg proposes that the movement should meet force with force: 'Violence must be met with violence' (p.97). His anarchism combines syndicalism with individualism: society should allow the individual as much freedom as possible by permitting economic control to rest with individuals. And it is as an individual that Lingg will strike at the heart of the bourgeoisie, with the aid of a powerful explosive device.

Schnaubelt throws the bomb, Lingg guides him to freedom, and is subsequently himself arrested. Sentenced to death, he offers as a defiance his theory of equal forces and of 'propaganda by deed':

> 'I believe in force just as you do. That is my justification. Force is the supreme arbiter in human affairs. You have clubbed unarmed strikers, shot them down in your streets, shot down their women and their children. So long as you do that, we who are Anarchists will use explosives against you.' (p.268)

After reaching England Schnaubelt himself endures an attenuated existence, living vicariously in the events of

Chicago: the trial and subsequent death of Lingg in prison by his own explosives. His final purpose becomes that of telling Lingg's story and establishing his fame as an anarchist martyr:

> One thing is past doubt. Louis Lingg was a great man, and a born leader of men, who with happier chances might have been a great reformer, or a great statesman. When they talk of him as a murderer, it fills me with pity for them, for in Lingg, too, was the blood of the martyrs: he had the martyr's pity for men, the martyr's sympathy with suffering and destitution, the martyr's burning contempt for greed and meanness, the martyr's hope for the future, the martyr's belief in the ultimate perfectibility of man. (p.309)

Anarchist violence is seen both as the outcome of a fanatical logic, and as a resistance to conditions of repression so harsh as to justify among the workers extreme measures of self-defence. Both the theory of anarchism and the practice of political violence are explored in the historical context of capitalist crisis and class struggle, and in the psychological context of unemployment and individual impotence in the face of bourgeois power. Frank Harris's treatment of the anarchist theme is certainly drawn towards the more mystical and quasi-religious dimension of anarchist thought, but at the same time located into contexts calculated to render anarchism intelligible rather than merely terrifying as a political force.

CONCLUSION

It is therefore possible to speak, despite my initial reservations, of a fiction of anarchism within the apparatus of late-Victorian/Edwardian British culture: a body of writing spanning the whole spectrum of artistic and ideological perspectives, from the established canonical 'great' writers who found the subject worth exploring, to the writers considered towards the end of this essay, who articulated in fictional form an engaged and appreciative response to anarchist philosophy and politics. What it was that attracted writers to anarchism, beyond the sensational appeal of terrorist outrages and the melodramatic possibilities lurking in dark illegal conspiracies, should now be clear. Anarchism offered an analysis and condemnation of society which in its totalising purity resembled the comprehensive moral visions of the imaginative artist. Some of the foundations of anarchist philosophy—their faith in the innate goodness of man, their belief in the possibility of ultimate individual liberty—are in themselves imaginative conceptions, mythical rather than materialist in form, and were inevitably attractive to those who chose to explore society by means of the imagination. Finally the artist who hopes to assist or secure through his art political or social change, finds himself in close kinship with the individualist anarchist, who also seeks the transformation of society by application of the individual will. I have identified in the novel of anarchism a species of political fiction: the relationships may well consist in the fact that anarchism is itself a species of fictional (which is not, of course, the same thing as non-existent) politics.

NOTES

1. See Jeremy Hawthorn (ed.), *The British Working-Class Novel in the Twentieth Century* (London, 1984); and H. Gustav Klaus (ed.), *The Socialist Novel in Britain* (Brighton, 1982).
2. See George Woodcock, *Anarchism* (Harmondsworth, 1963), p.414, which is the best introduction to the subject. Also useful are James Joll, *The Anarchists* (London, 1964); and David Miller, *Anarchism* (London, 1984).
3. See Robert W. Kern, *Red Years, Black Years* (Philadelphia, 1978); and J. Romero Maura, 'The Spanish case' in David Apter and James Joll (eds.), *Anarchism Today* (London, 1971).
4. Woodcock, *op. cit.*, p.414.
5. See for example Edward Jenkins, *A Week of Passion, or the Dilemma of Mr George Barton the Younger* (London, 1884); and cf. my discussion of Henry James's *The Princess Casamassima* (1886), see p.134.

6. See for example Grant Allen, *For Maimie's Sake: a Tale of Love and Dynamite* (London, 1886); George Griffith, *The Angel of the Revolution: a Tale of the Coming Terror* (London, 1893); and, for a rather clearer analysis, Joseph Conrad's *Under Western Eyes* (London, 1911).
   For the role of true anarchism in Russian conditions, see Paul Avrich, *The Russian Anarchists* (Princeton, 1967).
7. Emile Zola, *Germinal*, translated by Leonard Tancock (Harmondsworth, 1954), p.144. Subsequent page references are to this edition and will be included in the text.
   For Marx and Bakunin, see Paul Thomas, *Karl Marx and the Anarchists* (London, 1980).
8. See Woodcock, *op. cit.*, p.21; and Daniel Guérin, *Anarchism* (New York, 1970), pp.41 ff.
9. See Woodcock, *op. cit.*, p.14; Morley Roberts, Preface to Isabel Meredith, *A Girl among the Anarchists* (London, 1903); and Barbara Arnett Melchiori, *Terrorism in the Late Victorian Novel* (London, 1985), pp.123, 137-8. The latter study came to hand in the middle of research for this essay: I found its assistance invaluable, though I disagree strongly with some of Melchiori's conclusions, especially on Zola (see p.148n.) and Conrad (see p.81).
10. The residual sexism of the antithesis made here should not obscure Zola's remarkable portraits of working-class women, especially that of Maheude.
11. Quoted in Woodcock, *op. cit.*, p.166.
12. P. B. Shelley, 'Hellas' (1822); see *The Poetical Works of Shelley*, ed Thomas Hutchinson (London, 1905, reset 1943), p.477.
13. Sam Dolgoff (ed.), *Bakunin on Anarchy* (London, 1973), p.57.
14. Joseph Conrad, 'Author's Note' (1920) to *The Secret Agent* (1907). This quotation is taken from the Penguin edition (Harmondsworth, 1963), pp.8-9. Subsequent page references are to this edition and will be included in the text.
15. Cf. Ulrike Meinhof's ambition to 'provoke by violence the latent fascism in the state'.
16. Melchiori, *op. cit.*, p.81.
17. Letter of February 1899; in C. T. Watts (ed.), *Joseph Conrad's Letter to R. B. Cunninghame Graham* (London, 1969), p.117. I have translated Conrad's French.
18. W. H. Tilley, *The Background of 'The Princess Casamassima'* (Gainesville, Florida, 1961).

19. An ending which resembles that of Oscar Wilde's play *Vera: or the Nihilists* (1882).
20. Henry James, *The Princess Casamassima* (Harmondsworth, 1977), p.8. Subsequent page references are to this edition and will be included in the text.
21. E. Douglas Fawcett, *Hartmann the Anarchist: or the Doom of the Great City* (London, 1893), p.1. Subsequent page references in the text.
22. Meredith, *op. cit.*, p.vi. Subsequent page references in the text.
23. See Woodcock, *op. cit.*, pp.287-94.
24. Frank Harris, *The Bomb* (London, 1908), p.22. Subsequent page references in the text.

· 7 ·

French naturalism and the English socialist novel: Margaret Harkness and William Edwards Tirebuck

INGRID VON ROSENBERG

DEFINITIONS

In France as well as in Germany or in Scandinavia there has never been much doubt about what 'naturalism' was; it has always been understood to be literature produced under the influence of scientific observation methods which were so conspicuously advanced in the last decades of the nineteenth century, a literature that approached society and the human psyche in a similar way as the sciences approached natural phenomena—hence the term 'naturalism'. Zola, for his part, made the point quite clear in his famous programmatic article 'Le roman expérimental' (1879). In Britain, on the other hand, a certain shyness could always be observed about using the term 'naturalism'. Both contemporary and later writers and critics preferred terms that hinted at the subject matter or setting like 'slum literature', 'social novel', 'novel of misery', etc., or used the confusing label 'realistic', which had already been applied in earlier literary contexts.[1] Whether this uncertainty originally sprang from the authors' wish to avoid the discrimination which French literature was meeting with in Britain or whether it simply mirrored the fact that the new way of writing in Britain did not stand in such sharp contrast to earlier traditions as in France, need not bother us here. What seems essential is to abandon evasive terms and to define the object of investigation clearly. By naturalistic literature I mean works that are obviously influenced by the new continental mode of writing, works that show characteristic features such as a new precision in describing the details of a certain milieu, a preoccupation with the determining influence of social circumstances and heredity on people, and a new frankness in dealing with the dark sides of human existence, such as sickness, addiction and death, but also with human instincts, especially sexuality. The milieu described need not necessarily be a proletarian one; indeed, many continental writers turned in preference to bourgeois circles or rural communities rather than to the industrial proletariat, and even Zola set only three of his novels in working-class surroundings. But they were the works which by their subject and treatment inevitably appealed most to British writers with social or even socialist inclinations. As naturalism is not an ideology in itself, but merely a literary method bred under certain historical and epistemological conditions, it could be put to a variety of ideological uses, and this is what happened.

The term 'socialist novel' is not unproblematic either.[2] In order to cut a long discussion short I would like to describe socialist literature here simply as literature written from any kind of socialist viewpoint current at the time; and this, for the end of the century, means a large variety of diverse and not always stringent concepts. It would seem historically unfair, for instance, to demand compliance with the concept of socialist realism which was formulated only forty years later and within the context of a later development of socialist theory. Starting from these working definitions I shall look at the political convictions of the two authors to be considered here and examine to what extent and purpose they have used the new naturalistic writing techniques.

ZOLA AND HIS BRITISH DISCIPLES

The dramatic story of the reception of French naturalism in Britain is well known and need not be repeated here, but a few remarks may be apt.[3] Despite the hysterical public campaign against it, which culminated in the imprisonment of the publisher Vizetelly in 1889, British authors like George Moore and George Gissing had from very early on reacted with interest and admiration to the new mode of writing. Two naturalistic subjects commanded particular attention: the situation of the poorest levels of the proletariat, especially in the city slums; and the psychological deprivation of middle-class women. In this essay I am not concerned with the topic of female frustration; and I am not going to discuss the work of the better known authors of slum-fiction such as Gissing, Arthur Morrison or Richard Whiteing, though particularly Gissing in *The Nether World* (1889) and Morrison in *Tales of Mean Street* (1894) and *A Child of the Jago* (1896) gave descriptions of life in the London slums that in their clinically precise observation of the appalling environment and in their grim insistence on resultant phenomena like sickness, drink, violence and prostitution come closer to Zola than those of any other British writers. But their work has received quite a lot of attention from critics already; and, more importantly, none of them wrote from a socialist point of view. I want to focus on the work of two writers with definite socialist inclinations who also followed in Zola's steps, though it should be stated right from the beginning that they neither wrote pure naturalism nor ever reached the literary mastership of their great model.

In the case of Margaret Harkness we have two direct hints in her novels that she actually had read and admired Zola.[4] Tirebuck mentions Zola nowhere, but the traces of his influence are unmistakeable, as will be shown presently. There was in any case no language problem, for Vizetelly published translations of Zola's works in quick succession, and some novels like *Germinal* (1885) came out in England in the same year as in France.

Looking at the socialist literature of the 1880s and 1890s one may be surprised to find only few British writers making use of the new writing mode. John Goode has pointed out that the two 'writers of substance' who identified themselves with socialism, namely Morris and Shaw, 'felt compelled to work in a different aesthetic frame from that of a realist novel'.[5] Other writers of a lesser reputation did choose the novel as their frame, but also abstained from realism. Examples are Constance Howell's *A More Excellent Way* (1888) and J. H. Clapperton's *Margaret Dunmore: or a Socialist Home* (1888). In the former novel the hero, well-to-do but socialist nevertheless, finds his special field of work in spreading the 'gospel' to his own class; in the latter the heroine inherits a big house which she converts into a 'socialist home' for a group of her middle-class friends.[6]

It seems to me that the scarcity of realism in socialist literature may have something to do with the situation of the working class as well as of the socialist movement at the time. Proletarian writers were rare, due to the modest general level of education and very limited leisure time. Novelists with socialist ideas came as a rule from, or were close to, the still large and dominant middle-class membership of the various socialist groups and fractions and may have felt too remote from the everyday experience of the workers, particularly the poorest levels, to write about them. Margaret Harkness and Tirebuck were, as journalists, in an exceptional position. But there may have been a further obstacle to the use of naturalism on a larger scale: the concept of determinism is not easy to reconcile with the socialist conviction of the possibility of change through the victims of society themselves. If the living conditions of the proletariat were depicted in their true dark colours, it would be difficult to create characters growing up in this milieu who were convincingly strong and educated enough to fight back or even lead the struggle. This dilemma has puzzled left-wing theoreticians ever since the emergence of naturalism, and some, like Georg Lukács and Bertolt Brecht, rejected naturalism altogether as a suitable literary technique to promote socialism.

That despite such theoretical difficulties, a socialist perspective could very well be combined with the naturalistic writing mode had, however, been proved by Zola, and perhaps in no other novel better than in *Germinal* (1885), the story of a strike in one of the northern French coalfields.

MARGARET HARKNESS (1854-192?)

Margaret Harkness was a clergyman's daughter.[7] Having trained and worked as a nurse for some years, she became a journalist, doing research on, and writing about, the slums in the East End of London. Through her contacts with leading personalities of the left she quickly assimilated socialist ideas which gave perspective to her observations, but she was never able to develop a well-founded and stable political stance.

Though Harkness's work covers a wide range of interests, her five socialist novels stand out as central. In the first four of these she made a marked use of naturalism, and it is worth noting that she did so almost as early as George Moore, who is commonly regarded as Zola's first British disciple: Harkness's first four novels were published between 1887 and 1890, at the peak of the British controversy over the new mode.

The reader of these novels is immediately struck by the cool accuracy of the many descriptions of streets and interiors, of living rooms, kitchens, prison cells, workhouses, hospitals and pubs in the poor quarters of the industrial centres of London and Manchester. Some of these descriptions would fit well into one of the social reports of the time, by, for instance, Charles Booth. Take this passage from *Out of Work* (1888):

> He was taken into a cell that measured eight feet by four feet, at the end of which was a small dark hole called the stone-pit. The cell was lighted by a jet of gas . . . Jos sat down on the low bedstead, and looked at the cell. It had no furniture whatsoever, except the mattress and the rug on which he was sitting. An icy wind swept through the stone-pit, so he went to see if a door would shut out the draught. But no door was there, only a large iron window, with bars across, through which flints must be thrown . . . Large blocks of granite lay in the stone-pit, also a hammer. There was no seat, and the floor of the place dipped in the middle, so it was difficult to stand upright.[8]

With equally dry precision social habits, bred in the

circumstances, are reported: the drinking; the violence among the men and also among the women; the drug-taking to dull the hunger; the crude entertainment in pubs, music halls and penny gaffs; the crime, even murder. But Harkness also tells of mutual help and tentative signs of solidarity: the down-and-outs in the doss-house in *Out of Work* share their last scraps of food, and an old tramp watches from afar over the steps of the lonely young widowed mother in *A Manchester Shirtmaker* (1890).

As to the intensity of such naturalistic descriptions I see a development in Harkness's work in the form of a wave: Whereas in her first novel *A City Girl* (1887) naturalism is still strongly mixed with romance, it becomes dominant in *Out of Work* (1888), *Captain Lobe* (1889) and *A Manchester Shirtmaker* (1890), but is absent from *George Eastmont: Wanderer*, published fifteen years later in 1905. The latter work resembles such earlier novels of ideas as Howell's *A More Excellent Way*, telling the story of Harkness's disappointment with socialism in the form of a *Bildungsroman* with a young upper-class idealist as the hero. The stages of his disillusionment are more marked by theoretical discussions and intellectual 'insights' than by living experience of working-class reality.[9] Thus it seems as if Harkness's use of naturalism was closely bound up with her socialist convictions, and, indeed, at the time when she was writing her slum novels her political commitment was strongest: in 1888 she supported Keir Hardie in an (unsuccessful) by-election campaign in Ayrshire, and in 1889 she was involved in the organisation of the great London dockers' strike. Yet her handling of naturalistic techniques was not equally skilful in her four slum novels, the weakest being *Captain Lobe*, possibly due to a first shadow of doubt. In the fourteenth chapter there is some sharp criticism of all socialist groups existing at the time, which foreshadows her later break with the movement. A nameless 'lady', a thinly disguised mouthpiece of the author, says: ' "They are so jealous. They cannot work together. They split into small parties, and spend their time quarrelling . . .!" '[10] When in this novel the reader witnesses street fights, family rows or drunken bouts, he does so through the eyes of Salvation Army members, who are observers but not personally affected. As these scenes are not integrated into the plot, the novel is in danger of disintegrating into a loose series of unconnected tableaux seen from a distance.

The three other slum novels escape this danger as the naturalistic observations are to a large extent linked to the main characters, thereby forming constituents of the plot. So the violence in *A City Girl*, perpetrated by the heroine's brother, is directly aimed at her, and so is the cold indifference of the hospital nurses with whom Nelly has to leave her sick baby. In *A Manchester Shirtmaker* the heroine herself experiences the exploitation of sweat labour and kills her baby with drugs because she has no more food to give him.[11] And in *Out of Work* the reader is confronted directly with the growing hopelessness of the permanently unemployed through the hero's experience, though the general significance is underlined by the addition of a whole range of further sufferers.

The choice of a working-class hero or, more frequently, heroine also helped to strengthen the impact of Harkness's political message, notwithstanding a rather simple character psychology. As a complementary step she deliberately broke with a convention of the middle-class social novel, the angelic heroine. In *Out of Work* a pious young middle-class beauty makes her appearance in the person of Polly, the devoted Methodist, who is engaged to Jos, the jobless carpenter. But no unrealistic union between the classes through the medium of religion takes place. When Jos cannot find work and gradually sinks to the level of a tramp, Polly jilts him and marries her Methodist instructor, who has a safe and highly symbolic job at the Royal Mint. At the moment of final parting Jos unmasks not only Polly but a whole literary tradition when he calls her a 'little hypocrite', a judgement that keeps resounding in his memory.[12] Harkness skilfully juxtaposes the falling goddess of the past with the new working-class heroine in the person of Squirrel, a selfless little flower-girl, who becomes Jos's second love. When, in her weaker novel *Captain Lobe*, Harkness does make use of the conventional middle-class heroine, she does so only half-heartedly, for though Ruth means well and does no harm, her parasitical nature is exposed in the end: 'She was one of those creatures who cannot stand alone, who must fall to the earth if they have nothing to keep them upright. "A poor sort of creature," Jane Hardy said, "not much better than a young curate." '[13]

However, not even in Harkness's three strongest novels was the use of naturalism complete, and it remains to look at the limitations, which need not necessarily be artistic weaknesses. First, even though she did not only describe deplorable social conditions but also their degrading effects on the psyche, she went the whole way only with her minor characters. With her central figures she took great pains not to let them sink morally too low. Nowhere do they take part in violence or serious crime; none has an innate flaw of character like so many of Zola's protagonists. Jos in *Out of Work* does give way to his inherited tendency to drink and behaves selfishly to the loving Squirrel, but he is shown as generous at the beginning when he buys medicine for a friend's sick child with his first earnings after a long period of unemployment; Mary, the shirt-maker, may kill her own child, but only after she has starved herself for the baby's sake. Neither of them can really be condemned, not even by the strict standards of Victorian morality, so obviously are they merely driven by circumstances. This is also true of Nelly, the city girl guilty of extra-marital sex. Presumably Harkness wanted to make her central figures sympathetic to the reader on behalf of her socialist conviction: it was important to show the plight of the proletariat and even the moral dangers they were in, but it would not do to show them beyond hope of redemption, given different circumstances.

Another limitation may be due to less conscious and less positive reasons. Harkness is, in marked contrast to French naturalists, very secretive about the description of sexual feelings, let alone activities. The seduction in *A City Girl*, for instance, takes place in the space of two lines.[14] Besides, Nelly does not seem drawn to Mr Grant so much by passion, but because by his well-groomed appearance, smart clothes and fine speech 'he became mixed up with the ideal, nameless lover who played so great a part in her thoughts'.[15] He represents a brighter life to her, and there may be a faint echo of *Madame Bovary* here rather than of Zola. In Harkness's following books no more physical encounters happen at all: Jos in *Out of Work* has two platonic loves; the shirtmaker is a widow; and in *Captain Lobe* the seduction theme, though embarked upon, is dropped halfway, the heroine running away at the critical moment. Perhaps even more significant seems that, though Nelly, the city girl, is not condemned but pitied by the author, her physical surrender is, nevertheless, treated as a lapse and Nelly is, if not actually killed by the author, then at least punished by her child's death. This ambivalent treatment of physical love, still so much in conformity with official Victorian morals, may well have had something to do with a personal insecurity on the part of Margaret Harkness. Other new women writers, such as Olive Schreiner, had similar difficulties, and while George Moore, Grant Allen and 'George Egerton' (Mary Chavelita Dunne) were already breaking the taboos, the works of Schreiner, Sarah Grand and others bear witness to the same personal conflicts: theoretically they underlined a woman's right to sexual fulfilment in their books, but they dared not allow their heroines to enjoy it on the level of action.

But, as John Goode has pointed out, it is of some importance that Nelly—in contrast to so many other heroines of British naturalistic fiction such as Gissing's Thyrza, Moore's Kate, Hardy's Tess and also Tirebuck's Dorrie—is after all permitted to live on after her crisis. Though it may be slightly exaggerated to see in Nelly's endurance the vehicle of all the 'novel's political thrust', it can certainly be valued as a sign of budding feminism.[16] In George Moore's *Esther Waters* (1894), which was published seven years later, the feature is already much more pronounced: Esther does not merely survive, but is allowed to bring up her illegitimate son and even later to enter into a happy marriage with her former seducer.

It seems to me that the political message of the novel rests on the whole of the narrative fabric, that is Harkness's naturalistic picture of working-class life including the suffering as well as the brave endurance. Remembering that Harkness's use of naturalism was most stringent while her socialist commitment was strongest, one may draw the conclusion that it was just the power of pictures of poverty and degradation that she trusted to win over readers to a new world-view. In other words: Harkness obviously held naturalism to be an effective literary technique to convey socialist ideas, even without incorporating theoretical arguments into the text. If this was so, one can understand why she did not follow Engels's advice, who in his famous letter concerning *A City Girl* had taken issue with Harkness's portrayal of the working-class characters as a purely passive mass. For though she may have made her characters more 'typical' in the later novels, she never depicted workers who were active in the labour movement. Instead she went on drawing her grim pictures of the downtrodden, proving her faith in naturalism's power of persuasion.

WILLIAM EDWARDS TIREBUCK (1854-1900)

Born in Liverpool in 'humble circumstances', Tirebuck left school at the age of eleven to work in various offices.[17] Early literary inclinations made him turn to journalism, but his journalistic career, during which he worked for some time for the *Yorkshire Post*, was short, and he soon retired to live first in Scotland, later in Wales, his mother's homeland. During those years of withdrawal he wrote twelve books including art criticism, short stories, various romantic novels and the three novels dealing with problems of social reality that are of interest in our context. Two biographical points seem relevant for his view of the world: on the one hand his biographer Hogben testifies to a certain 'unworldliness' in him, on the other hand Tirebuck contributed an article 'On the verge of change' to an anthology *The New Party* (1894) containing essays by members and sympathisers of the newly founded Independent Labour Party. These two forces, Christian beliefs and socialist views, were to leave their characteristic stamp on his work.

Tirebuck's second novel and the first to include naturalistic traits, *Dorrie* (1891), can be read as proof that his socialism grew out of Christian convictions. Dorrie is a beautiful and buxom girl of seventeen. She keeps house with her less attractive, but pious and diligent sister Katherine (the pair are reminiscent of Hetty and Dinah in George Eliot's *Adam Bede*), and they have a lodger, the blind young lay preacher Nathaniel Brant, who spends his day quoting from the Bible on a street corner. Both girls are attracted by Nat who feels more drawn to Dorrie. But he suffers from pangs of conscience, for his feelings are more of the physical than of the spiritual kind. After some dramatic scenes Dorrie runs away to make a career in the theatre, while Nat meets a middle-class benefactor, Mr Franklin, the richest merchant in Liverpool, who not only takes him to Italy for an operation to restore his eyesight, but sets him up as a preacher with a house of his own in the village of his manor house. Some years later Nat who, though living with Katherine, has kept looking out for Dorrie, finally discovers her as a prostitute in a Liverpool brothel, mortally ill with syphilis. He takes her home, and together with Katherine nurses her in her last illness. At the very end a strange secret is revealed: Mr Franklin's wife, who has been unaccountably moody and ailing all through the action, confesses that she is Dorrie's illegitimate mother and had long ago left her child with a respectable working-class family. Mother and daughter die in a first and last embrace, while Nat and Katherine finally marry.

Naturalistic elements can be located in this novel not so much in faithful descriptions of Liverpool streets and places—though there are a few—as in the emphasis on the influence of heredity in Dorrie's story. In the end it is revealed that the vitality, restlessness and frivolity that had puzzled her sister and Nat so much, were in fact inherited from her mother, and so perhaps was her syphilis, though she may instead have contracted it from one of her lovers. Again and again the author stresses the influence of the past on Dorrie's behaviour: 'The fact was, though Dorrie herself did not know it, the greater part of her conflict was with the past, a past that insisted upon the present, a past that was at that moment moulding the possibilities of her future.'[18]

Dorrie's craving for the theatre and indeed some of the adventures in her bohemian life may well owe something to specific novels by Zola or to George Moore's *A Mummer's Wife* (1885). Dorrie resembles Moore's Kate—although she is not an adulteress, but an unmarried girl—in using the theatrical world as a means of escape from the drab domestic life of a respectable working-class home and the boredom of sewing for her living. Moore, in his turn, was indebted mainly to *Thérèse Raquin* (1867) and *Nana* (1880).[19] Some of the scenes in *Dorrie* in their precise observation of setting as well as of human behaviour remind one indeed of scenes from *Nana*. When Dorrie, for instance, manages to advance to the office of a theatre director for an audition but is rejected because she cannot read properly, the vividly painted scene reflects social realities. But there are equally many fantastic incidents—not just at the end of the novel—which are more reminiscent of Dickens than of Zola and hamper the realism of the story. For example, her career begins with a wildly romantic kidnapping: a Bengali restaurant owner holds her captive after a meal and forces her to dance on the stage of his music hall.

Where Tirebuck, like Harkness, does not follow his French models is in the treatment of sexuality. Though Dorrie has her lovers and becomes a prostitute, there is no explicit sexual scene; everything happens backstage. Tirebuck, of course, conforms to British Victorian morality like most other writers of his time who deal with the popular subject of the 'fallen woman'. But, interestingly, in this novel his conformity is not as complete as later in *Miss Grace of All Souls'* (1895). There are a number of situations when Dorrie's vivacity and hunger for pleasure are not treated as sinful, but appear as nothing more wicked than a natural and even charming liveliness. Such is the impression of some scenes in the country when Dorrie is looking for Nat, who is staying with the Franklins, and gets involved in a village dance or plays with children in the woods. At such moments she suddenly seems superior to Nat with his religious scrupulousness and primness, and it is this slight, but noticeable deviation from conventional morality that makes the novel interesting reading. To Rhoda, Mr Franklin's rather subdued daughter and Dorrie's half-sister (though neither know this), Dorrie even seems something of a heroine, and her secret thoughts have a surprisingly feminist touch:

> In both a remote and near way Dorrie's case seemed one of discontent like her own. Dorrie, Rhoda fancied, must have felt Brant rather serious, strict, and emphatic. *She* felt that he was so . . . Rhoda could quite believe that Dorrie had passed through something like her own cramped existence, only Dorrie had carried her ideas much further than she could—she had carried them out in fact.[20]

But, of course, this tone is only a subversive undercurrent, and in the end Dorrie, like so many other 'fallen women' in Victorian literature, is sentenced to death.

Yet Dorrie's story is only part of the plot; the reader actually loses sight of her in the middle of the novel to meet her again only near the end. It is Nat who dominates the scene, not just because his presence is the more continuous, but, more importantly, because his standpoint provides the transcendent perspective. Through him the religious perspective becomes the dominant message of the novel. His story, which, in contrast to Dorrie's punishment for her sins, is one of virtue rewarded, conveys the impression that religiousness is enough to overcome the differences between the classes. When Nat is first brought to Mr Franklin's office and is offered a position as a preacher in a Liverpool chapel, the author comments:

> There, in secret committee, sat four of the wealthiest men in the town . . . but in their midst was one of the poorest men in the town . . . And yet those five lives were warmly united by an unexpressed fellowship with a sixth—the mystical and yet assured fellowship of a spirit greater than theirs—the humbling and yet ennobling, the subduing and yet rousing fellowship of God. It was remarkable, it was beautiful, it was touching that they should meet as they did.[21]

It is striking that Tirebuck, though he accentuates the

contrast between the modest lifestyle of the sisters and the luxurious one of the Franklins, does not introduce any socialist ideas into this novel, particularly as in his first novel *Saint Margaret* (1888) there had been some discussion of political ideas. The hero, also a religious young man working in the mission hall of a Liverpool church, leaves the church out of disappointment that so little is done for the poor of the parish and joins the United Liberals in a small town. There he is disappointed, too—the leaders seem to him merely personally ambitious and the workers undisciplined and lazy—so that he returns to his church to renew his efforts there. Thus religion wins, but at least the question of a possible political path is raised.

In contrast to these two earlier novels *Miss Grace of All Souls'* deals with a historical event, the great lock-out of the miners in 1893, which affected large parts of the English and Welsh coalfields, particularly in the north and the Midlands. The reason for this choice of subject, unusual for Tirebuck, may well have been that, living in the north, he actually witnessed and was deeply impressed by what happened.

When Tirebuck set out to describe what he had experienced there was a literary model ready at hand, published and translated into English ten years earlier: Zola's *Germinal*. Though there are indeed some astonishing resemblances between the two novels, which suggest that Tirebuck very probably took Zola's work as a model, there are also marked differences. The most important similarity lies in the general message. Both authors describe the awakening of a group of miners, hitherto patient slaves of the coal-owners, to joint political action and self-confident class consciousness. The change is brought about under the pressure of a particularly ruthless attempt to curtail the already barely sufficient wages. In *Germinal* the strikers are—in accordance with historical events—in the end defeated, but their spirit is unbroken: the seed, the 'germ', is sown, as the title suggests. In Tirebuck's novel the miners are victorious in the material sense: the old wage is guaranteed. But more important seems the feeling of union and common strength that has grown among them and might be tapped in future struggles. The message of hope then is very similar in both novels and may indeed be called socialist—at least at a first glance.

Though there are very few minute descriptions of the work process and no Zolaesque pictures of domestic interiors, Tirebuck obviously borrowed a whole range of structural elements from *Germinal*, which helped to provide *Miss Grace* with a more unitary form than the still half-romantic *Dorrie*. Zola had personalised his subject by placing a typical working-class family of three generations at the centre of his novel, which gave him the opportunity to explore the full range of working-class experience from the young to the old and including women as well as men. In *Miss Grace* we find in the Ockleshaws a family almost exactly matching the composition of the Maheus in *Germinal:* there is a grandfather, a father, a mother, one grown-up daughter and two half-adult sons; only the younger brothers and sisters are missing. The growth of political consciousness through the generations is similar in both stories, and even the incident of the father's death by army bullets returns in *Miss Grace*. In addition, both authors contrast their central working-class family with a middle-class counterpart representing the employers. But while Zola, in order to symbolise the split of power and profit characteristic of an advanced stage of capitalism, introduced the two families of a rentier and of a managing director, Tirebuck needed only one family to mirror the more old-fashioned power-structure of the British coal industry: the Brooksters are owners as well as managers of the Beckerton pits. Both authors highlight the contrast between the two milieux by juxtaposing, for example, the frugal meals in the miner's kitchen with the luxurious dinner parties of the bourgeoisie. In both novels there is an additional network of minor characters, particularly a wide range of further working-class figures. But while in *Germinal* one may truly speak of the first emergence of a collective working-class hero, this is prevented in *Miss Grace* by the peculiar choice of the central figure.[22]

Structural similarities of the kind described need not necessarily indicate a true kinship of spirit, and, indeed, despite the similar political message the tone of the two novels is profoundly different. Zola's stance may perhaps be summed up as a blending of the sharp observation of the workers' appalling living conditions with hope for their own and humanity's future, based on a thorough study of socialist theory, the discussion of which is integrated into the framework of the novel. When Zola describes the miserable present he does not shrink from including also the distortions of character wrought by want and lack of education. He is very explicit about the envy and gossiping of the women, the ignorance and the violence of the men, and the raw, sometimes brutal sexual relationships between them. Political maturity is achieved at the end after many errors, disappointments and great efforts and only by very few people, perhaps only by Etienne, the strike leader, and Maheude, the widowed mother.

Tirebuck's novel, on the other hand, is tuned to a hopeful note right from the beginning. There is never any real doubt that the workers will win in the end, and this impression is generated not so much by the integration of a coherent socialist perspective as by the portrayal of the workers. They may be poor and approach the brink of starvation during the lock-out, yet they remain warmhearted and good, their solidarity never wavering. Here is a typical assessment of their reaction: 'The dumb endurance of the men in this and in other ways, their good temper, their self-control, their self-respect, their respect for others, were among the most appealing traits of the whole struggle.'[23] The miners share their last slice of bread, and the women help by taking on heavy physical work or by sacrificing their food to husbands and children. Solidarity even spreads to other groups of workers: 'railway-men, gas-men, iron-workers, tool makers, mill and factory hands of Beckerton and district were out by thousands' (p.189). This ubiquitous goodness, though certainly based on many actual observations, seems slightly idealised, as no exceptions are allowed.

The tendency is intensified by a further deviation from Zola. In his treatment of sexual relations Tirebuck again avoids the frank dealing with physical love, so integral a a part of Zola's picture of proletarian life. Physical feelings are mentioned even less than in *Dorrie*; everything is thoroughly romantic between the three couples heading for their happy ends, their stories being thus elevated to the lofty realms of romance. Perhaps scared by the scandal around Zola, but more likely himself still firmly adhering to Victorian morality, Tirebuck in this respect kept to the common course of Victorian writing.

His bonds with traditional nonconformist religion were indeed so strong that he seems to have based his socialism on Christian teachings. As mentioned before, Tirebuck was close to the ILP, a party in whose foundation the element of ethical socialism played an important part. Stanley Pierson has described it thus:

> Ethical Socialism was highly eclectic. Around the central Socialist goal of public ownership were gathered many of the diverse and often contradictory ideas which had entered the movement during the first decade. Spokesmen for Ethical Socialism might employ Marxist ideas of exploitation and the class struggle, or Fabian notions of rent and general enlightenment. But they were distinguished by their appeals to moral and religious sentiment and they promised a fundamental change in the quality of life.[24]

It seems significant that in *Miss Grace* there is little discussion of socialist ideas and that the little there is is frequently clad in Christian arguments. When Grace chides her father, the vicar who opportunistically sides with the coal-owners, she quotes the Bible: ' "While the many are working at the rods of the vine, the few are eating the grapes" ' (p.51). And she condemns her father's attitude: 'It was wrong—it was sinful—it was against both the spirit and the letter of the Church's own Scripture' (p.53). Not only the vicar's daughter, also the workers quote Christ in their support: ' "But our Saviour didn't say tak' twenty-five per cent off the poor to mak' them poorer, an' put twenty-five in the pockets o' the rich to mak' the rich richer" ' (p.154). It is in accordance with a basically Christian stance that within the scope of the novel not a complete reversal of the social order is envisaged as the final goal, but merely a correction of all too obvious injustices. When Grace in the face of an impending riot confronts Brookster, she appeals to his sense of responsibility, revealing the author's belief in the possibility of a paternalistic organisation of society: ' "As the proprietor of Beckerton pits, Mr. Brookster, it is in your power to save at least four thousand men, women and children from want . . ." ' And she asks: ' "Why will not employers admit . . . that masters and men are, after all, one in their interdependence upon each other?" ' (p.234). The workers argue from a similar basis when Sam Ockleshaw, the most politically articulate among them, does not demand common ownership as the struggle's aim, but, apart from some vague hints about a share in the control of the pits, merely a fair part of the wealth produced by the workers: ' "The man that gets, should at least be paid his meat" ' (p.155).

That religion is a weak basis for socialism and prevents a development of socialist concepts becomes obvious when Tirebuck, as in *Dorrie*, lets piety and moral goodness function as forces able to bridge the gulf between the classes. Although, like Zola, he applies a fair amount of sarcasm to his portrayal of the political tricks and business deals of his entrepreneur family and their accomplices, including the vicar, he allows individuals to feel remorse and even to change sides: Dora, the Brookster daughter, becomes a friend to the miners by marrying the young curate Rew, who had helped the miners at Grace's side and intends to live by Grace's ideals. Grace, as the vicar's daughter also a member of the middle class, has been an ally of the miners all through the struggle, and in the end actually joins the working class by marrying Sam Ockleshaw. This symbolical union, to my mind, impairs the final political message of the novel by substituting a Christian dream of the brotherhood of man for the socialist perspective.

The eponymous heroine requires a few final remarks. Surprising as it may seem that Tirebuck should have linked his lock-out theme to the central figure of an angelic middle-class girl, he could and probably did draw on a literary tradition. In some of the industrial novels of the

1840s and 1850s the same device was employed to make working-class topics digestible for a bourgeois reading public used to love stories about pure middle-class heroines: Mrs Gaskell's Margaret Hale in *North and South* and Disraeli's Sybil can be seen in this way. Their treatment reflects a real social function of middle-class women in the nineteenth century where it had become one of the acknowledged duties of the 'angel in the house' to exercise charity: Women were expected to 'do good' by giving alms to the individual poor while their husbands were often exploiting the working class on a large scale. If the author of a socialist novel applies a literary device reflecting this middle-class division of labour, even if he does so without fully realising the implications, the danger of weakening the socialist message arises. What finally saves *Miss Grace* from this danger is the novel's emphasis on the life and struggle of the miners.

Looking back at Tirebuck's social novels one must say that none of them, not even *Miss Grace*, can be called a purely socialist novel, and, equally, none of them is consistently naturalistic—and for the same reasons. Tirebuck's two strong driving motives, his real sympathy with the working class and his trust in true religiousness to overcome social evils, were, though widely spread at his time, inherently at odds with each other. Tirebuck's piety and Christian morality allowed him to include socialist ideas only in so far as they were reconcilable with Christian convictions. They also prevented a more daring use of naturalism, particularly in the field of sexual relations, but also with regard to characterisation. That he introduced naturalistic writing techniques at all was a happy circumstance, for it prevented his 'unworldliness' from entirely having the upper hand and gave his portrayal of working-class people a more realistic profile.

William Edwards Tirebuck and Margaret Harkness worked as pioneers in the field of applying naturalistic techniques to the ends of socialist fiction, and, as may have become apparent, their achievements cannot be called perfect. Their approach was in many ways half-hearted, and the traces of past values were still marked. When in

1914, more than twenty years later, Robert Tressell and Patrick MacGill made their appearance on the literary stage and included in their first novels admirably written naturalistic descriptions of the living and working conditions of house-painters in Hastings and potato-pickers and navvies in Scotland, they had a double advantage: being working-class themselves, they could draw on personal experience; but they could draw on naturalism too as a literary tradition that had already become well established. Harkness and Tirebuck were among those who helped to form this tradition.

NOTES

1. Margaret Harkness's novels *A City Girl* and *A Manchester Shirtmaker* were published with the subtitle 'a realistic story'.
2. For a detailed discussion of the term see H. Gustav Klaus (ed.) Introduction to *The Socialist Novel in Britain* (Brighton, 1982), pp.1-2.
3. See William C. Frierson, 'The English controversy over realism in fiction 1885-1895, *PMLA*, 43 (1928), pp.533-50; William C. Frierson, *The English Novel in Transition 1885-1940* (New York, 1965); and Clarence R. Decker, *The Victorian Conscience* (New York, 1952).
4. John Law (Margaret Harkness), *Out of Work* (London, 1888), p.204: 'That place [a prison cell] needs a Zola to do it justice.' John Law (Margaret Harkness), *George Eastmont: Wanderer* (London, 1905), p.125: 'He had just returned from a visit to the mines of Scotland and there he had found *Germinal* better than any guide-book.'
5. John Goode, 'Margaret Harkness and the socialist novel' in Klaus (ed.) *The Socialist Novel in Britain*, pp.45-66 (p.46).
6. For a discussion of Constance Howell's *A More Excellent Way* see chapter 2 by Brunhild de la Motte.
7. For more details of Harkness's biography see Goode, *op. cit.*, and Beate Kaspar, *Margaret Harkness: A City Girl* (Tübingen, 1984).
8. Harkness, *Out of Work*, pp.181-3.

9. For a discussion of *George Eastmont: Wanderer* see chapter 1 by Kiernan Ryan.
10. John Law (Margaret Harkness), *In Darkest London* [first published 1889 under the title of *Captain Lobe*] (London, 1891), p.153.
11. For a recent discussion of *A Manchester Shirtmaker* see T. Thomas, 'Representation of the Manchester working class in fiction, 1850-1900', in Alan J. Kidd and K. W. Roberts (eds.), *City, Class and Culture. Studies of Social Policy and Cultural Production in Victorian Manchester* (Manchester, 1985), pp.210-12.
12. Harkness, *Out of Work*, pp.221-2, 227-8.
13. Harkness, *In Darkest London*, p.280.
14. John Law (Margaret Harkness), *A City Girl* (London, 1887), p.84.
15. *ibid.*, p.63.
16. Goode, *op. cit.*, p.56.
17. For more biographical details see Hall Caine, 'Memoir' in W. E. Tirebuck, *Twixt God and Mammon* (London, 1903), pp.V-XXIII; and John Hogben, Foreword to W. E. Tirebuck, *Poems* (London, 1912), pp.5-15.
18. William Edwards Tirebuck, *Dorrie* (London, 1891), p.207.
19. See M. Chaikin, 'George Moore's *A Mummer's Wife* and Zola', *Revue de Littérature Comparée*, 31 (1957), pp.85-8.
20. Tirebuck, *Dorrie*, p.353.
21. *ibid.*, p.53.
22. For a different view of the novel's hero see chapter 4 by H. Gustav Klaus.
23. William Edwards Tirebuck, *Miss Grace of All Souls'* (New York, 1895), p.191. Subsequent page numbers given in the text are to this edition.
24. Stanley Pierson, *British Socialists. The Journey from Fantasy to Politics* (Cambridge, Mass., 1979), pp.35-6.

· 8 ·

Allen Clarke and the Lancashire school of working-class novelists

PAUL SALVESON

It is common to regard Tressell's great work, *The Ragged Trousered Philanthropists*, as the only novel of any importance written by a working-class socialist before the First World War. The purpose of this article is to show that there did in fact exist both a cohesive group of working-class novelists in the years between 1890 and 1914, and that they possessed a mass readership. They were based in Lancashire, and much of their writing reflects a strong regional, as well as class awareness. The central figure in this group was Allen Clarke (1863-1935) the son of Bolton mill workers, born at the height of the Lancashire cotton famine. At the age of twelve, he too went to work in the mills as a half-timer. His job as a piecer was a typical occupation for a working-class lad of his age in a northern mill town in the 1870s. It was both dangerous and exhausting, involving piecing up broken threads on the spinning mules, and cleaning the machinery (often when it was in motion). Clarke's mill career was mercifully short, although those early experiences undoubtedly provided him with material for his later industrial novels. He spent some years as a pupil teacher, trying to 'educate' the half-time kids such as he had once been, and, like many other humane members of his profession, became increasingly frustrated with the job. He had been writing, encouraged by his father, for many years and he dreamed of becoming a professional writer. He left his job as a teacher and started with the *Bolton Evening News* as a clerk—hoping that this would be the first step on the ladder of a writing career.

The hoped-for promotion never came, and he resigned in 1890 to start his own paper, *The Labour Light*. It was an uneasy combination of lengthy trade-union reports and speeches of working-class figures, together with humorous sketches of working-class life, written in Lancashire dialect. These were the *Tum Fowt Sketches*, recording the comic doings of Bill and Bet Spriggs and their friends. Although at first these were used as largely non-political light relief, Clarke (under the pseudoynm of 'Teddy Ashton') later developed these sketches into sharp political satire.

By the time Clarke started *The Labour Light* he was a convinced socialist. He had joined the Bolton branch of the Social Democratic Federation (SDF) in 1887, at the time of the great Bolton Engineers' Lock-Out, which he later used as the basis for his novel, *The Knobstick* (1893). Clarke could not, however, be described as a marxist. His political views found a better expression in the 'ethical' socialism of the early Independent Labour Party (ILP), seeing socialism as much a moral issue as a class one. This did not, however, mean that Clarke was unconcerned about working-class issues—for he was very much a part of that class—but he could still write:

> I would do justice to everybody—to shopkeeper, merchant and capitalist. I want fair play and fair opportunity all round. But the cause of the workers has first claim because the workers have been most unjustly treated and neglected.[1]

Clarke joined the Independent Labour Party, and stood as joint ILP–SDF candidate in Rochdale at the 1900 General Election. He polled 902 votes in a contest which included his 'Election Address to Th' Rachda Folk'—written, irreverently, in Lancashire dialect. The election experience also marked a turning point in Clarke's politics. As the ILP moved towards an alliance with right-wing trade-union leaders, Clarke became increasingly interested in libertarian politics, particularly the ideas of Tolstoy, and then the syndicalists. In 1903 he launched the 'Daisy Colony Scheme' for a working-class 'co-operative colony' near

Blackpool, and following its demise[2] used his paper, *Teddy Ashton's Northern Weekly*, as a mouthpiece for libertarian socialist groups, such as the Industrial Union of Direct Actionists. In later years he was an enthusiastic supporter of the Russian Revolution, and maintained this support until his death in December 1935. Clarke was an essentially non-sectarian socialist, who had no time for parliamentary manoeuvres and compromise, and no stomach either for the increasingly bitter inter-party feuds between the ILP and the SDF, and later between the Labour Party and the Communists.

THE THEMES OF ALLEN CLARKE'S NOVELS

This political and biographical background is essential for the understanding of Clarke's novels, and to appreciate his wider aims as a writer. In 1893 he expressed these aims in an editorial letter to his readers:

> I want to do something for all who are downtrodden and oppressed . . . I want to sing you songs of hope and tell you tales of truth. I want to picture faithfully in verse and prose the lives of the workers in towns and cities . . . Yet not merely do I want to delineate the life of labour but by so doing to draw attention to wrongs and evils, and if possible get them righted and remedied.[3]

There is no doubt then, that Clarke saw himself as a working-class writer writing about, and for, a primarily working-class readership. The subject matter of the majority of his novels is based on working-class life, mostly in Lancashire. Many of these have a contemporary setting, although some of his novels, including the first—*The Lass at the Man and Scythe* (1889)—about the English Civil war, are historical. Few of these novels were ever published in book form. Most were serialised in his newspapers such as *Teddy Ashton's Northern Weekly*, *The Cotton Factory Times*, and later, *The Liverpool Weekly Post*.

It would be impossible to given a complete survey of Clarke's novels in the space of this article; what seems most helpful in considering his role as a socialist novelist is to examine certain key themes in his work which show development in response to working-class struggles, and relate to the work of other members of the 'Lancashire school'.

The condition of Lancashire

This is the main theme which Clarke returns to constantly in his novels, as well as in his non-fiction (for example *The Effects of the Factory System*, 1899). It includes a strong historical awareness of how his native county was despoiled by industrial capitalism, and its independent-minded domestic workers, the handloom weavers, forced into highly regulated, large-scale factories. Allen Clarke described his sense of shock when he returned to Bolton after living for some years in Blackpool, the Lancashire holiday resort situated amidst the green pastures of the Fylde countryside:

> When I went back for a brief visit to the cotton town where I was born, I saw it as I never saw it when I dwelt therein. Living there, I had grown familiar with the ugliness, and familiarity oftener breeds toleration than contempt; I had accepted the drab streets, the smoky skies, the foul river, the mass of mills, the sickly worker, as inevitable and usual—nay, natural, and did not notice them in a probing, critical way.[4]

Much of Allen Clarke's writing is an attempt to 'shock' his own readers into a similar critical recognition of their surroundings—the men and women who had grown up like him in a dirty cotton town but who had not shared his good fortune to get out of it. He often does this by using the perceptions of an outsider, such as the middle-class socialist journalist Haddon Peer in *Driving* (1901). Peer is being shown round a mill in 'Drivenden' with some other friends, and he reflects on the drastic changes which Lancashire has undergone with the coming of industrial capitalism:

> What a marvellous transformation James Watt's steam engine, aided by the spinning and weaving inventions of Kay, Har-

greaves and Crompton had wrought in a hundred years; an agricultural and pasturing shire had been turned into a county of manufacture; Lancashire's wild moorland vales had become the smoky workshop of the world; and once sweet hillsides were now cinder-heaps and once-bright brooks were now stinking sewers.[5]

Clarke's historical sensibility frequently draws out the contrasts between pre-industrial and present-day Lancashire, suggesting that what exists is not 'normal' but a state of affairs engineered by men—and it was up to men, and women, to change it. Clarke is under no illusions that this will be easy, and seems at times almost to despair of the possibility. His pessimism is seen through the 'outsider' Harold in *Lancashire Lasses and Lads* (1906), where he observes the early morning trek by thousands of men, women and children to the mill:

> They're all mad, every one; man, woman and child. They must be mad to crawl out of warm beds, and shudder to horrid work through the cold. If they weren't mad they wouldn't do it; they'd stop in bed. They're mad to live as they do; to slave as if their very lives depended on killing themselves by work.[6]

Haddon Peer and Harold are clearly uttering the perceptions of outside observers; one a socialist who sympathises with the people, the other a rich man's son who has become a de-classed cynic.

Driving deals with one particularly unpleasant side of this industry—the 'driving' policy adopted in the weaving sheds. The term becomes a metaphor for life under capitalism. The overseers were under pressure (that is, driven) by their managers to increase production in the weaving sheds; the managers themselves were 'driven' by the owners who were in turn subject to the pressure of share holders to maintain and increase dividends. This led to intolerable bullying of the mostly female weavers, and the 'slate' system, in which the weavers with the lowest production figures had their names publicly displayed on a slate in the shed—often to the derision of their workmates. The suicide of weavers suffering under this system became almost commonplace, and the story is based on the real-life suicide of a young Darwen weaver who fell foul of the 'slate'. In the plot, Ann Draper is the young weaver, orphaned and friendless, who is bullied by the tackler, and eventually kills herself:

> She was in charge of four looms and she did her best with them. She worked the hardest in the weaving shed, and yet got the least pay. She did not care about the money; but she was tortured by the constant effort, under the 'driving' of the tackler, or overseer, to do more than it was possible for her to do, and she suffered under the sneers of those who ought to have pitied.[7]

Allen Clarke's second wife, Eliza, was a weaver from Chorley, and much of the sharp detail of his accounts of weaving was owed to her assistance. In *The Little Weaver* (1893), we get one of the most dramatic descriptions of a factory waking up to the day's toil that could be imagined—the mill becomes almost human, a slumbering giant yawning and stretching, then gaining speed and confidence. The scene is Maggie's first day at the mill; her young friend Jenny accompanies her into the weaving shed just before six o'clock when all is quiet:

> Then, slowly, at six o'clock precisely, there stole a huzzing murmur on the silence; the shafts began to revolve, the straps that chained the looms creaked, stretched and yawned, as if reluctant to begin their duty, and commenced to climb languidly up to the ceiling, quickening their speed with every turn; the huzzing murmur grew and grew; the weavers touched the levers of their looms one by one, and set them on. The murmur had now become a rattling roar; the sound swelled; the straps whizzed faster; the threads of the warp flowed into the loom like a slow broad stream, and the shuttle darted across them like a swallow, binding them together and making them into cloth; there was creaking and groaning of wheels; the hissing and spluttering of leather straps, as if the animal moaned painfully in its hide; the air grew warmer; the noise became deafening; you could not hear your own voice; and the weaving shed was in full swing.[8]

Clarke was fascinated, as well as repelled, by the factory system. He hated the driving system, the child labour, and the hours of monotonous, tiring work. Yet the sight of a weaving shed full of roaring looms, or spinning mules drawing backwards and forwards on the carriages, and still more the spectacle of a huge spinning mill lit up at night are recurring images in Clarke's writing. Dick Dickinson, the mill-owner's son who leaves to make a new and independent life in 'Spindleton', observes the mills lighting up early on a winter's morning:

> Lights began to show in the great factories of four or five stories, with their many windows. Soon they were all lit up looking like a vast illumination. 'Very pretty to look at from the outside, and at a distance on a black, frosty morning,' said Dick, 'but it's a different matter toiling inside them. My father's mills will be lit up now. I wouldn't like to be one of the poor wretches that salves for *him*, anyhow; I'm sure they're not allowed to work in any comfort.'[9]

Clarke was well aware that within the cotton industry, despite the increasingly de-skilled nature of the work, a strong sense of pride remained. In *Driving* the socialist Bertha Lindley is depicted as the most competent weaver in the shed, just as capable of repairing a mechanical fault on her looms as her more highly paid male tackler. Belton, in *The Knobstick*, proves himself to be one of the most skilled engineers in the factory where he commences work, and Clarke shows him admiring the human achievement which goes into modern technology, and what he sees as the ultimately religious nature of creativity:

> 'Great and wonderful is man', mused Belton, 'Who conceived and constructed the railway train! It is almost alive! It flies along of itself and carries its maker in its arms like a child! Mighty and sublime must be he who made the locomotive! Then how much more mighty and sublime must that power be which made him who made the locomotive! There must be a God!'[10]

Indeed Clarke's attitude towards machinery in novels like

The Knobstick and even *Driving* and *The Little Weaver*, is less severe than in his *Effects of the Factory System*, which reflects on modern factory production and advocates a return to craft industry and agriculture. Perhaps such a Utopian vision squared badly with the need to present a believable story which simply set the reader thinking about a future society, rather than advocating a programmatic remedy which would detract from the novel.

Trade unionism

Clarke's criticism of the factory system focused on the ill-treatment of women and young children. The most obvious form of redress would be through the trade union, but the unions in the cotton industry were dominated almost totally by men. The spinner's union was exclusively male, and waged strikes against attempts to use female labour in the spinning room. The mostly female weavers were less well-organised, and officials tended to be men; the young piecers had no organisation, and attempts to form piecers' unions were firmly resisted by the spinners—from whose wages the piecers were paid. In *The Red Flag* (1907) the central character, Jim Campbell, is forced to become a tramp after he is sacked for attempting to form a piecers' union—an actual struggle which Clarke, along with J. R. Clynes of Oldham, was directly involved in. He tells how he came to lose his job:

> The employers of the piecers are the operative spinners; and like most middle-men look after themselves. They have for themselves anything from two pounds to four pounds a week, while paying the piecers a paltry fifteen or sixteen shillings . . . Though terrible trade unionists themselves they objected to their piecers forming a trade union. They smashed our litle union up by intimidating the members and sacking the leading spirits. I was one . . . Not only was I dismissed by a trade unionist, instigated by a society of trade unionists, for no more offence than seeking to promulgate trade unionism, but I was so boycotted by the same noble army of trade unionists . . .[11]

Clarke is not being excessively harsh in his depiction of the spinners' conduct; as with most of his writing, he bases a fictional episode on a real event and there is little doubt that the spinners were classic examples of well-paid and highly organised trade unionists who practised a rigorous form of exclusiveness and had little or no interest in their less well-organised sisters and brothers in the card-rooms and weaving sheds. The piecers were expected to behave themselves until such time as they could get their own 'mules' when they could continue the tradition of underpaying their own piecers, as they had been underpaid and exploited themselves.

However, Clarke's characterisation of trade unionism is not confined to the conservative spinners. In *A Daughter of the Factory* (1898) one of the most sympathetic characters is Kate Marford, secretary of the 'Women's Trade Union Association', who is shown travelling the north of England organising the women workers. When she reaches 'Slagbourne' she addresses a small gathering including Rose, and plants the first seeds of political radicalism in Rose's mind:

> 'There is no help for the people,' said Miss Marford, 'but in brotherly and sisterly combination. You will never get better wages, my friends, nor better anything, till you join hands together and ask for it with the voice of the union.'[12]

Rose herself becomes Kate's closest ally, and a representative of the union in the weaving shed; she becomes one of the leading figures in a strike of the weavers and is described as 'singing the workers into insurrection' at a mass meeting chaired by Kate Marford.

Clarke's main criticism of trade unionism is against the established, conservative unionism of the skilled man. The organisation of women and young people is shown as a necessary and positive step forward to defend their interests. On its own, though, trade unionism is not enough. He criticised the attitude in which trade unionists on the one hand opposed their employer on the industrial front, yet often sent the same person to Parliament; only a a generalised political challenge to capital would bring any real change.

Socialism

The Red Flag represents a departure from the style of the earlier novels in being much more directly a propagandistic work for socialism. The struggle for political change is not introduced implicitly but in a much more direct manner, the bulk of the novel being based on the very strong socialist movement of Burnley ('Brunborough') and north-east Lancashire, in the early 1900s. The earlier part of the novel, set in the tramps' lodging houses and workhouses, is intended to represent the most acute human effects of capitalism. Whilst some of the inmates of the lodgings are depraved, many of the tramps are shown as ordinary, once-respectable people who have fallen on hard times—such as Jim Campbell, the victimised piecer. A feature of the story is the representation of the social reformer, Mary Higgs, as 'Mrs Wilkinson'. In real life Mrs Higgs, a well-to-do member of the Oldham middle class, disguised herself as a tramp to establish the facts about tramp lodgings and workhouses. Clarke uses this story in the novel, with Mrs Wilkinson accompanied round the lodging houses by the young ex-weaver May—who falls in love with Jim Campbell when they meet in Brunborough at a Labour Church gathering. Jim is converted to socialism from his previous trade unionism by listening to a socialist speaker in the Burnley marketplace, his own tragic experiences fitting in to a pattern of exploitation:

> He saw his own life passing before him, his hard struggle for bread, his willingness to work and no opportunity to get it, he saw his starving wife and child, he realised that all the misery and the death of his darlings had been brought about by this foul, murderous, competitive capitalist system which the speaker was so tremendously denouncing. He felt a wild anger against the rulers and authorities and employers, his soul rose in revolt, and he shouted out in excitement. 'By God you're right!'[13]

Someone reading this in the 1980s might find it a little incredible—people do not suddenly 'become socialists' by listening to a speaker, however fine an orator. Yet it should be remembered that the 'new socialism' of the 1890s frequently took on the semblance of being almost a religious crusade—converts were made in hundreds at meetings such as the one Clarke describes. First-hand accounts[14] of socialist propaganda meetings testify to the enormous appeal of speakers such as Caroline Martyn, Katherine St John Conway, Keir Hardie and others, who were expressing many of the subconscious hopes and fears of their audiences. Jim was not totally ignorant of working-class ideals—as a victimised piecer who had suffered direct personal tragedies he would obviously be receptive to the socialist message, as would many other people. Jim is befriended by the local socialists and given temporary accommodation in the Socialist Club House by Joe Summerfield, the socialist lecturer whom he had earlier been listening to. As Joe closes the club and goes home, Jim is left sitting in the club room, by the fireside. Above the fireside is a huge red flag; as he relaxes almost into sleep he sees a vision of all the poor and oppressed—his own parents, then thousands more people joining in a great procession: . . .'men, thin, pale, stunted; women, weary, white, worn down; little children pitiful to see, with sickly famished faces . . .' As the vision proceeds, this mass of the oppressed raise the red flag which stands before him, and they begin to sing:

> Raise the Scarlet Standard High,
> Within its shade we live or die . . .

The vision alters, and he sees an army of ghosts—men, women and children who had died of hunger and disease, of men and women who had killed themselves in despair, and those who had died in the workhouse. The vision changes yet again, and he sees thousands of living men and women joining the procession led by the Red Flag, people of all classes who had realised the evil of the present system; and then he even sees 'the heavens above the people in mystic motion . . . the stars marched with them'. And

> he saw a picture of the land of good fellowship, towards which the Red Flag was being borne—he saw industry and trade so arranged that there was food for all, shelter for all—no pauperism, no unemployed, no starvation . . . and land, not of human beings who allowed a few money-maniacs to make trouble for the rest, but a land where all that the co-operative nation produced was shared out equitably amongst all—and over this happy land of healthy men and fair women and joyous children, the Red Flag waved triumphantly.[15]

I think 'The Vision of the Red Flag' is one of the most moving pieces of imaginative socialist writing, combing a moral denunciation of capitalism, with a vision of the future, and a sense of the coming together of men and women from diverse social backgrounds to fight for a common cause. Clarke realises the vision is a long way from its final fruition, and as Jim Campbell throws himself into the socialist movement he finds that there are divisions and disagreements. The relative positions of the ILP, the SDF and the Labour Church are discussed; the merits of each are different compared to the observations of Haddon Peer in *Driving*, written in 1901. Seven years later the ILP had become more opportunist and was observed to be watering down its socialism through an alliance with the moderate trade unions. The SDF is shown as the uncompromising socialist organisation, with no criticism directed at its 'materialism'. The Labour Church is shown in the most positive light, expressing Clarke's own ethical socialist beliefs, without the corruption which the ILP's socialism had suffered.

In the Socialist Club Jim Campbell listens to arguments between the older, more experienced comrades, and the younger socialists who believe in violence. The main advocate of violence is Fordham, the villain of the story. Joe Summerfield argues strongly against Fordham's provocative suggestions, and afterwards warns that he is either a spy, or a lunatic. As the socialist movement was making rapid strides through peaceful struggle, Summerfield suggests that the authorities may attempt to discredit the cause through stirring up violence:

> 'Socialism is growing rapidly, and they're beginning to fear that the day of the blood suckers and money grabbers is at an end. Just be careful of Fordham, and have nothing to do with his schemes of violence. Our weapon is the ballot box and no other.'[16]

Fordham is not, in fact, a paid provocateur—he is simply embittered and degraded, a casualty of the system. Clarke suggests that such bitterness can lead people into irresponsible acts which damage the movement, and carefully uses the SDF stalwart, Summerfield, to warn against it. The way forward is shown through Jim Campbell being nominated by the SDF for the Board of Guardian elections—the body responsible for the administering of poor relief. Such elections, as well as the School Board contests, were seen as an important testing ground for the socialist movement's rise to power, and many ILP and SDF victories were won in Lancashire in the 1890s and early 1900s. The novel ends on a further apocalyptic note. This time, it does not come in a dream, but through the description of a huge socialist meeting on the summit of Pendle Hill, on May Day. Jim and May are happily united in marriage, and they join the crowd of thousands of working men and women, as well as teachers, doctors, clerks and other professional men and women:

> Then from the vast crowd, amid the still of the high moorlands, rose the chorus:
>
> Then raise the scarlet standard high;
> Within its shade we'll live or die;
> Though cowards flinch and traitors sneer
> We'll keep the Red Flag flying here.[17]

The revolutionary heroine

Clarke had heroines in many of his novels, though in some

cases they tended to be appendages to the male working-class hero. In *The Knobstick* Lizzie Banks is shown as an attractive, but innocent and unformed character until her relationship with Harry Belton turns her into a fiery defender of working people's rights. In his slightly later novel, *Lancashire Lasses and Lads*, Hannah Heyes, the young weaver, plays a similarly subsidiary role to the main character, Dick Dickinson. A major development takes place in *A Daughter of the Factory*, serialised in *The Northern Weekly* during 1898, although there is a curious twist to the characterisation of Rose Hilton as the female revolutionary. Her background is not that of a conventional working-class girl; she is the daughter of a gypsy woman, tricked into marriage and then deserted by a rakish mill-owner's son. Rose's incendiary rhetoric is shown as a result of the genetic combination of the gypsy and the young aristocrat, leavened by the experience of working-class life when she is brought up as an orphan by an ordinary family of Lancashire workers. There remains throughout the novel a suggestion of social distance between Rose and her workmates, illustrated by the following exchange between Rose and her friend Susy, about working-class apathy:

> 'Susy,' said Rose, 'the working people are idiots.'
> 'You shouldn't talk like that Rose,' said Susy, 'You're one of them.'
> 'I know that. That's what makes me madder than ever.'[18]

But the reader knows what Rose doesn't—by birth she isn't one of the workers, hence the irony of the discussion. Rose is 'different' not because she has developed a strong political awareness—but rather because of her 'gypsy and aristocratic blood'. In his book on the Fylde countryside, *Windmill Land*,[19] Clarke makes a similar observation in relation to the once-common practice of landowners seducing the village maidens—suggesting that this mixture of the supposedly 'noble' blood of the landowners with that of the 'common people' would result in a new breed of radicals by genetic means. Clearly, this is a considerable weakness in his writing as a socialist, if the only working-class leaders that can be found are the result of illicit sexual behaviour by members of the ruling class. Kate Marford, the union organiser, is apparently of more orthodox working-class parentage, but she, too, has had an unusual background; having lost her parents when a child, she was brought up by a progressive middle-class woman who instils advanced political ideas into her. She returns to her class as a propagandist but there is again the suggestion that revolutionary ideas only take root when imported from an 'outside' agency or by dubious genetic means.

The importance of *A Daughter of the Factory* is that it is a fellow working-class woman, Kate Marford, who exercises the key influence on Rose. After hearing her speak she begins to think about the world in a new way, about the exploitation of the working class and the immense contrast between the luxury of the rich and the degradation of the poor. The next time Kate Marford visits Slagbourne, Rose joins her on the platform, and makes an impulsive speech which takes the gathering by storm:

> 'We are not horses to be thrashed and sworn at, and spat upon and bullyragged out of all existence by little two-legged terrors in white slops, called tacklers and clothlookers . . . (Laughter). Ah you may laugh. I laugh too, but I feel I could cry. If I were an Irishman, I would say to you, "Now women, arise and be men!" (Laughter). But as the samples of men I daily come into contact with are not the kind for imitating, I will say "My sisters—be Women!" Join together—there is nothing like union—holy matrimony for instance (Laughter). But quite as good a union as holy matrimony—I nearly said better—is trade unionism. Wake up and pay your entrance fee.'[20]

Yet, ultimately Rose leaves her friends in the weaving shed. The 'happy end' of the story includes her marriage to Captain Lever—a politically progressive young officer who is able to give her the cultured life she inwardly craves for.

Clarke's women characters show significant developments over the period of his novel writing, from the early 1890s to the First World War. The early weaknesses of characters like Lizzie Banks are slowly overcome, at least so far as their dependence on the male hero. The obsession with genetics in *A Daughter of the Factory* mars what would otherwise have been a superb portrayal of the development of the woman revolutionary.

A LANCASHIRE SCHOOL

The success of Clarke's own novels, and the availability of a sympathetic outlet in his *Northern Weekly* encouraged other working-class writers to attempt novels on contemporary political themes. The following group of writers were all active in the socialist movement of the 1890s and early 1900s.

Arthur Laycock (1869-1957)

Laycock was Blackpool's first Labour councillor, and active in the unemployed movement, ILP and Clarion Club. He was the son of the famous Lancashire dialect poet Samuel Laycock and perhaps personifies the transition within Lancashire working-class literature from advanced liberalism to socialism. He wrote three novels which survived in published form. *The Young Gaffer* (1898) was his earliest, followed by *Steve the Outlander* (1900) and *Warren of Manchester* (c. 1906). *The Young Gaffer* was serialised in the *Northern Weekly* during 1898, in the aftermath of the national Engineers' Strike and is clearly influenced by that struggle. It deals with the forced migration of workers from country to town, and the demoralising effects of this on working people. Although rural 'Sunny Bank' is only separated from industrial 'Blastone' by a mere half-mile, they seem worlds apart:

> It was distant about half a mile from the fringe of the grimy town of Blastone, and with its snug, white-washed cottages standing out in bold relief against the sombre background of the great white moor, formed a striking contrast to the sombre, sooted habitations in the valley below.[21]

The contrast between town and country, and the morally corrupting nature of the latter, was a familar theme of working-class writers of the Lancashire School. In *The Young Gaffer*, Dick Haskett's family moves to Blastone, where he is unable to find work. As a result he becomes dissolute, neglectful of his family, and embittered. In contrast to Dick, Bob Sanders—the skilled engineer and trade unionist—remains in Sunny Bank and becomes a leading figure in the Engineers' Strike. His son, Lincoln— or the 'Young Gaffer'—is a socialist and falls in love with Sally, Dick Haskett's eldest daughter. As the lock-out drags on, the men become more desperate and violence is threatened.

Bob Sanders's hope of a negotiated settlement to the dispute comes under challenge at a mass meeting, from the labourers' spokesman—Dick Haskett.

> 'Let's ha less talk an more feightin,' shouted the first speaker.
> 'No!' said Bob Sanders, in a firm, clear voice which excited attention from the throng.
> 'No. We'll have no feightin, chaps—no physical force; leave that to th'brutes.'
> 'Masters are brutes,' cried the other, 'an' they threaten us wi physical force—police an sowjers. An we'll feight em an aw!'
> 'Goo lad Dick!' shouted some of the men gathered about the man with the shrill voice.
> 'No,' again said Bob, 'Let's feight fair lads, feight fair an be reasonable. Let us reason wi th'masters an no—'
> 'Reason be hanged!' cried the first speaker savagely. 'Yo cannot reason wi brutes; that's what th'masters are. They care nowt that our kids are clemmin . . .'[22]

Whilst Bob Sanders represents the 'respectable' artisans, the skilled workers in receipt of strike pay, Dick Haskett is the spokesman for the unskilled labourers, receiving no strike pay and forced to beg on the streets. Dick and his fellow-labourers turn to sporadic violence against 'the knobsticks', or strike-breakers, and falsely accuse the 'Young Gaffer' of aiding them.

The knobsticks themselves are shown to be figures of pity as much as scorn—they are capitalism's most pathetic victims. One of them is arrested by the police for assault and he splutters out his own path to becoming a 'knobstick':

> 'I'm sick o'the life I've been leadin lately. This is how I were fixed . . . I lost my job at Warrington through no fault of my own. Machines started doin the work that formerly I'd done. I were a steady, sober chap then, but I soon get to be th'other sort, for a chap gets every encouragement to become a "wastrel". Then th'lock out came on and there were no chance of a job at my trade or any other, nobbut knobstickin . . .'[23]

There are very close parallels with Allen Clarke's *The Knobstick*, even down to the engineering industry setting, and being based on an actual struggle. In Laycock's novel the knobsticks are, however, socially determined, whilst Clarke's 'knobstick' character is shown simply as a moral reprobate. Laycock also brings out more striking differences within the strikers themselves—the contradiction between the skilled and the unskilled, and the differing tactics espoused by the two groups.

An important sub-plot is the 'Young Gaffer's' technical ingenuity and the issue of the social effects of technology. Lincoln is shown attending night schools and becoming an ingenious inventor; however, he is conscious of how most modern machinery simply displaces labour and creates the sort of characters typified by the knobstick.

The main representative of the employing class, Darnton, is shown not as a villain—unlike his partner, White—but as someone who is just as much subject to the sort of social forces Clarke depicted in *Driving*, as are his workers. When the strike is finally settled, Darnton provides Lincoln with the necessary capital to set up a co-operative factory based on the advanced technology he has patented. Whilst Darnton obviously sympathises with Lincoln's idealism, he sees it as a potentially judicious business proposition. Lincoln, however, sees it as providing the basis for 'the factory of the future' such as William Morris had described:

Lincoln felt that at last he had work before him to which he could devote his best energies, whole-heartedly; work which would enable him to help his less gifted fellows. Heretofore he had often felt that prosperity for him, namely the success of his labour-saving inventions, meant ruin to other men. Under the new regime his inventions would be a blessing, not a curse, to the working man.[24]

Laycock's comments on the social effects of modern technology form an interesting contrast with those of Clarke's. Clarke, both in his novels and in *Effects of the Factory System*, dismisses the harnessing of modern technology to progressive uses, and instead calls for a return to an agriculturally based, labour intensive form of production. Laycock accepts the dehumanising effects of modern technology within capitalism, but shows that in a more advanced system of social relations of production, technology can be the asset, not the enemy, of the working class.

Whilst *The Young Gaffer* is rooted in industrial Lancashire, *Steve the Outlander* has an international dimension, providing a link between Lancashire and South Africa at the eve of the Boer War. The hero, Steve, emigrates to South Africa after he has been victimised in the spinning mill. The increasing tensions between the Boers and the non-Dutch whites are very skilfully developed, and the subsequent conflict is shown as a provocation by British imperial interests, aided by the greed of the 'outlanders'. There is a clear sympathy for the Boer people as well as for the Black African. The most negative character in the novel, Ralph Cartleigh—perhaps predictably a mill-owner's son— sails to South Africa in pursuit of Ella, the heroine, who is torn between her love for Steve and her self-interested attachment to Cartleigh. In South Africa Cartleigh catches up with Ella and, failing to persuade her to forget Steve, proceeds to assault her. He is also shown as viciously racist in his attitude towards the Blacks, depicting them as lazy, ignorant and dishonest—qualities which the author implies fit Cartleigh, rather than the Blacks. Laycock had first-hand experience of life in South

Africa, having worked there for a period in the 1890s. Whilst his sympathy for the Boers was thus based on personal observation, support for the Boer Republic was widespread amongst ILP members during the war and led to frequent attacks on them by 'jingoite' mobs.[25]

His last published novel, *Warren of Manchester* is less concerned with working-class life than his earlier two works. It is based on social life in Blackpool and the seaside town's close ties with the great commercial centre of Manchester and the cotton-manufacturing districts of Lancashire. The main characters tend to be of the middle class: boarding-house keepers, mill-owners fallen on hard times, dealers on the Manchester stock exchange. Blackpool's role as the working-class seaside resort *par excellence* is well shown, as a backdrop to the lives of the boarding-house keepers. Laycock describes Blackpool in August at the height of 'the season' and the thousands of holiday-makers:

> These strenuous toilers in workshop, factory, foundry and mine gave themselves up whole-heartedly to genuine enjoyment. The 'Wakes' week came but once a year, and one must merrily make the most of its fleeting hours. For a brief spell the clang of hammers, the roar of looms, the 'ping' of the coal pick in the coal seam were all forgotten, and the pleasant present remembered alone.[26]

Laycock lived in Blackpool for most of his life, and was well-attuned to the subtle differences in the resort—the north and central piers as social boundaries, dividing the 'better class' visitors off from the mass, and the distinctions between the mere 'day-trippers' and the families staying 'for the week'.

John Tamlyn (1859-1921)

The novels of John Tamlyn which were published in *The Northern Weekly*—*The Hermit of Cottondale* (1902) and *The Love of a Northern Farmer* (1903)—had both been rejected by established publishers because of their political content. According to Tamlyn himself[27] Heinemann's—

one of the largest British fiction publishers—were full of praise for the novel but refused to publish because 'it was unconventional and preached socialism'.

Tamlyn himself was highly unconventional. He left home as a boy and made a living as a sailor, parson, meat-pie salesman and mechanic. He departed from the SDF in Burnley, and left the ILP after a brief stay hoping to set up a new Christian socialist organisation. He was imprisoned during a free-speech campaign in Plymouth. *The Hermit of Cottondale* is the story of Madeline—a soldier's daughter, seduced by an aristocrat and left with a child. She travels to Lancashire where she has friends, and meets 'the hermit', Eli Harding, a socialist and a solitary tram-car conductor with intellectual tastes, living high on the moors above 'Cottondale'. Madeline attends a socialist meeting with the 'hermit', and is astounded at his remarkable oratorical power. Speaking on 'Socialism', the Glorious Gospels of Salvation', Harding sets out, in a lengthy passage, the essentials of Tamlyn's own brand of 'christian communism'. It is highly moralistic, and identifies the future society as one which will be attuned to 'Nature', not struggling against it under capitalism:

> 'Millionaires, aristocrats, brewer baronets, these are the noblemen which a competitive society likes to honour. Verily, this society knoweth its own. Survival of the fittest? Of course! For the thieves den, the best thief; for a profit-mongering society, the best bester. Nature is very just, awfully just! Run your society on the brute basis, and you shall reap the brute . . . So hurrah for the new socialism! The new basis! No trimming of that which is rotten at the root; the world for the workers, the means of production for social production—a common effort for a common ends.'[28]

Tamlyn uses the questions at the end of the speech as a means to counter anti-socialist arguments: would individual private property be confiscated? Would everyone, industrious or lazy be paid the same wage? Did competition not bring out the best in people? Would not socialism crush human liberty? Harding answers each point skilfully, and often humorously. Later, Harding is billed as the socialist speaker in a debate with a local priest. He exposes the contradictions of orthodox Christianity, and returns to the theme of human degradation being caused by capitalism. The means to the higher end is socialism:

> The poor are withered by poverty; the rich are rotted by luxury. The only way out is a return to the simple principles of Jesus—Life not Things. And the way to this? Free access to the same means of life! And the best way to secure this? The Socialist way. Let all work, land, machinery, and all other common things be for the work of all.[29]

The characterisation of socialists as isolated, Christ-like figures of derision by both oppressors and oppressed, returns in *The Love of a Northern Farmer*. Again the hero lives in an isolated moorland cottage. Again, the hero—John Heath—rescues the main female character, Kate Venn, from disaster. Kate, however, is no weak-willed girl. Whilst John Heath teaches her how to milk cows, she tells how she takes after her father in her political views:

> 'My father was a farmer like you. Oh, but he was an awful man. He used to harangue the men in the village public house upon politics—Republicanism, Socialism, all things common. Down with the parsons, squires, and all tyranny. I'm a bit like my father. I'd like to make a holocaust of kings, priests and all those who lord it over others.' 'Why, you're a full blown anarchist,' said John Heath.[30]

John Heath argues with Kate, suggesting that change must come through peaceful means, by socialist education. Kate stays with John, helping on the farm, and singing for countless local progressive groups, including performances in aid of strike funds. The relationship between John and Kate matures into romantic love, and Kate becomes the politically dominant partner—encouraging John to take an active part in the struggle, constantly appearing herself as a singer at socialist and union meetings. Her reputation as a militant socialist spreads, and the local reactionaries shun her—she is refused service in local shops, and many of the parishioners at the church where she sings urge the vicar to expel her. Yet her own strong-mindedness and socialist principles win out—even to the extent of persuading a reactionary coal-owner that socialism is the only answer for the future of humanity. Her powers of persuasion are such that the coal-owner wills her his coal-mines when he dies, and she proceeds to run them along 'enlightened' principles.

The story is an unlikely one, though it has considerable interest as a further example of a working-class male writer developing the character of the revolutionary woman, clearly more 'advanced' than the men around her. Tamlyn uses the novel to draw out what he sees as the crucial political issues—the moral basis of socialism, a belief that even the ruling class can be persuaded of the 'truths' of socialism, and the Christian basis of communism. *The Love of a Northern Farmer* appears to have been popular with *The Northern Weekly* readership, and in a short article Tamlyn mentions being asked many times by comrades at meetings he has addressed when it would appear in book form. He mentions the rejection of the script by Heinemann and offers to sell the copyright to anyone who wishes to publish it. He intends not to write any more novels, for, he says,

> in this age of exuberant patronage and appreciation of letters, I incline to the belief that a fish and chip business is more profitable . . . the following of literature entails too many doctor's bills, and I don't want to shorten my natural life, so I'll look out for a fish-and-chip shop.[31]

Tamlyn never got his fish-and-chip shop. He had to make do with selling half-penny meat pies on the streets of Burnley, and finally returned to Plymouth, where he was known as 'the communist parson'.

Fred Plant (1866-1925)

Tamlyn had little time for trade unionism. Where it does appear in his novels, it is usually in the context of a 'palliative' which stops the workers from identifying with the loftier aim of 'pure socialism'. The work of Fred Plant, which appeared in *The Northern Weekly* at around the same time as Tamlyn's novels, is much more rounded in its treatment of the relationship between trade unionism and socialism. Plant himself was an ILP activist and one of Stockport's first labour councillors. He worked for a time with Allen Clarke on *The Northern Weekly* and wrote scores of fascinating short stories of Lancashire working-class life. He also contributed dialect sketches under the pseudonym of 'Harry o'th'Hills'.

One of Plant's most directly socialist novels was *The Conductor's Sweetheart*, subtitled *A Tale of the Great Tram Strike* (1900-1). It appeared in *The Northern Weekly* as a serial beginning on 17 November 1900—less than a week after the end of the Ashton-under-Lyne tram strike on which it is directly based. Whereas Clarke in *The Knobstick*, and Laycock in *The Young Gaffer*, use an actual strike as a backdrop to their stories, the strike in *The Conductor's Sweetheart* is much more central to the action and very closely modelled on the actual events.[32] As was invariably the case in all these novels, a romantic love story structures the novel. The hero is Arthur Walton, one of the strike-leaders, who eventually wins 'his girl', Florrie, from the clutches of a dishonest suitor.

The strike's build-up is developed carefully by Plant, describing the injustices felt by the tramway workers, and the arrogance of the employers who dismiss the men's grievances with contempt; the one exception is Councillor Rathlane, a radical, who sits on the tramway board. The strike begins, and blacklegs are imported to run the trams. As with both Clarke's and Laycock's depiction of blacklegs, they are figures of pity and derision. However, Joe Radburn, a militant spinner, who is on short-time, argues that there are always alternative means of employment for someone who wants a job:

'There's other ways o'makin a livin without turnin blackleg. What did my brother Bill do when he were out o'wark after th' railway strike? Sooner than start wark as a blackleg he went to be a 'bobby' an has done well ever sin.'[33]

Other men argue with Joe Radburn that police are frequently used to break strikes, with unnecessary violence, although Joe sticks to his belief that his brother would never side with a 'knobstick' against a decent trade unionist. There is a bitter irony in Joe's sincere belief about his brother; in one of the most memorable scenes in the novel—and indeed of most other Lancashire novels of this period—the police attack a peaceful demonstration of strikers and their families:

> Policemen drew their batons and used them with terrific effect on those about them. A splash of blood fell on Joe Radburn's cheek and a young fellow went down with a groan . . . Joe turned when he heard the young man's cry, and gripping the policeman's wrist he roared 'Theau damned murderer! Tum Smith's done nowt wrung! He's one o'th' quietest lads i' Cottonly an theau's smashed his yead. Take that! . . . an that!' and Joe struck wildly but with revengeful force at the broad back of the policeman. The latter turned, with his blood-stained baton uplifted. Joe saw his face and his eyes rolled like a madman's. 'Oh my God—eaur Bill!' came from his lips in a long wail. 'Eaur Bill, an theau't a damned murderer yet!' and Joe's fist crashed into the face of the brother whom he had hitherto loved as himself.[34]

The violence of the police attack—based on a real incident during the strike—is shown not as the action of a group of reckless constables, but as a premeditated assault planned by the police and the tramway employers. The police are shown drilling baton charges each day, and playing card-games with the blacklegs, as well as riding on the tramcars that were manned by the blacklegs.

Plant shows the strike as a community struggle, as much as a simple trade-unionism issue; the trams are boycotted by the vast majority of the population, and women hiss and boo the strike-breakers. The violence of the police is answered by the violence of a group of strikers who stone the trams and attempt to derail them, assisted by other workers such as Joe Radburn, the cotton spinner. George Goldthorpe, president of the local Trades Council, intervenes in the struggle to advise against provocations which would jeopardise public support:

> 'Let us have no fighting . . . every blow struck will tell against the strikers. We mustn't give our opponents the opportunity to say we resorted to rowdyism . . . If the strikers let the public see they are conducting this struggle in legitimate fashion, and not out-stepping the law, the sympathy of the general public will be ours! If we get it, victory will lie with the tramwaymen; if we lose it, the issue is doubtful.'[35]

Whilst Plant shows the violence directed at the blacklegs as justified, he uses Goldthorpe to argue that tactically it is vital to avoid violence to maintain public support, in the form of the boycott and support for the strike fund. Ultimately, the strike is settled in the men's favour after Board of Trade arbitration, and the intervention of Councillor Rathlane.

The whole course of the strike is superbly described by Plant who clearly had first-hand insight into trade-union negotiation and strike action: it is not the superficial account of an outsider, but of someone who knows the movement inside out and has a clear grasp of class issues. His understanding of the relationship between capital and the state, particularly the role of the police, is also notable. Plant shows the strike as an instance of the battle between capital and labour, in an industry of, as he terms it, 'public usefulness'. The character of Councillor Rathlane is crucial in the ending of the strike and suggestive that such industries performing a socially useful purpose should be municipalised, rather than left at the behest of a group of grasping and irresponsible bourgeois. It is also interesting that Plant links the struggle to the war in South Africa, showing the strike beginning just as 'the final curtain of supremacy's tragedy was being lowered to the accompaniment of "Rule Britannia" '.[36]

Plant's other major work, *Tamsie—The Tale of a Hatting Town* (1899) also features an industrial dispute, in the hatting trade, based on the small town of Denton, near Stockport. *Tamsie* is more concerned with the everyday aspects of working-class life, than with the 'exceptional' such as a big strike. Details of the hatting industry itself are matched with careful description of working-class domestic life. Plant suggests that in the ordinary course of things, working people are more interested in the destination of next year's factory outing, 'than a parliamentary election or passing glimpses of royalty'. Standish Meacham's suggestion of working people inhabiting 'a life apart' from bourgeois society is dramatically illustrated.[37]

THE SIGNIFICANCE OF THE LANCASHIRE SCHOOL OF WORKING-CLASS NOVELISTS

Arthur Laycock, Tamlyn and Plant form the three main figures, alongside Clarke, in the 'Lancashire school of working-class novelists'. They were united in their general political approach, based on Independent Labour Party-style ethical socialism—though Laycock and Plant were more sympathetic to the limited aims of trade unionism than either Clarke or Tamlyn. The most obvious element was a common outlet for their work—Clarke's *The Northern Weekly*. Without this it seems unlikely that the Lancashire school would ever have appeared at all, given its highly political content, and the strong regional thrust, through its use of dialect and depiction of local customs and culture. The national labour movement papers may have found them too localised, and book publishers too controversial (as we have direct evidence of with Tamlyn's work). It is also important to remember that the four writers were close friends. At *The Northern Weekly* picnics in the Lancashire countryside, most of the circle would usually be present, though Tamlyn was less given to the social life of the movement than the others, preferring the solitary life of the ascetic which he glorified in his novels.

There were other writers on the periphery of 'the Lancashire school', such as James Haslam who shared Clarke's childhood experience as a piecer in the Bolton mills, and was taken on the staff of *The Northern Weekly* in the 1890s. He contributed several short stories of working-class life, and his novel *The Handloom Weaver's Daughter* (1906) was first serialised in the paper as *The Mill on the Moor* (1898).[38] Jospeh Whittaker, the Black Country ILP activist contributed many stories to *The Northern Weekly* which later appeared in collected form as *Tales of Tumble Fold* (1898). Peter Lee, the leading figure in the Rochdale ILP during the 1890s, was a friend of Clarke and contributed occasional dialect verse to his papers. His novel *Mystery O'Sunny Fowt* (1906) incorporates many of the central themes of 'the Lancashire school', such as the 'moral' rightness of socialism, the superiority of country living over the towns, and the cross-class appeal of socialist politics.

These writers, and novels, represent an unprecedented flowering of working-class socialist literature which has gone virtually unrecognised by socialists and students of literature today. It was a highly specific movement, well justifying the title of 'school'. The master was Allen Clarke—his pioneering working-class novels and short stories gave the necessary encouragement to other working-class people to write. The success of his paper, *The Northern Weekly*, in reaching a broad working-class readership in Lancashire provided the essential outlet for their work and the sort of readers they wanted. All the members of the 'school' were attempting to depict the life of the working class in Lancashire in a way which was realistic, but at the same time pointed the way to a socialist future. They tried to avoid being pedantic, and aimed to bring out the socialist message in a natural, common-sense way—as one amongst a number of points of view held by working-class people. The socialist hero or heroine is invariably the best worker, the most upright character, and loving comrade who proves by example that socialism is a qualitatively different way of life from the old, corrupting and immoral capitalist system. All the novels are strongly rooted in Lancashire and form an impressive literary image of the great Lancashire cotton industry and its people at the turn of the century. The use of Lancashire dialect in the dialogue between working-class characters, and also as an emblem of class difference, is used by all of the writers we have looked at.

Whilst this technique was also employed by middle-class novelists throughout the nineteenth century, in the novels of Clarke and Plant particularly, dialect is used as a distinctive form of working-class speech which the reader of *The Northern Weekly* could directly identify with. The working-class readership was encouraged to see bits of themselves in the characters—the mill girl struggling for a better life, the piecer frustrated at his lack of prospects and of the joyful aspects of life—in features such as romantic love, the trips to the seaside or the humour (displayed particularly by Clarke and Plant). The response of the *Northern Weekly* readers to these novels is one of the most interesting aspects of the history of the Lancashire school. The regular letters to the editor, commenting on particular novels—both critically and positively—was a feature of the working-class serial which was particularly important. The reader was not distanced in any sense from the novel—it was about their town (or a fictionalised town which could be anywhere in south Lancashire), and was about people like them. They could write in to 'their' paper commenting on particular episodes, and at *The Northern Weekly* social events could chat with the author of the current serial, and make face-to-face comments. I doubt very much whether any form of working-class literature has had such close interaction between reader and writer as this, and there is no doubt that Clarke and his school found it a particularly healthy feature of writing for *The Northern Weekly*.[39]

Judging by the letters sent to *The Northern Weekly*, these novels did have a strong impact on the Lancashire working-class families who read them each week. Stories like *The Knobstick, The Hermit of Cottondale, The Young Gaffer* and *The Conductor's Sweetheart* may have planted a few seeds in the minds of their readers which began to challenge the ingrained conservatism of the Lancashire cotton workers—their attachment to the bourgeois parties, the half-time system, the inequality of women, and their indifference to the grimy surroundings they had to live it. There is no doubt that the Lancashire school of working-class novelists was very much a part of that strong regional socialist culture which blossomed in the 1890s, and created 'a new world within our hearts'.[40]

NOTES

1. *Teddy Ashton's Northern Weekly* (hereafter given as the *Northern Weekly*), 20 October 1900.
2. See Paul Salveson, 'Getting back to the land. The Daisy Colony experiment', *North West Labour History*, 10 (1984).
3. *The Bellman*, 15 September 1893.
4. Allen Clarke, *The Effects of the Factory System* (London, 1899), p.38.
5. *Northern Weekly*, 27 July 1901.
6. Allen Clarke, *Lancashire Lasses and Lads* (Manchester, 1906), p.11.
7. *Northern Weekly*, 6 July 1901.
8. *The Bolton Trotter*, 16 June 1893.
9. Clarke, *Lancashire Lasses and Lads*, p.11.
10. C. Allen Clarke, *The Knobstick. A Story of Love and Labour* (Manchester, 1893), p.108. For a discussion of this novel see chapter 4 by H. Gustav Klaus.
11. Allen Clarke, *The Red Flag* (London, 1907), p.19.
12. *Northern Weekly*, 14 May 1898.
13. Clarke, *The Red Flag*, p.76.
14. See Stephen Yeo, 'A new life: the religion of socialism in Britain 1883-1896', *History Workshop*, 4 (Autumn 1977).
15. Clarke, *The Red Flag*, p.89.
16. *ibid.*, p.107.
17. *ibid.*, p.106.
18. *Northern Weekly*, 21 May 1898.
19. Allen Clarke, *Windmill Land* (London, 1916), pp.36-8. Referring to the custom of 'maiden rent', that is the seduction of the tenant's daughter by the lord of the manor on her wedding night, Clarke comments:
    > Yet even that vile custom would bring about its own retribution, even by this wicked old custom was introduced into the peasantry some aristocratic blood, with its everloving instincts, its resentment of domination, with perhaps a touch of culture.

    For Clarke, this is not simply a genetic process—it is partly mystical. The sub-heading of the section quoted above is 'Karma', the eastern mystical philosophy of cause and effect.
20. *Northern Weekly*, 9 July 1898.
21. *ibid.*, 12 March 1898.
22. *ibid.*, 21 May 1898.

23. *ibid.*, 25 June 1898.
24. *ibid.*, 6 August 1898.
25. See R. Price, *An Imperial War and the British Working Class* (London, 1972).
26. Arthur Laycock, *Warren of Manchester* (London, n.d. [c. 1906]), p.97.
27. *Northern Weekly*, 16 May 1903.
28. *ibid.*, 31 May 1902.
29. *ibid.*, 12 July 1902.
30. *ibid.*, 20 December 1902.
31. *ibid.*, 16 May 1902.
32. See S. Carter, 'The ILP in Ashton-under-Lyne 1893 to 1900', *Bulletin of the North West Group for the Study of Labour History*, 4 (1976-7). The article relates events of the Tram Strike to the ILP locally.
33. *Northern Weekly*, 24 November 1900.
34. *ibid.*, 19 January 1901.
35. *ibid.*, 17 November 1900.
36. *ibid.*
37. Standish Meacham, *A Life Apart. The English Working Class, 1890-1914* (London, 1977).
38. For a discussion of James Haslam's novel, see chapter 5 by J. M. Rignall.
39. A photograph of one of the 'Northern Weekly Picnics' appears in Allen Clarke, *Moorlands and Memories*, third edn (Blackpool, 1924), p.134.
40. A longer version of this chapter is available for inspection at Bolton Reference Library. A number of Allen Clarke's works have been reprinted recently, including *Teddy Ashton's Lancashire Scrapbook. Selections from Allen Clarke* (Bolton, 1985), ed Paul Salveson; *The Effects of the Factory System* (Littleborough, 1985); *Moorlands and Memories* (Littleborough, 1986); *Windmill Land* (Littleborough, 1986). All these works contain introductions by the present writer and are available from G. Kelsall, 22 Church Street, Littleborough, Lancashire.

· 9 ·

Henry Lawson's radical vision

MICHAEL WILDING

In March 1902 Edward Garnett wrote 'An Appreciation' of the work of Henry Lawson in *Academy and Literature*, reprinted in his *Friday Nights* (1922) as 'Henry Lawson and the Democracy':

> Nothing is more difficult to find in this generation than an English writer who identifies himself successfully with the life of the working democracy, a writer who does not stand aloof from and patronise the bulk of the people who labour with their hands. This no doubt is because nearly all our writers have a middle-class bias and training, and so either write down to or write up to their subject when it leads them outside their own class, and accordingly their valuations thereof are in general falsified . . .
> It is therefore an immense relief to the unsophisticated critic, after looking East and West and North and South for writers untainted by the ambition to be mentally genteel, to come across the small group of able democratic writers on the 'Sydney Bulletin', of whom Mr Lawson is the chief.[1]

Lawson's first collection of stories, *While the Billy Boils* (1896) received English distribution and *The Times* found it 'a little in Bret Harte's manner, crossed, perhaps, with that of Guy de Maupassant'.[2] His second collection, *On the Track and Over the Sliprails* (1900), was similarly well received. Francis Thompson wrote in the *Daily Chronicle* that it 'will sustain the reputation its author has already won as the best writer of Australian short stories and sketches the literary world knows'.[3] Encouraged by his reception Lawson came to London in 1900. Blackwood's published a selction from the two previous prose volumes, *The Country I Come from* (1900), and a new collection *Joe Wilson and His Mates* (1901) and Methuen published a further collection *Children of the Bush* (1902). Lawson returned to Sydney in 1902 but his work was remembered. Will H. Ogilvie wrote of him in the *Scotsman*, 2 May 1914:

> He became a confirmed Socialist in his early manhood, setting a high value on the brotherhood of man, and seeing nothing but virtue in the attitude of Trade Unionism in its long war against capital. Against the blue sky of the infinite Bush spaces fluttered for him for ever the red flag of Revolt. The gipsy in his nature, and his deep-rooted and romantic sense of fair play, made him a ready convert to the camaraderie of the river roads; and his talent for verse-writing made him the accepted and much-loved spokesman of the brotherhood.[4]

Henry Lawson (1867-1922) was born on the Grenfell goldfield in New South Wales. His father was a Norwegian seaman who had jumped ship in Australia. His mother was the daughter of English immigrants. 'They were supposed to have come of English gipsies and were hop pickers in Kent,' Lawson wrote in his uncompleted autobiography.[5] His parents separated and Lawson worked with his father as a carpenter and painter, and then went to live with his mother in Sydney:

> I worked about in various private shops and did a bit of house-painting too. I knew what it was, when I was out of work for a few days in winter, to turn out shivering and be down at the Herald office at four o'clock on bitter mornings, and be one of the haggard group striking matches and running them down the wanted columns on the damp sheets posted outside. I knew what it was to tramp long distances and be one of the hopeless crowd of applicants. I knew what it was to drift about the streets in shabby and patched clothes and feel furtive and criminal-like. I knew all that before I wrote 'Faces in the Street'—before I was twenty.[6]

In 1887 the Mayor of Sydney called a public meeting to plan celebrations for Queen Victoria's jubilee. The meeting and its immediate successors were taken over by republicans and freethinkers. 'Recent immigrants from the English working classes and the petty bourgeoisie touched with socialistic principles, aided by the old convict leaven, had humiliated the loyalists,' writes Manning Clark.[7] A Republican Union emerged, attracting British-born radicals such as Thomas Walker, George Black and John Norton as well as native radicals like J. D. Fitzgerald and Louisa Lawson.[8] Republicanism was a very broad category. It could express or conceal a number of political attitudes. It could be both robber baron capitalist or socialist revolutionary. The first issue of *The Republican* appeared on 4 July 1887—independence day for the United States of America, a country that had broken free of British imperialism and become a dynamic, capitalist nation. Both capitalist and communist could use republicanism as a catch-cry. Much of the radical reputation of *The Bulletin*, established in 1880, derived from its republicanism. Disrespect for Queen Victoria, or Westminster, could be the assertiveness of the colonial businessman or the class hostility of the working person or unemployed. The displacement of class-aware radical activism from confronting the social and economic situation within Australia to inveighing against the imperial rule of Australia was one of the achievements of the *Bulletin*. Whereas anti-bourgeois or anti-capitalist sentiments were threatening the social order, the same feelings could be displaced into anti-monarchical or anti-imperialist expression and have a certain nationalist respectability.

The socialist direction of Lawson's republicanism was quite clear in the political ballads that he now published in *Bulletin*: 'The Song of the Outcasts' (12 May 1888), 'Faces in the Street' (28 July 1888) and 'The Hymn of the Socialists' (24 August 1889). 'Song of the Outcasts' was reprinted in the Brisbane *Worker*, and under the title 'The Army of the Rear' widely reprinted in the USA. 'The Hymn of the Socialists' was reprinted in William Morris's *Commonweal* (30 November 1889).[9]

The especial force of these ballads lay in their showing poverty and oppression existing in this new world just as they existed in the old. The dominant myth was that Australia offered a new world free from those exploitations. 'The workingman's paradise', Henry Kingsley had called Australia in *The Recollections of Geoffrey Hamlyn* (1859). This mystification is confronted in 'The Song of the Outcasts':

> I looked upon the mass of poor, in filthy alleys pent;
> And on the rich men's Edens, that are built on grinding rent;
> I looked o'er London's miles of slums—I saw the horrors there,
> And swore to die a soldier of the Army of the Rear.[10]

And in case there was any remaining ambiguity that might claim these English conditions were not replicated in Australia, he opened 'Faces in the Street':

> They lie, the men who tell us in a loud decisive tone
> That want is here a stranger, and that misery's unknown;

the answer Lawson offers is unambiguous:

> But not until a city feels Red Revolution's feet
> Shall its sad people miss awhile the terrors of the street.[11]

The encouragement of nationalism of an Australian republican variety was a strategy that served to break down the powerful transnational working-class alliances that were being established, notably in the £31,000 collected in Australia and sent to support the London dockers. Lawson wrote:

> I have seen the stern-faced unionists of Sydney gather in thousands (forming a meeting that had to be divided into three portions) and stand for five long hours arranging plans of campaign and subscribing funds to carry them out, simply because a body of men, whom they had never seen and who were separated from them by fifteen thousand miles of sea, sought their assistance against a bitter wrong. I refer to the great dock laborers' strike.[12]

Lawson's first story, 'His Father's Mate' (*Bulletin*, 22 December 1888) has as its central incident the death of a child helping his father on the gold workings. A subsidiary theme is the fate of the elder brother who got into trouble with the police and has disappeared. Drawing on a true incident told him by his grandfather[13] Lawson presents the tragedy as emblematic of the wretchedness of working-class life, with its limited choice of useless toil, death, or criminality. This same range of possibilities structures the group of stories he wrote about urban working-class conditions and child labour: 'A Visit of Condolence' (*Bulletin*, 23 April 1892), 'Jones's Alley' (*Worker*, Sydney, 1, 8, 15 June 1892), 'Arvie Aspinall's Alarm Clock' (*Bulletin*, 11 June 1892) and 'Two Boys at Grinder Bros.' (*Worker*, Sydney, 7 October 1893). Drawing on his own experiences working for a firm of coach-builders when he first arrived in Sydney, Lawson turns the experience of humiliation and exploitation into the weapons of political action. Bill, Arvie's young workmate, calls to find out why he's not at work, and is told he's dead. Talking to Arvie's mother he asks 'How old was Arvie?'

> 'Eleven.'
> 'I'm twelve—going on for thirteen. Arvie's father's dead, ain't he?'
> 'Yes.'
> 'So's mine. Died at his work, didn't he?'
> 'Yes.'
> 'So'd mine. Arvie told me his father died of something with his heart.'
> 'Yes.'
> 'So'd mine; ain't it rum? You scrub offices an' wash, don't yer?'
> 'Yes.'
> 'So does my mother. You find it pretty hard to get a livin', don't yer, these times?'[14]

The paralleling of shared experiences generalises the individual tragedy into a larger class oppression. These are not individual calamities resulting from individual failure, but the consequence of the social order. Lawson uses the same device of parallelism in Bill's dialogue with Arvie in 'Two Boys at Grinder Bros.'. This is the technique of socialist education, of awakening the oppressed to the nature of their conditions, to the shared exploitations. These stories have generally been labelled Dickensian and sentimental by Lawson's commentators;[15] as if infant mortality, the exploitation of child labour, and slum life were somehow literary tropes and not all too common, everyday realities. That they were everyday realities was a provocation to political action. Lawson was developing a political consciousness that could work strategically, that could see in the individual suffering the basis for a shared sense of outrage. This was exactly William Lane's strategy in *The Workingman's Paradise* (1892), where the child born at the beginning of the novel dies at the beginning of part II, a victim of the poverty and unhygienic conditions of Sydney's slums. 'The Slaughter of the Innocents', Lane titled the chapter in which the child dies.[16] The dying child is not at all an easy sentimental trope but a directed, political symbol for Lawson, as for Lane. The death of Arvie Aspinall is the triggering or concluding incident for four stories: Lawson is not being wanton with death. Quite remarkably and significantly he does not give us a succession of deaths like a Jacobean dramatist or contemporary thriller writer. That he uses the one incident for a number of stories suggests a shocked reverence in its economy.

Arvie's work is described in the final section of the last story of the group, 'Two Boys at Grinder Bros.':

> Arvie was late out of the shop that evening. His boss was a sub-contractor for the coach-painting, and always tried to find twenty minutes' work for his boys just about five or ten minutes before the bell rang. He employed boys because they were cheap and he had a lot of rough work, and they could get under floors and 'bogies' with their pots and brushes, and do all the 'priming' and paint the trucks. His name was Collins, and the boys were called 'Collins' Babies'. It was a joke in the shop that he had a 'weaning' contract. The boys were all 'over fourteen', of course, because of the Education Act. Some were nine or ten—wages from five shillings to ten shillings. It didn't matter to Grinder Brothers so long as the contracts were completed and the dividends paid. Collins preached in the park every Sunday. But this has nothing to do with the story.[17]

These details are presented almost perfunctorily, as if to say: these are the normal conditions of urban exploitation, why make anything of it, how can you be surprised? The perfunctory presentation of Arvie's death that concludes the story is in part a necessary strategy since Lawson had already published the three other Arvie Aspinall–Jones's Alley stories, so the event cannot be given in any full-blown way. But this suited Lawson's skill in the oblique, the understated. The perfunctory account of exploitation and death, undramatised, flatly recorded, serves as an explosive conclusion to the earlier dialogue between Bill and Arvie, the development of a relationship, from persecution to comradeship and solidarity. The story opened with Bill calling out ' "Here comes Balmy Arvie" ' as he sat with 'five or six half-grown larrikins'.[18] But this first section ends with an expression of friendship, comradeship, mateship: 'Look here, Arvie!' he said in low, hurried tones, "Keep close to me goin' out tonight, 'n' if any of the other chaps touches yer or says anything to yer I'll hit 'em!" '[19] What provokes the solidarity is Bill's perception of a shared pattern of class exploitation in the experiences of their two families. He realises, silently but so clearly—such is Lawson's art—that these are no serendipitous coincidences, but the demonstration of their shared situation as workers, as proletarians. Nothing is spelled out—there is no generalising, no theory, no moral-drawing. The bare facts, presented in parallel, reveal the socio-political truth:

'I say, Arvie, what did yer father die of?'
'Heart disease. He dropped down dead at his work.'
Long, low intense whistle from Bill. He wrinkled his forehead and stared up at the beams as if he expected to see something unusual there. After a while he said, very impressively: 'So did mine.'
The coincidence hadn't done striking him yet; he wrestled with it for nearly a minute longer. Then he said:
'I suppose yer mother goes out washin'?'
'Yes.'
'N' cleans offices?'
'Yes.'
'So does mine . . .'[20]

The details of 'Collins' Babies' that seem so artlessly tacked on to the story are tacked on to take their true place. Lawson's theme is not restricted to presenting working-class conditions, the victims of exploitation. That is known, that is familiar. What Lawson is dealing with is the ending of divisions within the working classes. The bullying and teasing that make Arvie's life a misery, the factionalism of the oppressed in picking on someone else to oppress, is here brought to an end by Bill's promise of solidarity. The story shows how the lumpenproletarian, semi-criminal, wanton agression of the larrikins can none the less turn into supportive mateship. This is a socialist fable, and it was first published in the union paper the Sydney Worker. The larrikins don't suddenly become respectable bourgeois citizens. The action describes the transformation of random, divisive provocative aggression into shared mateship. The further political point is that it is too late. Arvie dies before he can return to work and appreciate this new mateship with Bill, this first experience of class solidarity. The Queensland shearers had been defeated in their 1891 strike by non-union working-class labour recruited from the huge pool of unemployed. The lack of solidarity amidst the exploited, divided amongst themselves, led to a larger class defeat. When the Australian Workers union risked strike action in 1894 in NSW, it was defeated.

Simultaneously with these stories of urban working conditions, Lawson was publishing his stories of conditions outside the towns. These were not seen as separate concerns, though Lawson is generally presented as a writer of up-country and outback materials. 'The Drover's Wife' (*Bulletin*, 23 July 1892) offers a vision of outback life and a tribute to the courage and resilience of the women in the bush. It tells simply of a woman's vigil to protect her children when a snake gets under the house. She waits all night, and past events are recalled, flood and fire, giving the story a mythic dimension. Out of these recurrent experiences of pioneering life Lawson extracts the representative. In part the snake and woman confrontation is of course Edenic, an Australian Genesis, which is why the story has had such a powerful impact. But the Edenic is itself a political myth. When Adam delved and Eve span, who was then the gentleman? When the snake has been killed the dog 'shakes the snake as though he felt the original curse in common with mankind',[21] the curse of labour, and suffering in childbirth. Henry Kingsley's phrase that Australia was a workingman's paradise provides the social specificity for the archetypal reference. Lane's novel re-examines *The Workingman's Paradise* from a socialist perspective. Lawson is doing the same in brief.

The situation the woman is in is quite specifically established. She is alone because her husband is away working: the economic cause underlying the break-up of the family, the enforced separations. He is also set in a precise social category. He is an ex-squatter. The squatter who has lost his land either to the banks or through alcohol or both, is a recurrent figure in Lawson's work—'Middleton's Rouseabout', and 'Telling Mrs Baker' are characteristic. The situation is clearly related to current social reality. The archetypal quality of Lawson's work comes from its precise observation of social class particularity. It is not a mystifying, unplaced, never-never land pastoral with figures unlocated in history or class that Lawson creates.

Lawson like Lane was concerned with class co-operation. Socialist propaganda required getting the middle classes sympathetic to the rights of labour, and showing them they too were vulnerable to the destructive effects of capitalism. Consistently in his work he tries to break down divisions: to show the parallels of the city and the country working-class life; to show the destructive effects of the system on working and middle classes. 'The Big Brassingtons came down in the world and drifted to the city, as many smaller people do, more and more every year,' he writes in 'The House That Was Never Built'.[22] In the background is the process remarked in the *Communist Manifesto*: 'the lower strata of the middle class ... sink gradually into the proletariat ...'[23]

A recognition of the situation of women and a concerted effort to press for women's rights was part of the developing socialist consciousness of the union movement. The isolation, the loneliness, the hardship are succinctly evoked. Here is the drover's true mate, his marriage mate, his wife, separated from him by the work situation. At the same time another sexual politics emerges, and the woman's clubbing the snake to death suggests a revenge on the phallic, a refusal of the procreative. The dryness of the outback has dried out the sexuality of its struggling pioneers and left only resentment, resentment at being brought to and left in such an isolated place. The eldest child, who tries to get out of bed when the snake is killed 'but his mother forces him back with a grip of iron', offers an Oedipal conclusion to the story:

> 'Mother, I won't never go drovin'; blast me if I do!'
> And she hugs him to her worn-out breast and kisses him; and they sit thus together while the sickly daylight breaks over the bush.[24]

With its absent drover, 'The Drover's Wife' poignantly presents the broken family, 'the practical absence of the family among the proletarians' as the *Communist Manifesto* puts it;[25] the drought, as well as a naturalistic portrayal of conditions, represents too the drought of sexual absence; and this in its turn issues in the destruction of the masculine, the killing of the snake and burning it. Yet even so, dawn still breaks, there is still a positive note. Edward Garnett wrote:

> If this artless sketch be taken as the summary of a woman's life, giving its significance in ten short pages, Maupassant has never done better. Lawson has re-treated this subject at length in the more detailed picture in 'Water them Geraniums'; I leave it to mothers of all ranks and stations in life to say how it affects them, and whether it has not universal application to the life of working women wherever the sun goes down. Art stands for much, but sincerity also stands for much in art, and the sincerity of Lawson's tales nearly always drives them home.[26]

Garnett was well aware that the artlessness was in itself the mark of Lawson's art. He hedges his bets on how great art it is, or nearly is, yet recognises the genius in this work that was so unlike the English norm. In the same way Garnett encouraged those other outsider, marginal figures—Conrad, W. H. Hudson, D. H. Lawrence.

> Read 'The Union Buries its Dead' . . . if you care to see how the most casual, 'newspapery' and apparently artless art of this Australian writer carries with it a truer, finer, more delicate commentary on life than do the idealistic works in any of our genteel school of writers. It isn't great art, but it is near to great art; and, moreover, great art is not to be found every 'publishing season'.[27]

'The Union Buries Its Dead' (*Truth*, 16 April 1893) is another classic picture of bad times in the bush. It opens with a delicate suggestion of Maupassant, and then the Seine is quickly redefined as a billabong:

> While out boating one Sunday afternoon on a billabong across the river, we saw a young man on horseback driving some horses along the bank. He said it was a fine day, and asked if the water was deep there. The joker of our party said it was deep enough to drown him, and he laughed and rode further up. We didn't take much notice of him.
> Next day a funeral gathered at a corner pub and asked each other in to have a drink while waiting for the hearse. They passed away some of the time dancing jigs to a piano in the bar parlour. They passed away the rest of the time sky-larking and fighting.
> The defunct was a young union labourer, about twenty-five, who had been drowned the previous day while trying to swim some horses across a billabong of the Darling.[28]

Manning Clark captures the tone of the story: 'he was telling Australians that the bush barbarians had their own way of showing they knew just as well as the author of the book of Ecclesiastes what life was all about'.[29]

The story has a more specific socialist purpose than this, however.

He was almost a stranger in town, and the fact of his having been a union man accounted for the funeral. The police found some union papers in his swag, and called at the General Labourers' Union Office for information about him. That's how we knew.[30]

The unionism is part of the subject. The General Labourers Union (GLU) of Australia had been established two years earlier in February 1891. The Australian Shearers Union (ASU) had organised the New South Wales shearers, the GLU 'took up the work of organising the woolshed laborers'.[31] W. G. Spence, who was president of the ASU and secretary of the GLU, recalled:

> A great deal of good work was done by the GLU. It made experiments in the shape of carrying out road work and sewerage contracts under co-operation, the Union finding the deposit, plant, etc., and the men dividing the result of their labor. The Union also engaged Mrs Summerfield to organise the women workers.[32]

The progressive socialist position was to create one big union of an alliance of all working people. But class society permeated the working classes as well as the middle classes. The distinctions between skilled labour and unskilled labour persisted, not only in pay differentials but in status and union organisation. Although it was proposed to amalgamate the Australian Shearers Union with the General Labourers Union in 1892 and again in 1893, a majority of the shearers voted against the proposal; in 1892, 5,862 were for, 5,997 against. In 1893 4,825 were for, 5,686 against. However the New South Wales branches gave a majority of 576 in favour, and its branches were allowed to amalgamate. 'Practically amalgamation was agreed to at the Conference of 1894, but the new constitution was only adopted at the special convention held in Albury in February, 1895.'[33] The amalgamated organisation was called the Australian Workers Union. In 1904 the Queensland and New South Wales AWUs amalgamated.

These class divisions within the working classes are part of Lawson's story:

> The procession numbered fifteen, fourteen souls following the broken shell of a soul. Perhaps not one of the fourteen possessed a soul any more than the corpse did—but that doesn't matter.
>
> Four or five of the funeral, who were boarders at the pub, borrowed a trap which the landlord used to carry passengers to and from the railway station. They were strangers to us who were on foot, and we to them. We were all strangers to the corpse.
>
> A horseman, who looked like a drover just returned from a big trip, dropped into our dusty wake and followed us a few hundred yards, dragging his pack-horse behind him, but a friend made wild and demonstrative signals from a hotel verandah—hooking at the air in front with his right hand and jabbing his left thumb over his shoulder in the direction of the bar—so the drover hauled off and didn't catch up to us any more. He was a stranger to the entire show.[34]

The separations between those on horseback and those on foot are class separations. 'A barrier which became equally marked was the one separating those who worked on horseback from those who did not,' G. A. Wilkes has noted, and he offers representative evidence from the literature.[35] The horseman does not have solidarity with the labourers on foot. A sympathy, yes, but mateship and the society of alcohol draw him off. Similarly the shearers pay their alcoholic respects to the procession but do not join in.

> On the way to the cemetery we passed three shearers sitting on the shady side of a fence. One was drunk—very drunk. The other two covered their right ears with their hats, out of respect for the departed—whoever he might have been—and one of them kicked the drunk and muttered something to him.[36]

What Lawson represents are the class divisions within the working classes; at the same time the solidarity of the labourers is stressed in their attending the funeral of the unknown man. So we have Lawson's characteristic bitter-sweet plangency, that celebration of the impulse towards solidarity, and the notation of the forces opposed to solidarity.

The divisions between labour had been considerably broken down, but progress still had to be made, before the horsemen would continue to the funeral, and the shearers get off the fence and join in with the rouseabouts. Lawson remarked on the sense of superiority of the shearers that underlay the class divisions between shearers and labourers in 'A Word in Season' in *The Worker* (Sydney) in 1894:

> Get rid of the idea that the shearers are the only wronged men on earth and the squatters the only tyrants.
> Remember that the hardship of bush life at its worst is not a circumstance compared with what thousands of poor women in cities have to go through.
> Remember that there are bitterer struggles and grander battles fought by the poor of cities than ever in the country.
> Remember that the fathers, the heroes of modern Liberty, fought and threw away their lives on barricades in the streets of cities.[37]

The opening of Harte's 'Tennessee's Partner'—'I do not think that we ever knew his real name'—[38] and the disquisition on the names people went by is taken up by Lawson and rewritten with political implication. Apart from being the representative unknown outback worker, the dead man's anonymity carries suggestions of the necessarily pseudonymous nature of early radical activity. The Queensland shearers' strikes had meant that many union activists had changed their names to avoid arrest or to gain re-employment. Mitchell remarks in 'The Man Who Forgot' 'and as for a name, that's nothing. I don't know mine, and I've had eight.'[39] Lane edited *The Worker* and wrote *The Workingman's Paradise* under a pseudonym, John Miller. Lawson regularly used the names Joe Swallow, Cervus Wright, and Jack Cornstalk to sign political pieces. Larry Petrie, the Scots-born secretary of the General Labourers Union, had been christened George Frederick Augustus Howard Carlyle Petrie, he said, and as G. F. Howard he booked a passage on a non-union crewed ship and was arrested for causing an explosion aboard, in July 1893.[40]

In July 1893 the first 220 members of the New Australia Co-operative Settlement Association under the chairmanship of William Lane sailed for Paraguay. Lawson wrote a poem in support, 'Something Better'.[41] But the movement was seen by many as a further weakening of socialism within Australia. A second batch sailed in December, but by then the first group had already been split and the movement destabilised. Lawson stood in as editor of the Sydney *Worker*, hoping to be given the permanent position, but someone else was appointed, and he went to New Zealand looking for work. The voyage steerage issued in the poem 'For'ard', published in the *New Zealand Mail*, the Sydney *Worker*, and Keir Hardie's *Labour Leader*.[42] On the offer of a position on the new *Daily Worker* Lawson returned to Sydney, only to find the paper had collapsed. The unions were once again under attack from the pastoralists in the attempt to cut wages and the consequent strikes and violence of 1894. At this period Lawson seems to have been close to Mary Cameron (later Mary Gilmore), who was living in a boarding house kept by William Lane's wife, Annie, preparatory to joining Lane's Colonia Cosme, the second communist settlement in Paraguay. The other radical centre Lawson frequented was McNamara's bookshop in Sydney, a library and centre for international radical journals and discussions. In 1896, with his first book of poems *In the Days When the World Was Wide* published, he married McNamara's step-daughter, Bertha.[43]

This radical world had been Lawson's milieu for ten years. But now radicalism was in retreat; the unions had been badly defeated, membership dropped disastrously. Collecting his contributions from the papers of those years for book publication, he had to endure considerable subeditorial emendations. The texts collected in his books often lack the political specificity of the original magazine publication. But encouraged by the critical reception of these books in England, Lawson made plans to go there, and sailed in April 1900.[44] The attempt to launch himself on a literary career in London was part of Lawson's attempt to take remedial action and halt his descent into the vortex of depression and alcoholism. The political movement to which he had committed himself and which had provided the rationale and aesthetic of his work was in disarray. So that attempt at positive thinking, launching off on the next stage of a literary career, was one shrouded in the context of pervasive pessimism. Turning from the political to the private he had only his increasingly unhappy marriage, and the memory of his parents' stormy and unhappy marriage to confront. The four long stories about Joe Wilson and his wife Mary, an archetypal (Joseph and Mary) pair of young settlers, show the destructive effects of economic hardship and the struggles of the life of the small settler in the bush on marital relationships. The theme is there not only in Joe's and Mary's marriage, but reinforced in the lives of the few neighbours. Far longer than those early *Bulletin* sketches, these stories aspire to a fully-fledged realism of recorded detail, rather than that earlier allusive impressionism. ' "Water them Geraniums" ' opens with an inventory of Joe Wilson's furniture and possessions. But this realism is something of an illusion. Just as Lawson had produced material aceptable to the *Bulletin's* rigid preconceptions—short, boiled down, spare—now he could simulate the more discursive mode of mainstream British magazine realism. Much of the force of these stories, however, lies on their margins. The effects are as oblique as ever. The glancing, the tangential, the implied, the allusive, are the tactics Lawson uses to capture his material. The ostensible direction or mode of the story is not the 'point': rather it is a strategy employed by Lawson in order to slip in the unacceptable—the material the editors and publishers would refuse if they thought that was the central concern. The innocence of Joe and Mary is a way of introducing the sexual threats that could not be written about in a direct way, at a time of repressive censorship of sexual materials in the printed word. The story tells of Joe's slow, bashful courting. There is a delicately idyllic episode where Joe helps Mary hang out clothes, a celebration of ordinary, daily activity at that time not ordinarily experienced by those who could afford servants. 'I took the line from Mary, and accidentally touched her soft, plump little hand as I did so: it sent a thrill right through me.'[45] The idyll turns into embarrassment as Mary shoos Joe away so she can hang up unnamed things he is not allowed to see. The sexual implications in the sheet hanging are now drawn attention to; not exactly made explicit because they are unmentionable. But the unmentionable exerts its strong force of absence, appropriate for Joe's unfulfilled inexpressible sexual yearning. Later Joe's 'handkerchiefs and collars disappeared from the room and turned up washed and ironed and laid tidily on my table' and, 'I felt so full of hope and joy.' Then Jack tells him, 'I see you've made a new mash, Joe. I saw the half-caste cook tidying up your room this morning and taking your collars and things to the wash house, (p.25). Not only is there the simple humour of love's delusions, there is also the racial categorising which again marks an unbridgeable gulf for Joe. All the racist complex of attitudes is brought into play here. The issues are also class issues. Mary, as Jack describes her early on is

> a nice little girl in service at Black's . . . She's more like an adopted daughter, in fact, than a servant. She's a real good little girl, and good-looking into the bargain. I hear that young Black is sweet on her, but they say she won't have anything to do with him. (p.7)

She is described in terms that make her appear of marginal working-class status. Though 'in service' she is treated like a daughter. The station owner's son could be just wanting sexual diversion, or it could be marriage; it is left unclear. Joe's relationship with Mary would be upwardly mobile; with the half-caste cook, unnamed, downwardly mobile. Racial and national and class characteristics are recurrently indicated in this story. Mary's father had

> been an old mate of Black's, a younger son of a well-to-do English family (with blue blood in it, I believe) and sent out to Australia with a thousand pounds to make his way . . . They think they're hard done by . . . I wish I'd had a thousand pounds to start on!

Mary's mother was the daughter of a German immigrant.
(p.262)[46]

All these issues of sexuality and race and class are brought into play in the fight Joe has with Romany. The Romany, the gypsy, presents the classic sexual threat to the Anglo-Celtic.

> He was a big shearer, a dark, handsome fellow, who looked like a gipsy: it was reckoned that there was foreign blood in him. He went by the name of Romany. He was supposed to be shook after Mary too. He had the nastiest temper and the best violin in the district. (p.26)

It is the alter ego of Joe Wilson–Henry Lawson. Joe's 'I reckon I was born for a poet by mistake' (p.3) incites the identification of Joe with Lawson, while Lawson continually recurred to his foreign blood, to his Norwegian father and his gypsy grandfather. The innocent naïve bush poet Joe fights the sexual, gypsy, bohemian violinist Romany; Romany represents that sexual, decadent, bohemian milieu Lawson was trying, maybe not wholeheartedly, to escape.

In fighting Romany, of course, Joe is displacing the aggression he feels for the jackaroo, who has turned up at Black's and is interested in Mary. Romany manages to stir up Joe's sexual anxiety about the jackaroo, but Joe cannot fight the jackaroo directly. The class divisions prevent it. Lawson shows how an inexpressible aggression to the ruling class produces an expressed aggression to the scapegoat racial minority, the gypsy. This is no mere metaphor. The gypsies no less than the Jews were victims of the extermination camps, and continue to be harried and harrassed in England and Europe today. Out of a simple, purportedly innocent, clean, positive love story, Lawson produces an oblique sexual-political-radical exploration.

The socialist aspects of the *Joe Wilson* volume had been subdued and implicit. The years of writing for the radical press had ensured the development of Lawson's radical vision, whether political themes were explicitly proclaimed or not. The verses 'The Never-Never Country' that conclude the volume, however, pay explicit tribute to 'Oh rebels to society!' and 'The communism perfected!' (p.333). In *Children of the Bush* the socialist and unionist is foregrounded. *The Athenaeum* commented:

> one finds it right and natural that a strong democratic note should ring through these pages. But it is rather a pity that the note should be quite as insistent as it is, that it should be aggressive, and that, on occasion, it should sound bitter.[47]

Here he collects stories about unionists, stories about the meaning of socialism.

'Lord Douglas' proclaims its political context with its opening:

> The Imperial Hotel was rather an unfortunate name for an out-back town pub, for out-back is the stronghold of Australian democracy; it was the out-back vote and influence that brought about 'One Man One Vote', 'Payment of Members', and most of the democratic legislation of late years, and from out-back came the overwhelming vote in favour of Australian as against Imperial Federation.[48]

And the hotel is described in its place in outback politics.

> The Imperial Hotel was patronised by the Pastoralists, the civil servants, the bank manager and clerks—all the scrub aristocracy; it was the headquarters of the *Pastoralists' Union* in Bourke; a barracks for blacklegs brought up from Sydney to take the place of Union shearers on strike; and the new Governor, on his inevitable visit to Bourke, was banqueted at the Imperial Hotel. The editor of the local 'Capitalistic rag' stayed there; the Pastoralists' member was elected mostly by dark ways and means devised at the Imperial Hotel, and one of its managers had stood as a dummy candidate to split the Labour vote; the management of the hotel was his reward.
> (p.45)

The manager is representative of a recurrent type in Lawson—the immigrant with nothing known about his background. After his arrival in England Lawson developed his presentation of this type with a new sense of English class differentials.

> Jack Mitchell reckoned, by the way he treated his *employés* and spoke to workmen, that he was the educated son of an English farmer—gone wrong and sent out to Australia. Someone called him 'Lord Douglas', and the nickname caught on. (p.46)

The story details some of the confrontations between unionists and 'Lord Douglas' up until the manager disappears and is gaoled for embezzlement, but the focus is on his return from gaol, when some are in favour of boycotting him, kicking him out of town, tarring and feathering him. But Mitchell insists on passing round the hat to help the manager get back on his feet. And is proved right; the final paragraph notes he opened a shop 'and the *Sydney Worker, Truth*, and *Bulletin* and other democratic rags are on sale at his shop' (p.57). It is a straightforward parable of samaritan socialism, class collaboration, though this bare outline of its conscious socialist content does not do justice to the subtlety, irony, comedy and self-awareness of the writing. It is not a naïve fable. It concludes:

> He is scarcely yet regarded as a straight-out democrat. He was a gentleman once, Mitchell said, and the old blood was not to be trusted. But, last elections, Douglas worked quietly for Unionism, and gave the leaders certain hints, and put them up to various electioneering dodges which enabled them to return, in the face of Monopoly, a Labour member who is as likely to go straight as long as any other Labour member.
> (p.57)

In 'Barney Take Me Home Again' in *Children of the Bush* the destructive aspects of migration are examined. This has never been a recognised theme in English language culture in the way it has in modern Greek culture, the loss and tragedy implicit in having to leave one's homeland in order to find work. Later the narrator visits the Johnsons who have returned to London and Lawson records his appalled reaction to English working-class conditions.

> It was a blind street, like the long, narrow yard of a jail, walled by dark houses, all alike. The next door but one to that at which I knocked to inquire was where the Johnsons lived; they lived in a four-storey house, or rather a narrow section of a four-storeyed terrace. I found later on that they paid the landlord, or nearly paid him, by letting lodgings. They lived in one room with the use of the parlour and the kitchen when the lodgers weren't using them, and the son shared a room with a lodger. The back windows looked out on the dead wall of a poorhouse of some kind, the front on rows of similar windows opposite—rows of the same sort of windows that run for miles and miles in London. In one a man sat smoking in his shirt-sleeves, from another a slavey leaned out watching a four-wheeler that had stopped next door, in a third a woman sat sewing, and in a fourth a women was ironing, with a glimpse of a bedstead behind her. And all outside was gloom and soot and slush.
> (p.183)

And he remarks as much as the material conditions, the defeat of spirit. 'I would never have recognised the Johnsons' he said, 'I found Johnson an old man—old and grey before his time' (p.183):

> When I left Johnson I felt less lonely in London, and rather humbled in spirit. He seemed so resigned—I had never seen such gentle sadness in a man's eyes, nor heard it in a man's voice. I could get back to Australia somehow and start life again, but Johnson's day had been dead for many years.
> (p.185)

The fullest expression of Lawson's English experience is collected in *Triangles of Life*, a volume proposed and prepared in 1907 but not published until 1913. The 94-page title story offers a comparative study of Australia and England, a theme broached with 'Barney Take Me Home Again'. There it was the woman who could not adjust to the rawness of pioneering life, and the account of her dissatisfactions are the substance of the first part of the story. In 'Triangles of Life' it is the young man, Billy, who has developed the horrors and is shipped back to England. The first part set in Australia describes his collapse, and the other two parts deal with what happens to him on his return. The story takes its title from old Higgins's meditations on an old elementary book of Euclid. ' "Life," he'd say, after some preliminary shuffles, coughs, and grunts, "is wot I call made up of triangles—ekal hatteral triangles.' But this is given a political gloss by 'Brennan, the silent semi-foreman' (a *Reynold's Newspaper* reader): ' "You're right there, Higgins, and you and me and the rest of us in hundreds of English villages are shoring up the props. And they're comin' down, Higgins!"⁴⁹ 'The triangles' are also one of the infamous punishments of Australia's convict days, the frame to which convicts were bound, to be flogged. And so Lawson assembles this ambitious three-part story, the first part in the bush, the second part seemingly irrelevant, digressive observations on village life near London, and then the third side in which Billy, returned from Australia, settles down with Lizzie, who has had a child and various liaisons in London. Bob, Billy's old mate from Australia who had nursed him through the horrors, returns to England and stays with them, and the gossip within the village generates and creates the very situation it fantasised, Billy breaking up with Lizzie who goes to live with Bob. It is an examination of the complexities of mateship and communality, of the failures of communication and of misunderstandings. It shows the alienation and isolation of the workingman's life in the bush; and then it shows the repressive nature of English life—class ridden, controlled by the expectations of class roles monitored by gossips. And nobody wins. Bob doesn't want Lizzie, and at the story's end Billy is sailing out to Australia again on the *Gera*,' and Bob was aboard the *Karlsruhe*, a fortnight ahead'⁵⁰ with Lizzie left in England.

In 'The Letters to Jack Cornstalk' (*Argosy*, October 1900, January and February 1901) Lawson presents himself as an 'Australian' for his critical perspective on England, not a vanguard socialist or a proletarian. It leads to a quasi-Mark Twain bumptiousness, a cocksureness that now seems more defensive than anything else. It is the tone of the upstart colonial, the proletarian larrikin mutated into the colonial tourist, modelled on the American. Yet the blustering critique of St Pauls retains a socialist basis: its 'atmosphere suggestive of wide spaces' 'is one of the apparently useless lies of civilisation—but I suppose it's born of commercialism, like most other lies—a little branch line lie of commercialism'.[51] Something of the indictment of the university D.H. Lawrence delivers in *The Rainbow* is captured here. But in general the assertive note suggests that Lawson is not totally at ease with the tone. It isn't his tone, but a tone he is adopting, a persona, an image. As a foreigner in England he is treated as a gentleman, but he knows he is a proletarian. But he knows the risks of a proclaimed proletarianism or a proclaimed socialism. He mentions the absence of politics in the English village. His own lack of politics he does not mention. But it is indicated by mention of this other, parallel, absence. The inexpressible politics are displaced into nationalism. The 'colonial' was an acceptable caricature, a mask. The problem, however, is that masks like nationalism can suffocate their wearers. The necessity of subterfuge meant that inside the mask Lawson was with difficulty holding on to his real identity.

Alcohol can be seen as the response to the crisis of his art in which his political commitment became increasingly inexpressible. The climate of repression with the defeat of the unions by the mid-nineties had made revolutionary sentiments unacceptable in the press. Lawson's poetic vision of revolution mutated into a vision of war, enemy unspecified. It could be the class enemy; but it could be taken as a national enemy and the solidarity that of patriotism or race, not class. The left itself was fragmented. The parliamentary labour party had little appeal for Lawson. While the failure of Lane's New Australia enterprise, with Lane himself leaving it in 1899, afforded little hope of alternatives to the parliamentary model.

But turning to personal themes of domesticity and sexuality, Lawson soon found these equally inexpressible. The political put him in impossible conflict with society, an author dependent on acceptance by the commercial media. The domestic-sexual-familial put him in impossible conflict with his wife, and his mother. His mode of transparency, of exploration and recollection of interrelationships, allowed few disguises. His aesthetic was based on drawing from life, on a realism he identified with his socialist commitment. In *Triangles of Life* he goes as far as psychically he dared push himself in writing about the collapse of his marriage. It is there in two powerful stories, 'Drifting Apart' and 'A Child in the Dark of a Foreign Father'. The failing marriage in that latter story suggests too the marriage of his parents, and his own childhood resentments of his mother.

Lawson's work is comparatively unknown outside Australia today. Within Australia, his profile adorning the ten-dollar note, he has become a nationalist icon, and his specifically socialist vision has been obscured, though not forgotten. It is something his friend, English born Fred Broomfield, stressed in 1930:

> Lawson's name is refused a place on the scroll of Australian literature by the superfine critics, on the ground that he voiced the emotions of a class—the rank and file of 'My Army, O My Army'—rather than of a nation—or, at least, that is one of the reasons given, apart from the alleged rudeness and crudity of his verse-form. But what a class! What a toiling universe of sorrow-smitten men and women found an utterance through his verse! It has been said that Lawson, when a lad, was caught in the spell of socialism. That may be, but he never altered. In one of his poems written in later life he declared that he was 'too old to rat'.[52]

NOTES

1. Edward Garnett, *Friday Nights: Literary Criticism and Appreciations* (London, 1922), pp.181, 182.
2. Quoted in advertisements in Angus & Robertson publications: for example Henry Lawson, *When I Was King* (Sydney, 1905), appendix of announcements of other books, p.5. Emile Saillens compared Lawson to Gorky in *Mercure de France*, 1 October 1910; reprinted in Colin Roderick (ed.), *Henry Lawson Criticism 1894-1971* (Sydney, 1972), p.147.

3. Francis Thompson, *Daily Chronicle* (London) 29 March 1901, reprinted in Roderick (ed.), *Henry Lawson Criticism*, p.108.
4. *ibid.*, p.163.
5. Henry Lawson, *Autobiographical and Other Writings 1887-1922*, ed. Colin Roderick (*Collected Prose*, volume 2) (Sydney, 1972), p.193. This edition is subsequently quoted *CP*.
6. *CP*, pp.209-10.
7. Manning Clark, *Henry Lawson, The Man and the Legend* (Melbourne, 1985), p.36.
8. Thomas Walker, born Preston 1858, had arrived via San Francisco as a spiritualist lecturer. George Black, born Edinburgh 1854, was a sub-editor on the *Bulletin* and later edited the *Workman* and the *Worker* and wrote *The Labor Party in New South Wales* (Sydney, 1917). John Norton, born Brighton, 1858, became proprietor of *Truth* and is one of the subjects of Cyril Pearl, *Wild Men of Sydney* (London, 1958) and Michael Cannon, *That Damned Democrat: John Norton an Australian Populist, 1858-1916* (Melbourne, 1981). On Henry's mother, Louisa Lawson, see Brian Matthews, 'Dawn crusade' in Eric Fry (ed.), *Rebels and Radicals* (Sydney, 1983), pp.148-62.
9. Anne Cranny-Francis, 'Pacifying the socialist: the "reform" of Henry Lawson's "The Hymn of the Socialists",' *Australian Literary Studies*, 10 (1982), pp.511-15.

    On the influence of Morris in Australia see Bruce Mansfield, 'The socialism of William Morris: England and Australia', *Historical Studies Australia and New Zealand* (1956), pp.271-90.
10. Henry Lawson, *Collected Verse: Volume One: 1885-1900*, ed. Colin Roderick (Sydney, 1967), p.11. Subsequently quoted as *CV*.
11. *CV*, pp.15-17.
12. *CP*, p.17.
13. Colin Roderick, *Henry Lawson, Commentaries on his Prose Writings* (Sydney, 1985), p.5.
14. Henry Lawson, *While the Billy Boils* (Sydney, 1896) p.211. All quotations from this edition. An English edition from Simpkin, Marshall appeared in 1897, jointly with Angus & Robertson, Sydney. E.V. Lucas reviewed it enthusiastically in *The Academy*, 17 July 1897:

> He shows us what living in the bush really means. By force of sketch, dialogue, story and yarn, he brings before us the Bohemians and wastrels of that vast island: their humour, their way of thought, their vocabulary, their comradeship. The result is a real book, a book in a hundred.
>
> In 1903 Angus & Robertson published a joint edition with Humphrey Milford, Oxford University Press, London. In 1927 it was issued in two volumes in Jonathan Cape's 'Traveller's Library' (nos. 38 and 39), London. See George Mackaness, *An Annotated Bibliography of Henry Lawson* (Sydney, 1951), pp.14-16.

15. A.G. Stephens, *Bulletin*, 29 August 1896, reprinted in *A.G. Stephens: Selected Writings*, ed. Leon Cantrell (Sydney, 1977) p.225; Brian Kiernan (ed.), *The Essential Henry Lawson* (South Yarra, 1982), p.14; John Barnes, *Henry Lawson's Stories* (Melbourne, 1985), p.13.
16. 'John Miller' (William Lane), *The Workingman's Paradise: An Australian Labour Novel* (1892), facsimile reprint (Sydney, 1980).

    See Michael Wilding, 'William Lane's *The Workingman's Paradise:* pioneering socialist realism', in Stephen Knight and S.N. Mukherjee (eds.), *Words and Worlds: Studies in the Social Role of Verbal Culture* (Sydney, 1983) p.44.
17. Henry Lawson, *On the Track and Over the Sliprails* (Sydney, 1900), p.127.
18. ibid., p.123.
19. ibid., p.127.
20. ibid., pp.125-6.
21. *While the Billy Boils*, p.138.
22. Henry Lawson, *Children of the Bush* (Sydney, 1910), p.167.
23. Karl Marx and Frederick Engels, *Manifesto of the Communist Party*, translated by Samuel Moore (1888) (Moscow, 1973), p.53.
24. *While the Billy Boils*, p.138. Xavier Pons offers the fullest psychoanalytical approach to Lawson in *Henry Lawson: l'homme et l'oeuvre* (Paris, 1980), and *Out of Eden: Henry Lawson's Life and Works—A Psychoanalytical View* (Sydney, 1984).
25. *Manifesto*, p.68.
26. *Friday Nights*, p.184.
27. ibid., p.183.
28. *While the Billy Boils*, p.91.

29. Clark, *op.cit.*, p.78.
30. *While the Billy Boils*, p.91.
31. W. G. Spence, *History of the A.W.U.*, (Sydney, 1911), p.47.
32. *ibid.*, pp.47-8.
33. *ibid.*, p.80.
34. *While the Billy Boils*, p.92.
35. G. A. Wilkes, *The Stockyard and the Croquet Lawn: Literary Evidence for Australia's Cultural Development* (Melbourne, 1981), pp.43-4. 'There is not a horse in the book from title page to imprint—not one horse!' David Ferguson (1896) in Roderick, *Henry Lawson Criticism*, p.48.
36. *While the Billy Boils*, p.93.
37. *CP*, 2, p.28.
38. *The Complete Works of Bret Harte*, II (London, 1903) p.135.
39. *While the Billy Boils*, p.34.
40. Lawson quotes the ballad Mary Cameron wrote on Petrie in 'A Hero in Dingo Scrubs'; see Roderick, *Commentaries*, pp.206-9. Petrie later went to Lane's Paraguayan settlement: see Gavin Souter, *A Peculiar People: The Australians in Paraguay* (Sydney, 1968), pp.170-1, and E. H. Lane, *Dawn to Dusk: Reminiscences of a Rebel* (Brisbane, 1939).
41. *New Australia*, 24 March 1894; *CV*, 1, 256-7. On New Australia, see Lloyd Ross, *William Lane and the Australian Labor Movement* (Sydney, 1937) and Souter, *A Peculiar People*.
42. Anne Cranny-Francis, 'Henry Lawson and the labour leader', *Australian Literary Studies*, 11 (1983), p.266.
43. The standard biographies are Denton Prout, *Henry Lawson: The Grey Dreamer* (Adelaide, 1963) and Colin Roderick, *The Real Henry Lawson* (Adelaide, 1982).
44. John Barnes, 'Henry Lawson in London', *Quadrant*, July 1979, pp.22-35; 'Henry Lawson in England: The "high tide": a revaluation', *Quadrant*, June 1984, pp.28-43.
45. Henry Lawson, *Joe Wilson and His Mates* (Sydney, 1902), pp.17-18. Subsequent page numbers given in the text are to this edition.
46. Lawson's wife, Bertha Marie Louise Bredt, was the daughter of two German immigrants. 'Remember I was brought up in a German district', (*CP*, 2, p.227) he wrote in 1913.
47. *The Athenaeum*, no. 3907, 13 September 1902, p.347.
48. *Children of the Bush* (Sydney, 1910), p.44. Subsequent page numbers in the text are to this edition.

49. *Triangles of Life* (Melbourne, 1913), pp.36, 37.
50. *ibid.*, p.92. Lawson's wife and two children sailed from England to Australia on the Karlsruhe on 30 April 1902 and Lawson followed on the *Gera* on 21 May (Clark, *op.cit.*, 133).
51. *ibid.*, p.119.
52. Fred J. Broomfield, *Henry Lawson and His Critics* (Sydney, 1930), p.37. On Broomfield see Ann-Mari Jorden, 'Fred J. Broomfield', *Australian Literary Studies*, 9 (1980), 468. The poem quoted is 'The Old Unionist', *CV*, 3 (1969), pp.94-5.

· 10 ·

Tressell in international perspective

RONALD PAUL

From 1905 to 1914 the international labour movement experienced one of its most decisive and conflicting periods of political crisis and organisational growth. The pivotal year of 1905 in Russia not only marked an important stage in the maturation of the Russian working class but its stormy events reverberated throughout the world accelerating the impending rupture between the reformist and revolutionary tendencies within socialism. At the same time, also in the wake of the first Russian revolution were written some of the greatest pioneering works of socialist fiction—Maxim Gorky's *Mother* (1907), Jack London's *The Iron Heel* (1907), Upton Sinclair's *The Jungle* (1906), Martin Andersen Nexö's *Pelle the Conqueror* (1906-10) and Robert Tressell's *The Ragged Trousered Philanthropists* (c. 1906-10, pub. 1914). Clearly, the almost simultaneous appearance of these landmark novels reflected a level of consciousness and confidence within the working class of being capable of putting its own specific stamp on both the political and literary spheres of class society.

However, the most immediate political consequence of the defeat of the 1905 revolution was a strengthening of the reformist leaderships of the labour movements. The use of the mass strike as a revolutionary weapon for social change was subsequently rejected by many labour leaders in favour of a further parliamentary accommodation to capitalism, which finally led to their total capitulation at the outbreak of the First World War in 1914. Although all of the above novelists were personally associated with the left wing of the socialist movement—Gorky with the Bolsheviks, London and Sinclair with the Socialist Party of America, Nexö with the then radical Danish Social Democrats, while Tressell was an active member of the Social Democratic Federation—only London seems to have been sensitive to the reformist watershed and used his novel to polemicise against both the increasing bureaucratic control of the movement as well as its fatal underestimation of the virulence of capitalist reaction faced with a fundamental threat to the system.[1] In the other works, this crucial juncture of organisational consolidation and concomitant political retreat from revolutionary principles is only distantly registered in their more restricted and basic preoccupation with the effects of capitalist oppression on the lives of individual protagonists. Perhaps in an attempt to close ranks against a state of growing ideological confusion, these novels are all thematically defined by the lowest common denominator of working-class consciousness at a very early point in its formation—the fundamental need to unite and struggle for political and trade-union rights. Tressell, for instance, basing himself on his own experience of the building trade in a small town on the south coast of England, confronts the reader with a picture of a political backwater—'Mugsborough'—where the prime obstacle is not so much the power of the local capitalists as the reluctance of the workers themselves to recognise their own class interests. This lack of even a limited trade-union militancy causes Frank Owen, Tressell's socialist alter ego in the novel, to express feelings of bitterness and despair over the conservatism and indifference of his workmates:

> As Owen thought of his child's future there sprung up within him a feeling of hatred and fury against the majority of his fellow workmen.
> *They were the enemy.* Those who not only quietly submitted like so many cattle to the existing state of things, but defended it, and opposed and ridiculed any suggestion to alter it.
> *They were the real oppressors*—the men who spoke of themselves as 'The likes of us', who, having lived in poverty and

degradation all their lives considered that what had been good enough for them was good enough for their children they had been the cause of bringing into existence. He hated and despised them because they calmly saw their children condemned to hard labour and poverty for life, and deliberately refused to make any effort to secure for them better conditions than those they had themselves.[2]

In his ideological battle against this reactionary spirit of inertia, Owen's only apparent support comes from a rich middle-class socialist—Barrington—who has gone slumming in the guise of a housepainter, which seems to further undermine the image of the working class as the active instrument of its own emancipation.

In all of the novels, the actual realisation of socialism is projected in a very long-term perspective, to be reached either via the ballot box or through the peaceful but effective expansion of the state-owned industrial sector. Once again, the exception to this is *The Iron Heel*. Although writing in the Utopian mode himself, London, nevertheless, exposes this reformist tactic in his novel and it is significant to note that it was the only one of the five works that was originally greeted with hostility by the socialist press reviewers who, according to Robert Barltrop, 'attacked it for its pessimism and its preoccupation with violence'.[3] However, Barltrop also notes that the novel's 'reputation as a socialist classic derives from its first half, in which the case against capitalism is expounded dramatically'[4]—and in politically more orthodox terms. In contrast, the final volume of Nexö's sequence of novels about Pelle—*The Dawn*—manifests perhaps the most idyllic co-operative illusions of transforming capitalism, something which compelled Nexö later in the 1930s to write a sequel—*Morten the Red*—in which he exposes Pelle's reformist betrayal and counterposes the revolutionary communist politics of Pelle's childhood friend, Morten.

Despite the uneasy and in most cases unresolved relationship between these novels and the critical ideological debate within the labour movement at the time, it was their intrinsically didactic aspect that gave them an immediate popularity and lasting appeal. Obviously, the propaganda impact of socialist ideas realised in an imaginative fictional setting could be a compelling formative support to both sympathisers and activists alike. In the case of all five novels, the fusion of politics and literature came at opportune moments when the balance of class forces was being shifted and where a work of fiction could make a powerful and even decisive intervention. Thus, Lenin's famous characterisation of Gorky's novel could, in fact, be applied to each of them: 'It is a book of the utmost importance; many workers who have joined the revolutionary movement impulsively, without properly understanding why, will benefit from reading *Mother*. It is a very timely book.'[5] It is remarkable just how 'timely' the publication dates of these novels have been. Although the initial response to the appearance of Tressell's book in 1914 was quickly swamped by the jingoistic euphoria over the outbreak of the war, Grant Richards, its astute-minded publisher, while privately admitting the novel to being 'damnably subversive',[6] understood its political and market value when he reissued it in 1917. This cheaper second edition was published to cash in on the revolutionary fervour of strikes and the creation of workers' councils that occurred after the February insurrection in Russia. The novel's function as one of the most effective and appreciated texts in the ideological arsenal of the British labour movement continued to grow with each new, albeit heavily expurgated edition. When the mood of the population once again became radicalised by the defeat of fascism in 1945, Alan Sillitoe recalled that Tressell's book was reputed to have lain behind the Labour victory in the general election in Britain later that year.[7] Similarly, Gorky's novel, as Lenin had predicted, acted as an essential morale booster for the Russian masses, although perhaps more importantly as a much needed political antidote to the widespread defeatism among the intelligentsia who were abandoning the revolution after 1905. In the case of *Pelle the Conqueror*, although centred around the events of the general strike and lock-out of 1899, Nexö's monumental work represents in fact a literary tribute to the reformist coming-of-age of the Danish Social Democratic Party which was shaping itself for its future role as benevolent administrator of the modern Danish state. With the same symbolic span as Lewis Grassic Gibbon's *A Scots Quair*, Nexö sought to portray the social transformation of the Danish peasantry into a concentrated and politically organised industrial class, first in the small-scale manufacturing community on the island of Bornholm and later in the great industrial centre of Copenhagen itself. This sweeping socio-economic transition is personified by the main character of Pelle as he moves from a farm labourer to a shoemaker and finally factory worker. Pelle's struggle to 'conquer' a place in the sun for himself is the mainspring for the novel's psychological tension between his own individual rise to consciousness and the strivings of the working class as a collective. Thus, Nexö's epic has become established as the archetypal *Bildungsroman* of the whole Danish labour movement.

In America, London and Sinclair were actively engaged both as writers and agitators for the socialist cause. Sinclair himself later admitted that he had been inspired by his reading of his fellow author's sociological account of slum life in the East End of London, *The People of the Abyss* (1903). The avowed purpose of the two writers was to utilise the novel form in order to rally support for the rising Socialist Party of America, though the subsequent appearance of their novels had rather disparate results. The effect produced by *The Jungle* was immediate and tangible, after which Sinclair was forced to admit that while aiming at the hearts and minds of his readers, he had mainly succeeded in hitting them physically in their bellies. His efforts in the radical muckraking tradition of American journalism to expose the horrific working conditions and pestilential filth of the Chicago meat-packing industry led to such a public outcry that a Pure Food and Drug Act was rushed through the Senate. In contrast, the significance of London's book, *The Iron Heel*, was not fully appreciated until much later, in the 1930s in fact, when the political validity of some of his fundamental predictions had become painfully obvious. At an early stage, London had shown a profound understanding of the reactionary role of the labour bureaucracy in the eventual collapse of the American socialist movement. Furthermore, his dystopian image of a capitalist oligarchy whose overriding ethic was to maintain its position of power at whatever cost proved a fateful insight into the psychology of fascism:

> In roar of shell and shrapnel and in whine of machine guns will our answer be couched. We will grind you revolutionists down under our heel, and we shall walk upon your faces. The world is ours, we are its lords, and ours it shall remain.[8]

Despite their distinctive political and historical influence, there remain some crucial literary weaknesses which the majority of these novels share as works of art. One such obvious limitation, common to all propaganda fiction, is the danger of character oversimplification. It has been, for example, a recurring problematic in the socialist literary tradition to depict a fully developed working-class protagonist in a psychologically convincing way. Only in a few cases have authors succeeded in avoiding the distorted projection of heroically romanticised, larger-than-life characters set against a realistic context of social and class environment. This exaggerated, idealised and hardly credible heroic enlargement is most visibly expressed in Jack London's novel where the main figure—Ernest Everhard—epitomises both physically and intellectually the image of the working-class superman:

> the cloth bulged with his muscles . . . His neck was the neck of a prize-fighter, thick and strong. So this was the social philosopher and ex-horseshoer my father had discovered, was my thought. And he certainly looked it, with those bulging muscles and that bull throat. Immediately I classified him—a sort of prodigy . . .
> He was a natural aristocrat—and this in spite of the fact that he was in the camp of the non-aristocrats. He was a superman, a blond beast such as Nietzsche has described, and in addition he was aflame with democracy.[9]

The didactically constructed early scenes in the novel are

manipulated set-pieces in the form of dinner gatherings, lectures etc., whose sole function is to reveal Everhard's crushing intellectual superiority over the mealy-mouthed or apoplectic representatives of the bourgeoisie. This overwhelming predominance of such a magnified working-class hero has, of course, political as well as aesthetic implications for the novel. The assertive individualism is, for example, in sharp contrast to the qualities of collective strength which the novels seek to underscore. In *Pelle the Conqueror*, also, Pelle's autodidactic development is not only the almost exclusive emotional pole around which the interest of the story revolves, but his own embodiment of the struggle of the labour movement makes it impossible to distinguish the person from the cause he is leading. In the end, Nexö's novel of class conflict dissolves into a portrait of a charismatic leader at the head of an anonymous grey mass:

> Pelle walked in the front rank beside the standard-bearers. He looked straight on, over the heads of those out walking . . . He had only one thought in his mind: the tread of fifty thousand men behind him. He had experienced it in his dream as a child, heard it as a roar from outside when he laid his head against the pillow. It was the great people's migration and now he was leading the multitude into the country.[10]

In Everhard's as in Pelle's case the implicit conclusion seems to be that the fate of the movement succeeds or fails with them as individual leaders. This blurring of political and personal identification is also true of the characters of Jurgis in *The Jungle* and Pelagea Nilovna in *Mother*. A large part of Pelagea's motivation merely seems to stem from a need to receive personal endorsement for her son's political involvement. Moreover, their almost superhuman efforts against enormous odds lifts them to the level of romantic heroes which, in respect to Jurgis's fate is not only implausible but has the inverted effect of appearing almost comic. Several Russian Marxist critics, including Plekhanov, while recognising the propaganda value of Gorky's novel, were more sceptical of his handling of the literary and aesthetic aspects and a debate developed on the 'typicality' and 'individualism' of his main characters. Gorky himself indirectly accepted the justice of this criticism through his constant revision of the work during his lifetime. Six different versions were published and a seventh was in preparation at his death. Gorky is, of course, rightly hailed as the father of Soviet socialist realism and it is a short step from his portrayal of Pelagea's son, Pavel, to the stainless steel bolshevik heroes in many of the proletarian novels of the 1930s. This magnified stereotyped image of working-class heroes did not cease, however, but continued to be uncritically reproduced in the novels that formed part of the vogue of working-class writing during the post-1945 period, where it was given an aggressively individualist, sexist and often careerist expression in the early novels of Alan Sillitoe, John Braine and David Storey.

Of all these internationally outstanding works of socialist fiction, the one that was most successful in negotiating this literary pitfall was *The Ragged Trousered Philanthropists*. Here the author achieves a consistently anti-heroic emphasis which is finely balanced against the genuinely collective portrait of class experience. It is true, of course, that Tressell's narrative is primarily concerned with the character of Frank Owen, an intellectual workingman who seems rather isolated within the group of house painters. However, although somewhat out on an ideological limb, Owen is a measure of the social and political breadth of the working-class milieu in which he is so firmly placed as a character. It is this very tangible sense of community and collective strength that makes the book more politically optimistic than it first appears. Much of the sympathy which Owen engenders as a character stems from his basic qualities of human solidarity as well as the very ineffectiveness of his role as socialist agitator. Paradoxically, this weakness in a propaganda novel turns out to be one of its greatest psychological strengths. It is significant that Tressell chose to underscore this aspect and to counterpose a healthy scepticism among the workers to Owen's intellectualism and often abstract level of debate. Tressell took care to give the compulsory set-pieces of socialist agitation a much more realistic, natural and lively context by constantly injecting the deflating comments of the workers themselves, thus preventing any tendency in the novel to project Owen as the superior socialist hero. Owen's now classic lecture—'The Oblong'—delivered during one of the dinner breaks, on the causes of poverty and exploitation is given the following introduction, for example:

> 'One of the finest speakers I've ever 'eard!' remarked the man on the pail in a loud whisper to the chairman, who motioned him to be silent.
> Owen continued:
> 'In some of my previous lectures I have endeavoured to convince you that money is in itself of no value and of no real use whatever. In this I'm afraid I have been rather unsuccessful.'
> 'Not a bit of it, mate,' cried Crass, sarcastically. 'We all agree with it.'
> ' 'Ear, 'ear,' shouted Easton. 'If a bloke was to come in 'ere now and orfer to give me a quid—I'd refuse it!'
> 'So would I,' said Philpot.[11]

On a more personal level, Owen is doomed to a life of oppressive poverty and sickness, despite his obvious talents and craftsmanship as a painter. This physical frailty only serves to increase the novel's emotional persuasiveness and to fundamentally emphasise the complete lack of any possible individualist perspective. In terms of the underlying political conclusions, the negation of any personal solution to Owen's predicament, either through professional promotion or collaboration with the bosses, confirms the total interdependence of individual and class which informs Tressell's novel throughout. The outcome of Owen's fate is bound firmly and finally to that of his fellow house painters. There is, however, one concession which Tressell makes, clearly under the influence of Dickens, to the sentimental drama of the story by allowing Barrington, the middle-class socialist, to intervene at the end with his money and Christmas presents. At this point also, Barrington has succeeded Owen as the didactic voice in the novel, and his Beano speech contains a comprehensive picture of the future realisation of socialism. Despite this, the figure of Barrington is never allowed to distract in any decisive way from the collective celebration of the stoical strength and vitality of the working-class community which, for all its ideological limitations and contradictions, Tressell sees as providing the basis for the new society.

Tressell's warm sense of human fraternity is rarely transmitted in the same positive and compassionate way by his contemporaries, the socialist writers mentioned above who, instead, tend to underscore the idealised image of a working-class hero with a similarly distorted overemphasis on the brutalisation of the mass of workers. This latter aspect was clearly a lingering echo from the naturalist movement of the 1880s and 1890s which had, for instance, impelled English novelists such as George Gissing and Arthur Morrison to represent the population of London's slum underworld as brutish, demoralised and semi-criminal. In Jack London, perhaps the most aesthetically instinctive and autodidactic of all the great pioneer writers of socialist fiction, the working-class blond beasts are contrasted with the frightening abyss of a degenerate lumpenproletariat which threatens to well up and swamp the rest of society. Moreover, this reactionary mass is shown as being not only easy prey to the repressive forces of capitalist state power but also as one of the biggest obstacles to the success of the revolution itself. In *The Iron Heel*, Everhard's facile intellectual victories in lectures and debates give way in the later climactic chapters of the book to the harrowing scenes of bloody massacre during the Chicago Commune where London, with brilliantly dramatic skill, envisages the premature rising of the slum dwellers, significantly described as 'The People of the Abyss'. Here, London's taut narrative style comes into its own as he evokes this 'roaring abysmal beast' with a fascination and vigour that is in total contrast to the wooden characterisation and simplistic psychology of the individual portraits of the leaders. However, despite the heroic supportive rearguard actions of Everhard and his comrades, the blind explosion of these slum dwellers does not provide any progressive political impetus but acts instead as a reactionary provocation that only incites the iron heel of the oligarchy to drown the whole revolutionary movement in blood. To London, the jungle of the city seems only to spawn a demoralised subhuman mob of rampaging yahoos:

> men, women and children, in rags and tatters, dim ferocious intelligences with all the godlike blotted from their features and all the fiendlike stamped in, apes, and tigers, anaemic consumptives and great hairy beasts of burden, wan faces from which vampire society had sucked the juice of life, bloated forms swollen with physical grossness and corruption, withered hags and death's heads bearded like patriarchs, festering youth and festering age, faces of fiends, crooked, twisted, misshapen monsters blasted with the ravages of disease and all the horrors of innutrition—the refuse and the scum of life, a raging, screaming, screeching, demoniacal horde.[12]

The slums of Chicago are also seen as an epitome of a capitalist hell on earth in *The Jungle*, where the scenes of Jurgis's descent into the inferno of the meat-packing industry rival those of Dante's circles of torment. Moreover, the condition of urban brutalisation is rendered in exactly the same animal terms as Jack London uses— 'hideous, beastly faces, bloated and leprous with disease, laughing, shouting, screaming in all stages of drunkenness, barking like dogs, gibbering like apes, raving and tearing themselves in delirium'.[13] At the same time, Sinclair's symbolism of the slaughterhouse of class society is obviously meant to be extended even further to include the actual working masses themselves, as much passive victims of the system as the cattle and hogs trapped in the factory pens outside. In an attempt to broaden the political scope of the novel, Sinclair manipulates the calamitous fate of Jurgis and his family so as to scan the whole barbaric spectrum of social oppression by moving through and highlighting a totality of human experience from worker to convict, capitalist to criminal. Unfortunately, such an ambitious literary sweep and didactic concern often stretches the credibility of the novel's coincidences of plot to the limit. This is especially the case when Jurgis meets up with the drunken son of the owner of the whole Chicago meat-packing industry who takes him to their palatial residence so that the reader may gain an ideologically salutary insight into how the decadent, top-hatted bourgeoisie really live.

A further recurring convention adopted by several of our novelists in order to increase the moral indignation of their readership was to portray the seduction or forced prostitution of a workingman's wife or girlfriend, usually by a representative of the capitalist class or one of their hangers-on. The prostitution of Jurgis's wife to a factory foreman is, for example, the incident that destroys his dream of making good in the new world. After his prison sentence for assaulting the man and his own wife's death from shame, he loses all sense of social and class orientation and gradually sinks into criminal demoralisation until saved after a decidedly revivalist enlightenment at a socialist meeting near the end of the book. In *Pelle the Conqueror*, almost exactly the same moral complication is reproduced when Ellen, Pelle's wife, faced with Pelle's neglect of their family during the great lock-out, goes streetwalking in order to keep the children in food.[14] This, and his subsequent imprisonment for attempted forgery, also causes a profound emotional crisis in Pelle which impels him away from the revolutionary heart of the labour movement. From this point onwards, there is a marked shift in thematic emphasis towards a more exclusively individual preoccupation which becomes even further restricted in the final volume of Nexö's work, where Pelle's now limited reformist efforts towards social emancipation begin to coincide fully with Ellen's petit bourgeois dreams of family bliss in a home of their own. Moreover, Nexö's psychological exploration of the tension between the personal and the political in the novel is fundamentally weakened by this romantically Utopian solution of Pelle's country cottage and shoemakers' co-operative. As the titles indicate, the glowing pastoral vision of *Dawn* has by this time completely replaced the grim and sombre realism which characterises the earlier parts of *The Great Strike* when Pelle first arrives in Copenhagen and lives in a slum ghetto called 'The Ark'. However, even here, it is possible to discern an underlying romantic tone which takes the edge off the poverty and brutality and reveals Nexö's pervadingly idealistic theme of the basic human goodness of all his characters—slum dweller or shopkeeper, worker or capitalist—and, more politically, his overriding faith in their social-democratic potential.

A tangible feeling of the community and humanity of the oppressed is also prevalent both in Gorky and Tressell although their images of brutalisation are applied solely to representatives of the capitalist class. The single exception is in the opening scene in *Mother* where Gorky suggests a level of working-class brutishness which he then totally banishes from the heroic sphere of the story:

> Worn out as they were by hard work, the drink went quickly to their heads, and some uncountable irritation rankled in their breasts, demanding an outlet. And so they seized the slightest opportunity to relieve their painful feelings by flying at one another with bestial ferocity. Bloody fights were the result. Sometimes they ended in serious injuries and occasionally in killings.[15]

This significant distinction in artistic treatment is what makes Gorky and Tressell differ from the other novelists discussed here. Despite a similar need to criticise and expose the ideological limitations of the workers, both novelists seem to have made a conscious literary choice to portray their working-class characters as straightforwardly sympathetic as possible while representing the class enemy as the embodiment of all that is brutal and corrupt. These were the really 'useless men' in Gorky's eyes. In *Mother*, for example, Pelagea's lingering doubts and political misgivings are finally dispelled when she comes face to face at Pavel's trial with the actual physical representatives of law, order and religion. The comparison between the parasitical duplicity of the court officials and the transparent honesty and nobility of her son and his comrades exorcises the last remnants of her instinctive class fear and respect for authority:

> The mother kept her eyes on the judges and noticed that their excitement increased as they talked together . . . the young men roused in the old judges the gnawing, vengeful fury of worn-out beasts who see fresh food before them and lack the strength to seize it. Beasts who are no longer capable of taking their fill of other creatures' strength, but only growl and whine on seeing a means of satiety escaping them.[16]

It is also when he deals with the local echelons of capitalism in Mugsborough that Tressell turns on the full force of his ironic satire in order to caricature the bosses as savages totally lacking any redeeming qualities. They are exposed, as Jack Mitchell points out, as a class of 'Yahoos, as human beasts of prey'.[17] At the same time, it is important to note that Tressell, like Jack London, is careful to show that these people do not act merely as individuals but are forced to behave according to their position within the economic system:

> They all hated and blamed Rushton. Yet if they had been in Rushton's place they would have been compelled to adopt the same methods, or become bankrupt: for it is obvious that the only way to compete successfully against other employers who are sweaters is to be a sweater yourself. Therefore no one who is an upholder of the present system can consistently blame any of these men. Blame the system.[18]

Such a conscious socio-economic connection between character and context represented an important advance on the radical bourgeois novel tradition—as exemplified by Dickens's *Hard Times* or Elizabeth Gaskell's *Mary Barton*—where the capitalist is often shown experiencing a change of heart at the end, which not only strains the psychological plausibility but seriously blunts the critical edge of such novels. Nevertheless, Tressell himself does include a number of other literary stereotypes. He uses, for example, the same convention of a seduced workingman's wife to strengthen the moral force of his religious critique, when Ruth is made pregnant and then abandoned by the hypocritically pious foreman, Slyme. The sometimes quite virulent attacks on organised religion form, in fact, a manifest and integral part of Tressell's ideological preoccupations throughout the novel and reflect, perhaps, a lingering reaction against his own Irish Catholic upbringing.[19] Moreover, as in all the other cases mentioned, Tressell's inclusion of the fallen woman theme as a very emotive moral indictment of the system reveals the socialist novel at this stage, despite the avowed revolutionary politics in the public sphere, still upholding very traditional bourgeois family values in the home. In Gorky's *Mother*, there is an even clearer separation of the personal and the political, the ties of the family and the wider struggle, in Pavel's rejection of ever realising his love for Natasha, a comrade militant, as it would interfere with their work for the cause.

Most certainly, it was the whole context of oppression—the descriptions of poverty and the accompanying threat of degradation—that sustained the explicitly didactic function of these socialist novels. However, the object was not only to awaken the conscience of their readers but, more decisively, to transform an initial emotional response into a consciousness of the need for political involvement. Thus, the socialist novelists sought to fuse the pessimistic realism of the naturalist novel, which had depicted the poor as passive victims of cruel circumstances, with a more optimistic image of working-class heroes actively striving to break through such social and economic constraints. This uneasy transition was provided for by the other essential novel ingredient—the intellectual appeal of the ideas of socialism and the labour movement transmitted usually in the form of a speech, a polemic or lecture. Tressell's biographer, Fred Ball, states for instance that Tressell started writing a series of agitational pamphlets at first but soon found himself with the embryo of a novel on his hands.[20] Despite the artistic elaboration, a chapter such as 'The Oblong' can still easily be extracted as a classic set-piece in this didactic category, dealing as it does with a very practical lesson in the theory of surplus value. Apart from this immediate agitational function, all of the novels seek to project the longer-term perspective of a total transformation of society. But here a somewhat surprising ideological displacement of the working class occurs. In an attempt to give the concept of socialism more authority and persuasiveness, both Tressell and Sinclair assign middle-class characters to present the vision of change. Similarly, they also draw heavily on the Utopian theories of Edward Bellamy's *Looking Backward* (1888), which envisage a peacefully expanding state sector.[21] In exactly the same conciliatory way, although more pragmatically, Pelle, in *The Dawn*, is shown trying to realise this co-operative dream, using the private capital backing of a middle-class philanthropist. Despite Pavel's crushing indictment of the system of private property during the court scene in Gorky's *Mother*, the immediate prospect for the militants in the novel is one of imprisonment and exile—a realistic appraisal of the state of revolutionary ebb in Russia at that time. In Jack London's case, his vision of bloody repression is even more total and devastating, while the actual achievement of socialism is relegated to a series of Utopian footnotes which counterpose a three-hundred-year history of violent struggle against oligarchic reaction.

The different emotional and intellectual strategies of the novels remain, in most cases, on a rather mechanical, contrived and hardly integrated level, once again illustrating the perennial problem of the socialist novel of successfully fusing fiction and politics. The sense of militant pathos which these novelists sought to engender was, obviously, based on the deadly seriousness of their unremitting exposé of working-class poverty and misery. The exception to this is Tressell who complements the emotive and ideological effect of his message with the disarmingly sarcastic and affectionate humour of his working-class house painters. It is this key use of the comic ironic tradition of Dickens and, further back, the morality plays, which endows his novel with such a uniquely popular and appealing quality. As Tressell himself modestly expresses it in his preface to the book:

> 'The Philanthropists' is not a treatise or essay, but a novel. My main object was to write a readable story full of human interest and based on the happenings of everyday life, the subject of Socialism being treated incidentally . . . As far as I dared I let the characters express themselves in their own sort of language and consequently some passages may be considered objectionable. At the same time I believe that—because it is true—the book is not without its humorous side.[22]

Thus, Tressell is the only one of the socialist writers compared here who consciously and effectively employs a whole range of humour from the bitingly ironic to farcically satiric as an integral part of the narrative tone of his novel. It is this essential quality which lifts his work above the sombre political gravity and strained didacticism that dogs much of the writing in the other novels in discussion. Partly, it also goes to explain the genuine affection which his book has engendered over the years amongst a mass audience of working-class readers both in Britain and abroad. Activists in the British labour movement, for example, may often refer to the works of Jack London and Upton Sinclair as having played an influential role in their own early political formation, but Tressell's fictional characters have become endowed with that mythical essence that has secured them a place in the industrial folklore of the working class. As Brendan Behan recalled in his own fictional autobiography:

> It was our book at home, too, and when my mother was done telling us of the children of Lir and my father about Fionn MacCumhaill they'd come back by way of nineteen sixteen to the *Ragged Trousered Philanthropists* and on every job you'd hear painters using the names out of it for nicknames, calling their own apprentice 'The Walking Colour Shop' and, of course, every walking foreman was called Nimrod, even by painters who had never read the book, nor any other book, either.[23]

In the context of Tressell's comic narrative technique, it is significant to note that, although the title of his novel contains an ironic comment on the misplaced charity of the workers in donating the surplus profit of their labour to the capitalists, there is little or no sustained satire directed against the working-class characters within the story itself. Here, Tressell's personal and political sympathies are clearly and consistently manifest, while artistically he obviously did not want to confuse the issues of his message. On the contrary, as has been mentioned, it is his own socialist alter ego—Frank Owen—who bears the fraternal brunt of the workers' chaffing scepticism. Instead, the full force of Tressell's humour and satire is played upon the figures of the capitalists and their hangers-on—Rushton, Sweater, Slyme—all of whom, as their names suggest, are remorselessly caricatured. Tressell's exposure of these representatives of the class enemy is as ruthless and unequivocal as it is devastatingly comic. Perhaps nowhere else in the novel does he succeed better in didactically realising the personification of oppression than through this rogues' gallery of outrageous portraits in the great radical tradition of Bunyan and Dickens. One such example of the mythical proportions of Tressell's burlesque satire is the fate of the hugely overfed and spiritually inflated preacher, the Reverend Mr Belcher of the Shining Light Chapel, who is literally exploding with hot spicy air:

> 'Who is this last party what's dead?' asked Harlow after a pause.
> 'It's a parson what used to belong to the "Shining Light" Chapel. He'd been abroad for 'is 'ollerdays—to Monte Carlo. It seems 'e was ill before 'e went away, but the change did 'im a lot of good; in fact, 'e was quite recovered, and 'e was coming back again. But while 'e was standin' on the platform at Monte Carlo Station waitin' for the train, a porter runned into 'im with a barrer load o' luggage and 'e blowed up.'
> 'Blowed up?'
> 'Yes', repeated Philpot. 'Blowed up! Busted! Exploded! All into pieces. But they swep' 'em all up and put it in a corfin and it's to be planted this afternoon.'[24]

Tressell's novel, with its celebration of working-class humour and compelling narrative of resilience and defiance, stands as one of the most remarkable achievements of that fruitful convergence of socialist politics and literature which occurred at the beginning of the twentieth century. The social tension which the growth of the labour movement generated within capitalism provided the creative climate for a group of writers who sought to extend the function of critical realism through the active intervention of their works of fiction as weapons for socialist change. Whatever their artistic limitations, the novels of Maxim Gorky, Jack London, Upton Sinclair, Martin Andersen Nexö and Robert Tressell firmly and irreversibly launched the theme of working-class struggle into the mainstream of world literature.

NOTES

1. In 1915, a year before his death, London broke with the American Socialist Party because, as he wrote in his letter of resignation, 'of its lack of fire and fight, and its loss of emphasis on the class struggle'. Quoted in Robert Barltrop, *Jack London: the Man, the Writer, the Rebel* (London, 1976), p.163.
2. Robert Tressell, *The Ragged Trousered Philanthropists* (London, 1971), p.46.
3. Barltrop, *op. cit.*, pp.127-8.
4. *ibid.*, p.123.
5. Quoted in B. Bursov's Preface to Gorky's *Mother* (Moscow, 1983), pp.9-10.
6. Quoted in F. C. Ball, *One of the Damned* (London, 1979), p.167.
7. See Sillitoe's Introduction to the Panther edition (1965), p.7.
8. Jack London, *The Iron Heel* (London, 1975), p.63.
9. *ibid.*, pp.7-8.
10. Martin Andersen Nexö, *Pelle the Conqueror* (Stockholm, 1976), vol. 3, p.388. (My translation—RP).
11. Tressell, *op. cit.*, p.280.
12. London, *op. cit.*, p.207.

13. Upton Sinclair, *The Jungle* (Harmondsworth, 1974), p.277.
14. In his autobiographical novel from the same period, *Children of the Dead End* (1914), Patrick MacGill includes both the convention of the seduction and prostitution of Norah, a working-class girl, and the matriarchal figure of Gourock Ellen, a prostitute with a heart of gold.
15. Maxim Gorky, *Mother* (Moscow, 1983), p.19.
16. *ibid.*, p.444.
17. Jack Mitchell, *Robert Tressell and the Ragged Trousered Philanthropists* (London, 1969), p.73.
18. Tressell, *op. cit.*, p.217.
19. See Ball, *op. cit.*, pp.67-8.
20. *ibid.*, p.147.
21. Sinclair was later to use the proceeds from his novel, *The Jungle*, to open Helicon Hall, a Utopian co-operative-living venture in Englewood, N. J.
22. Tressell, *op. cit.*, p.12.
23. Brendan Behan, *Borstal Boy* (London, 1975), p.302.
24. Tressell, *op. cit.*, p.269.

· 11 ·

Ethel Carnie: writer, feminist and socialist

EDMUND AND RUTH FROW

The years 1909 to 1915 were Ethel Carnie's apprenticeship. She learned, during that time, to express her inherent and instinctive loathing of the capitalist system in political and positive terms; she found that her expressive needs could not be met by writing poetry and she became aware of herself as a woman, consciously and conscientiously writing with women as the pivot of her stories. She became an active socialist demanding a change in the system as well as the participation of workers in the determination of their lives.

CHILDHOOD AND FIRST POEMS

Ethel Carnie was born in Oswaldtwistle on 1 January 1886. Her parents were both cotton weavers and by the time Ethel was six years old they had moved to the growing textile town of Great Harwood near Blackburn in search of work. There, she attended the British School for a few years where she showed promise in composition and often had her essays read out in class, but otherwise displayed no outstanding ability.

Ethel Carnie's father was a member of the Social Democratic Federation (SDF). Great Harwood is within easy distance of Burnley which had one of the strongest SDF branches in the country. There was a club house and a lively programme of social and political activity. In Blackburn there was an SDF branch and a branch of The

Independent Labour Party (ILP). They worked amicably together in a friendly relationship. Mr Carnie took his daughter to political meetings and helped her to clothe her instinctive socialist attitudes with scientific understanding. In one of Ethel Carnie's later stories, a little girl is portrayed as being late for work because she cannot get up in time because of raging toothache. As she finally manages to make her preparations and rushes out of the door, she says 'Damn!' in a loud voice. This causes the girl's father to laugh and explain to his wife that the girl had been at a meeting the night before to hear Dan Irving speak. 'She looked so funny and it sounded so queer to hear her say "damn" like that. An' she's goin' to be a rebel, an' aw'm glad.'[1] Dan Irving was for many years Secretary of the Burnley SDF. He contested Board of Guardian and Town Council Elections when Ethel was a teenager.

At the age of eleven Ethel went half-time as a reeler in the nearest cotton mill. The following year she was taught the art of winding. At thirteen her formal education ended and she went full-time to the mill. She continued to work as a winder until she was eighteen when she was promoted to become a warper and beamer. The indignities of factory life bit deep into her consciousness and although she respected and admired her fellow workers, she hated factory life.

While still a winder at St Lawrence Mill, Ethel started composing poetry at work. According to her own testimony: 'From a child I found myself expressing my thoughts in rhythmic forms, and deriving great pleasure from so doing, accompanied though it was with a sense of restraint—that I must do so.'[2] Her first writing was published in the two Blackburn weekly papers. Blackburn had a strong radical and poetic tradition. The earliest local paper, *The Blackburn Mail*, had, from its inception, a column devoted to poetry, a practice that was continued over the years. As one commentator said: 'Although Blackburn cannot claim to be a town of outstanding literary associations, it is fortunate in possessing a tradition of native poetry far outrivalling many of its larger contemporaries.'[3]

The poem that drew attention to Ethel Carnie's talent was called 'The Bookworm':

> I own no grand baronial hall,
> No pastures rich in waving corn;
> Leave unto me my love for books,
> And rank and wealth I laugh to scorn.
>
> The world of books—how broad, how grand!
> Within its volumes, dark and old,
> What priceless gems of living thought
> Their beauties to the mind unfold.[4]

When Ethel read this poem before Blackburn Authors' Society to which she had been invited, its members were astonished that a mill girl of nineteen should be capable of such verse. Mr Barnett of the Society encouraged her, and a small volume of her poetry was issued as *Rhymes from the Factory* in 1907. The first edition of 500 copies sold out within a month. A second edition of a thousand followed, and in her preface Ethel Carnie reported that enquiries had come from all parts of the country and even from abroad and that she had dealt with as many as forty orders in one day.[5]

The second edition was reviewed by Keighly Snowdon in *The Woman Worker*. Snowdon pointed out that Ethel Carnie's poems were not about factory life, but thought poems reflecting wide reading[6] and a warm concern for her fellow workers:

> If death be equal, why not also life?
> Why should the toil, the suffering and the strife
> Fall but to some?[7]

Snowdon commented that Ethel Carnie 'comes in quietly and takes her place among the poets one loves', but he recognised that the poetry varied in quality and that much of it was unpolished: 'Schooled critics can point out many a fault in Ethel Carnie's verse. Most likely they will refuse for a long time to notice her.'[8] That was an understatement. They allowed her to sink without trace as so many working-class authors have done.

At first, however, the review had dramatic consequences. Robert Blatchford, editor of *The Clarion* and one of the founding fathers of the Independent Labour Party, took advantage of a visit to Lancashire to call on the author. He wrote an account of his interview in *The Woman Worker*. Although his style is patronising and paternalistic, he was obviously impressed by the young worker poet. He called Ethel Carnie 'an inscrutable, inexplicable, impossible fairy' and added that

> The Lancashire fairy lives at Great Harwood! Great Harwood is a monstrous agglomeration of ugly factories, of ugly gasometers, of ugly houses—brick boxes with slate lids. There is neither grace nor beauty in Great Harwood. It is the last place in which one would expect to find a poet.[9]

Blatchford described Ethel Carnie as a small quiet young woman, with quiet grey eyes, a quiet smile, and a dimple in her chin.

> There is not a single spark of conceit in Ethel Carnie. She is as free from affectation as a seagull; she has as much common sense as a policeman; she dresses plainly, speaks with a downright homely Lancashire accent; and is a real lady in the best sense of that ill-used word . . . There is no decorative copy to be made out of the Lancashire fairy. Her appearance is in no wise striking; she is not brilliant, nor eccentric; she does not say fine things about 'literature', nor about 'nature'; she never used the word 'art'.[10]

EDITING THE WOMAN WORKER

Following that interview, Ethel Carnie took the momentous decision to leave the factory and try to earn her living through her writing. Little is known about the arrangements which enabled her to do this. But it is quite clear that Blatchford had persuaded her to move to London to work for *The Clarion* and, especially, *The Woman Worker*. Probably in July 1909 she took over as editor of *The Woman*

Worker, whose original editor Mary Macarthur had given up the post in order to concentrate on trade-union work. From March until July of that year either Blatchford or one of the *Clarion* team may have written the editorials. There is no indication as to exactly when Ethel Carnie took over as editor. Blatchford indicated in the issue of 14 July 1909 that he was retiring. There was no editorial in the following issue, but that of 28 July 1909 contained a polemic against the 'yellow' press. For the next six months, the editorials and the tone of the journal bear Ethel Carnie's imprint. Reading between the lines, it can be assumed that she left Lancashire early in 1909 and spent some months learning the business of running a journal which she was unlikely to have experienced in Great Harwood. She was persuaded to write prose and fiction during that time and when she came to write the first editorial comment, her style had developed sufficiently to be recognisable. Her name did not appear as editor on the title page as Mary Macarthur's and Julia Dawson's had done. But the paper reflected her class consciousness and gained readers from her realistic approach. The editorial heading had claimed 31,000 circulation. Her influence probably accounted for the more likely figure of 26,500 in July and made her claim of an additional hundred in the issue of 8 September more plausible.

Reading her editorial comments indicates how her thinking developed over the six months. In her first editorial, she inveighs against the 'yellow press':

> It panders to the lowest tastes. It prostitutes itself in the cause of commercialism. Its gods are the trinity of £.s.d. . . . and its supreme justification is that it supplies what the great public desire. Yet if the public paused to think, even for a moment, they would realise that they were subsidising the people who insult them by placing such a low value upon their intelligence.

And she added: 'These papers treat women as puppets—as playthings—as mere adjuncts to man. The insolence of the whole thing!'[11]

The following week she presents the week's news as if it

were on a cinema screen. She makes her anti-war feelings clear in a comment on the war in Spain:

> Oh, it is a pretty business—this war of brothers. And all because men are living not in brotherhood but in anarchy. Because, under an iniquitous social system, life is a terrible struggle in which only a minority can hope to survive with advantage to themselves.[12]

A constantly recurring theme is the universal brotherhood of man. 'The greatest ideal which has ever been preached', she called it and suggested that Europe would only be prevented from invasion from the Far East by 'their conversion to the international ideal which recognises no distinction of class, or creed, or clime, but would have the men and women of the world live together in loving comradeship'.[13] Returning to the theme later in the month she said:

> There is, however, another factor today in the world-game. That factor cannot be ignored; It is the factor of the international spirit. Remember, today there is a great army throughout the world. The Red Army. The Army which recognises the red standard as their flag—first last and all the time.[14]

On the Budget, she assured Lord Rosebery, the Chancellor, that

> for every concession given by the exploiting classes we will demand two, that the wedge shall be driven up to the hilt, and that the women and men of this country will never rest satisfied until there is no hungry child crying for bread, no woman forced to sell her honour to keep her body alive, no man compelled to go cap in hand to a master for permission to maintain himself, which is the common right of humanity.[15]

She also charged Lord Grey, the Minister for Foreign Affairs, with having covered himself and his Government with infamy because he had refused to intervene in a Russian pogrom in which twenty-nine Jews were killed and over a thousand injured.

The topic which exercised her attention almost every week in one way or another was the position of women. 'The demand of "Equal Pay for Equal Work" is being gradually forced upon the attention of all thinking people', she asserted and added that 'neither men nor women can work out their salvation as sexes—they must march hand in hand to the conquest of the world.'[16] Calling attention to women in the news who had climbed a peak in the Himalayas, swum fifteen miles of the Thames, and traversed the continent of Africa, she said: 'And there are still men who persist in "chivalrously" regarding women as frail creatures, unfit even to vote.'[17] She also rejoiced at the University of London results in which girls had been exceptionally successful.[18] But she warned that

> the only thing woman has to fear is stagnation—the interchange of ideas can only help her on her road to emancipation; for those of both sexes who would keep woman in her traditional shackles, fear only one thing, and that is her intellectual development.[19]

Calling for juries to be composed of both sexes, she pointed out the unjust course taken by the Liberal Government who, instead of giving women the vote, imprisoned them for demanding it and then, having driven them to extreme measures, 'as though to complete an impossible and Gilbertian situation, they endeavour to forcibly feed them by the use of the stomach pump'.[20]

Throughout her editorials, Ethel Carnie drew attention to the technological changes taking place. She was obviously greatly impressed by the cinema and referred to it on several occasions. She also reported on the developments in flying and forecast an exciting future for women who were willing to try their hands at the less conventional exploits.[21]

Unemployment and poverty were rarely far from her mind.

> If you women [she informed her readers] were in deadly earnest you could, by propaganda, compel legislators to legislate for those who need legislation—the exploited—

instead of bolstering up a wretched system which is rapidly making life intolerable and impossible. Concentrate, as I have said before in these columns, on a Right To Work Bill. Once get that through, and force the State to take the unemployed off the market, and it is the beginning of the end for our present anarchic and archaic system.[22]

Ethel's own literary output accelerated once she had entered the atmosphere of the literary circle around *The Clarion*. By November 1909 she had contributed poems, articles and stories to *Woman's World, The Red Letter, Horner's Weekly, English Illustrated Magazine, Woman, Co-operative News, The Millgate Monthly, The Clarion* as well as the two Blackburn weeklies, *The Weekly Telegraph* and *Blackburn Times*.[23] In addition, of course, she contributed to each issue of *The Woman Worker*.

Ethel Carnie's editorial comments indicate her increasing politicisation and feminism. She brought a thread of realism to the paper. During her six months it certainly adopted a 'left' approach to the situation, in spite of Blatchford's reiteration that '*The Woman Worker* is not a class paper, its aim is to unite women of all classes: to get women into line with men.'[24] Such chauvinism would not have accorded with the growing feminism and personal confidence of the young editor.

By the middle of December 1909 there was a hint that Ethel Carnie had not fulfilled Blatchford's expectations of how the paper should develop. In the editorial, mention was made of readers thinking that the editor had been too emphatic in her condemnation of the Liberal–Labour alliance.[25] In January 1910 the paper changed its name to *Women Folk*, its editor to Blatchford's daughter, Winifred, and its policy to a much less pronounced socialism. Winifred's first editorial set the tone: 'And I hope we shall represent, so far as in us lies, those various states and professions, well balanced and impartially.'[26] Then there was 'An Open Letter to MISS ETHEL' by Pa B (Robert Blatchford?). The letter was a typical rambling mixture of paternalistic advice and inconsequential information. But one sentence gives a clue to what had happened: 'Ethel, they told me, had contracted an acute form of home sickness, and had floated out of their ken upon a tempestuous and saline sea of tears.'[27] For reasons beyond our knowledge, Ethel Carnie left London, returned to Great Harwood and resumed her work as a warper and beamer in a cotton mill.

She tried to continue writing and almost every issue of *Woman Folk* has a contribution from her. But getting up even earlier than she needed to get to the mill and retiring after midnight hardly made ideal conditions. In spite of that she managed to publish a second volume of poetry, *Songs of a Factory Girl*,[28] only a year after her return home. It was dedicated to her mother and it is possible that her floods of tears may have been occasioned by the news that her father had died—but that is speculation. In an interview with a journalist from the *Blackburn Weekly Telegraph*, Ethel told him that her return to the mill was not necessarily for all time and that she might leave it again to work with her pen instead of at a winding machine. 'And as for my poetry', she continued, 'there is plenty of inspiration in a room full of girls at a mill—all with different characters and temperaments and experience.'[29] She commented on work in a mill and said that it was

> a lamentable obstacle to the development of true womanly character. This is no matter of sentiment. It is unnatural; but in many cases it is necessary because the husband's wage is not sufficient to keep the home together. They have grit and cheerfulness, and this quality keeps them superior to their conditions, but it is none the less true that the life of many a woman with a family, who has to work in the mill, is the life of a slave.[30]

She determined to escape once again. With her mother she took a small shop in Ancoats, Manchester, where she was in touch with students from the University. But living in Ancoats did not suit her and she failed to establish rapport with the students, so she turned to writing again. She returned to London to work at Bebel House encouraging working women to express themselves in writing. When that job folded she returned to Lancashire and tried her hand at selling ribbons and laces on Blackburn Market. Meanwhile she continued writing. Regular articles and stories of hers appeared in *The Wheatsheaf* as well as *Woman Folk* and *The Clarion*.

THE STORIES

Ethel Carnie's stories reflect her powers of observation and her sympathy with the poor and exploited. They are seldom revolutionary in content nor didactic in tone. She seems content to mirror scenes as she saw them and leave the reader to draw conclusions. Her constant standby is the life of the textile workers. Illness and poverty occur frequently but how else could she have portrayed factory workers?

Hannah is a weaver who has to keep her mother. She obtains a good place in a new mill, but soon becomes ill. ' "Tha morn't go, Hannah", said Mrs Smith firmly. "Never mind t'looms. Life is o' moor consequence than brass." "But brass means life for sich as us", said Hannah, turning over.'[31]

In nearly all her fiction, Ethel Carnie presents women as the central characters. They are not always ideal models, but they are always human. In 'The Giver' Mary is left to fend for herself as she has watched her mother's household bits and pieces sold for a pittance. She lodges with a desperately poor family who, however, manage to maintain a cheerful exterior. Mary is determined to ensure that she will not be caught in the poverty trap. She saves and denies her better instincts to give. Her mother gives her advice: ' "If I had all the half-crowns I've given in my lifetime—aye I could ha' covered this quilt wi' 'em . . . Mary lass, stick to thy half-crowns." ' Mary does just that. She banks her coppers weekly and by the end of the first year has acquired a bank balance of twenty pounds. She continues to save and is eventually able to purchase a house and to buy a woman a bracelet that she admired only to find herself caught in a trap of generosity.

The thin edge of the wedge grew thicker. Soon she was no better off than the average worker, but the look of strain had gone from her eyes . . . She felt richer than she had done in the doorway of the bank . . . born a giver, she remained a giver, and giving is the soul of love, of life, of the progress of the world.[32]

'The Unbeliever' is interesting because it is not only one of the few stories of Ethel Carnie which has a male central character but also indicates her attitude towards religion. In the story, the woman believes in a supreme being and wants to marry a man who shares her creed. But the man she encounters turns out to be an atheist. When challenged on this account, he replies, however: ' "Unbeliever, Janet? Why there isn't a man, woman or child in the village that I don't believe in." ' Janet pursues the argument by telling him that her father said he had never seen him in church. While she is talking she pulls a flower to pieces for which he remonstrates with her.

"Don't, Janet!" he said, sharply. "What?" "Destroy that poor flower—you couldn't make one." She looked up eagerly. "That's what I can't understand about you, Fred," she began. "Look at the beauty of the earth—the stars, and the sun, and the violets coming back every spring, just to the time. You can see all the wonder of it, but you can't believe in a maker for it all!"

In the end she walks away from him and he is left with the dog who looks at him with adoring eyes.[33] Since the atheist is portrayed as much the more sympathetic character, Carnie leaves no doubt as to where her own feelings lay.

She was extremely fond of children and often wrote about the fate of the little half-timers in the mill which she knew so well from her own bitter experience. In one story she looks at the situation of a woman who has acquired a ready-made family by marrying a widower with five children. 'Plain, homely Susan' has accepted the responsibility and made an immediate success of it. But her husband is killed in a pit accident less than a fortnight after the wedding. Susan's uncle arrives to give her the benefit of his advice, which is to parcel the children out amongst the family. At this she gets furious.

> 'These children are my children, do you hear, and they are not going to be separated and given away amongst Stephen's relatives like so many pups of a litter. Besides, when I married Stephen I married him chiefly for the children's sake . . . I wouldn't leave Bobby for all the world. That child needs a mother's care . . . So here I stay.'

Uncle retired discomforted. Susan brought up the family with success and Bobby repaid her devotion by looking after her in her old age.³⁴

To complete the picture mention must be made of Ethel Carnie's children's stories. Several were published by Mr Stead in his series *Books For Bairns* which were penny booklets for children. Others were published in *The Wheatsheaf* and *The Woman Worker*, and a collection came out in 1911 under the title of *The Lamp Girl*.³⁵

MISS NOBODY

T. A. Jackson once remarked that

> any sort of proletarian novel by a proletarian is welcome, if only as an attempt . . . Even if the book is not, taken as a whole, a masterpiece, or anything like one, it is in much of its detail much better done and much more readable than many 'best sellers' from people of established reputations.³⁶

Much the same can be said about Ethel Carnie's first novel *Miss Nobody*, which came out in 1913. It shows one of the strengths of Ethel Carnie's fiction—an insightful and sympathetic representation of working women.

Books written by men often portray women in relation to men; and their moral worth is evaluated by how they cope with these relationships. By placing the relationships centrally around a working woman, the stage is set for working women to relate to the novel. As one reviewer stated: 'One welcomes in Miss Ethel Carnie a writer possessing an instinctive sympathy with her sisters, whether they work in mills or factories or in the thousands upon thousands of little homes of the industrial towns.'[37] In preference to the large canvas Carnie chose to portray the local scene and the ordinary women and men in it. However, her class consciousness was an integral part of the story. Miss Nobody[38] is Carrie, an orphan, who with her brother and sister is brought up in an orphanage. She is a cheerful and sensible person who accepts life as it comes. But she comments along the way on other people and events from a working-class point of view. She marries a farmer and has to adjust to life in the country where she finds a different set of values from those in the town to which she has been accustomed. She copes with a jealous sister-in-law, a dissolute brother and with leading a strike in a flax mill, with equal equanimity.

Mary Ashraf commented:

> In *Miss Nobody* socialism is, as it were, hovering just out of range of these little people, who have not yet arrived at any clear class consciousness . . . Ethel Carnie takes people as they are and shows their hopeful side, the positive values and power of growth in spite of crippling disadvantages of upbringing and environment.[39]

For a first novel, *Miss Nobody* certainly showed promise. It is written in a lively style directed at a general readership. It is not polished, but it has a verve and fluency which indicate a desire to communicate. The plot is possibly contrived, but at the level at which it is pitched, it does not seem outlandish. The dialogue is generally terse and suitable. She does occasionally labour and over-accentuate situations in her effort to make certain the reader understands. This is particularly so in her descriptions of life in the remote village where the farm is situated. The town scenes are true to life and more credible.

Some of her characters have endearing qualities: the girl in the Ardwick slum who has been bedridden much of her life and is able to have an operation to give her back the power to walk only after Carrie inherits a small fortune from her unknown father; the man who gives Carrie a lift when having set out to walk back to the village she changes her mind when she is half way and turns back to Manchester, and who explains his action as his belief in Socialism; the joy of the poor village idiot, Peter, in listening to Hans Andersen's stories; and the washerwoman who imitates animal noises to keep the soap suds out of her mind.

The petty, ingrained village life is contrasted unfavourably with the warmth and friendliness of the Manchester slum. It is, perhaps, overdrawn. Surely no one would sit up half the night to spy on her neighbours as Jane Wilkins is portrayed as doing; and the picture of Sarah, the jealous sister-in-law who finds herself ousted by the young enthusiastic wife, is hardly convincing. Even less so is her eventual change of heart and reconciliation.

Although *Miss Nobody* has the faults of a first novel written by an unsophisticated, down-to-earth woman with a comparatively limited perception of life, it has a vigour and depth which gives promise for her future work. *Miss Nobody* was the only Carnie novel published before the First World War but it is more than possible that some of her other work was actually written or prepared in her apprenticeship period. In 1917 her most successful novel, *Helen of the Four Gates*, was published with a print run of 25,000, and was subsequently made into a film. *The House that Jill Built* came out in 1920 and was followed in the same year by *The Marriage of Elizabeth*. Four years later, *General Belinda* was published and her only overtly socialist novel, *This Slavery*, came out in 1925. Her last publication was *Eagles Crag* in 1931.

At the foot of a story in *The Wheatsheaf* in April 1915 was a note saying that Miss Ethel Carnie and Mr Alfred Holdsworth had been married at Burnley on Saturday 3 April.[40] Shortly after the wedding, Ethel marched with Alfred to the railway station to see him off on his journey to his military call-up. She carried the Red Flag.[41]

Ethel Carnie's apprenticeship as a writer, as a woman and as a socialist had ended. She graduated with a record of work in the movement and a creditable collection of published work. She had the knowledge that she had satisfied a need for literature which class-conscious workers and especially women workers could recognise as the experiences of their own lives and struggles from the working-class point of view.

NOTES

1. 'Tissie Wakes up', *Women Folk*, vol. 4, no. 35 (2 March 1910), p.755.
2. Preface to *Rhymes from the Factory* by a Factory Girl (Blackburn, 1907).
3. G. C. Miller, *The Evolution of a Cotton Town* (Blackburn, 1951), p.228.
4. 'The Bookworm', *Rhymes from the Factory*, p.1.
5. *ibid.*
6. Among authors with whose work Ethel Carnie was familiar were: Hillaire Belloc, Charlotte Brontë, Thomas Carlyle, Edward Carpenter, Coleridge, Dante, Defoe, Dickens, Ebenezer Elliott, Emerson, Bret Harte, Victor Hugo, Jerome K. Jerome, Ernest Jones, Keats, Lamb, Meredith, Scott, Shelley, Swinburne, Thackeray and Wordsworth.
7. 'The Rich and the Poor', *Rhymes from the Factory*, p.22.
8. Keighly Snowdon, 'A Book of the Hour', *The Woman Worker*, vol. I (new series), no. 5 (3 July 1908), p.135.
9. Robert Blatchford, 'A Lancashire Fairy', *The Woman Worker*, vol. I, no. 6 (10 July 1908), p.155.
10. *ibid.*
11. 'The Editor's Chair', *The Woman Worker*, vol. IV, no. 4 (28 July 1909), p.84.
12. *ibid.*, no. 5 (4 August 1909), p.108.
13. *ibid.*, no. 6 (11 August 1909), p.132.
14. *ibid.*, no. 8 (25 August 1909), p.180.
15. *ibid.*, no. 11 (15 September 1909), p.252.
16. *ibid.*, no. 18 (3 November 1909), p.418.
17. *ibid.*, no. 7 (18 August 1909), p.156.
18. *ibid.*, no. 23 (8 December 1909), p.518.
19. *ibid.*, no. 20 (17 November 1909), p.458.
20. *ibid.*
21. *ibid.*, no. 17 (27 October 1909), p.296.

22. ibid., no. 16 (20 October 1909), p.372.
23. PEM, 'A Factory Girl Poet', *Millgate Monthly*, V (November 1909), pp.70-2. PEM is Priscilla E. Moulder.
24. Editorial, *The Woman Worker*, vol. III, no. 10 (10 March 1909), p.228.
25. 'The Editor's Chair', *The Woman Worker*, vol. IV, no. 24 (15 December 1909), p.538.
26. 'The Editor's Chair', *Women Folk*, vol. IV, no. 31 (2 February 1910), p.678.
27. Pa B, 'An Open Letter To Miss Ethel', *ibid.*, p.685.
28. Ethel Carnie, *Songs of a Factory Girl* (London, 1911).
29. *Blackburn Weekly Telegraph*, 15 April 1911.
30. ibid.
31. 'Weaver', *The Wheatsheaf* (October 1911), p.60.
32. 'The Giver', *The Wheatsheaf* (December 1913), p.101.
33. 'The Unbeliever', *The Woman Worker*, vol. II, no. 17 (28 April 1909), p.390.
34. 'His Family', *The Wheatsheaf* (October 1912), p.61.
35. Ethel Carnie, *The Lamp Girl and Other Tales* (London, n.d.).
36. T. A. Jackson in *The Sunday Worker*, 21 April 1929.
37. 'Miss Nobody and Its Author', *The Wheatsheaf* (November 1913). p.85.
38. For a full assessment of *Miss Nobody* see P. M. Ashraf, *Introduction to Working-Class Literature in Great Britain*, Part II: Prose (Berlin, 1979), pp.178-86.
39. *ibid.*, p.185.
40. *The Wheatsheaf* (April 1915), p.173.
41. Oral evidence from the late Bessie and Harold Dickenson of Nelson.

Chronological Table

The following tables provide a conspectus of the period, relating the fiction discussed in this book to principal events in the history of the British labour movement, and to mainstream English fiction. It should be clear that the lefthand section contains neither an exclusive nor a comprehensive list of socialist narratives.

	Fiction discussed in this book	Events in labour history	Some mainstream English Fiction
1880			Butler, *The Way of All Flesh* (in progress)
1881		(Social) Democratic Federation founded	James, *The Portrait of a Lady*
1882			
1883		SDF turning socialist Marx died	
1884	Allen, *Philistia* Shaw, *An Unsocial Socialist* (serialised)	Third Reform Act SDF split Socialist League founded Fabian Society founded *Justice* started	
1885	Zola, *Germinal* Morris, *The Pilgrims of Hope* (ser.)	*Commonweal* started	

	Fiction discussed in this book	Events in labour history	Some mainstream English fiction
1886	Morris, *A Dream of John Ball* (ser.) James, *The Princess Casamassima*	Trafalgar Square riot	Gissing, *Demos*
1887	Harkness, *A City Girl* Rutherford, *The Revolution in Tanner's Lane*	'Bloody Sunday'	
1888	Howell, *A More Excellent Way* Bramsbury, *A Working Class Tragedy* (ser.) Harkness, *Out of Work*		
1889	Leslie, *How the Strike Began* Harkness, *Captain Lobe*	Great Dock Strike Second International founded *Fabian Essays*	Gissing, *The Nether World*
1890	Morris, *News from Nowhere* (ser.) Harkness, *A Manchester Shirtmaker*		
1891	Tirebuck, *Dorrie* Leslie, *The Seed She Sowed* Oakhurst, *The Universal Strike of 1899*	*Clarion* appeared	Hardy, *Tess of the D'Urbervilles* Wilde, *The Picture of Dorian Grey*
1892			
1893	Clarke, *The Knobstick* Fawcett, *Hartmann the Anarchist* Adderley, *Stephen Remarx*	ILP founded 'Coal War' Blatchford's *Merrie England*	
1894	Black, *The Agitator*		Moore, *Esther Waters*

	Fiction discussed in this book	Events in labour history	Some mainstream English fiction
1895	Tirebuck, *Miss Grace of All Souls'* Fletcher, *Lost in the Mine* Brooke, *Transition*	Engels died	Hardy, *Jude the Obscure* Wells, *The Time Machine*
1896	Lawson, *While the Billy Boils*	Morris died	Morrison, *A Child of the Iago*
1897	Voynich, *The Gadfly*	*Social Democrat* started	Maugham, *Liza of Lambeth* Stevenson, *Weir of Hermiston*
1898	Clarke, *The Daughter of the Factory* (ser.) Laycock, *The Young Gaffer* (ser.) Sykes and Walker, *Ben o' Bill's*		
1899	Plant, *Tamsie*	Boer War	Conrad, *Heart of Darkness* (ser.)
1900	Laycock, *Steve the Outlander* Plant, *The Conductor's Sweetheart* (ser.) Lawson, *On the Track and over the Sliprails* Birrel, *Love in a Mist*	Labour Representation Committee founded	
1901	Clarke, *Driving* (ser.) Lawson, *Joe Wilson and His Mates*	Taff Vale decision	Kipling, *Kim*
1902	Tamlyn, *The Hermit of Cottondale* (ser.) Lawson, *Children of the Bush*		James, *The Wings of the Dove*

	Fiction discussed in this book	Events in labour history	Some mainstream English fiction
1903	Rossetti, *A Girl among the Anarchists* Tamlyn, *The Love of a Northern Farmer* (ser.)	Women's Social and Political Union founded	
1904	Haslam, *The Handloom Weaver's Daughter*		Conrad, *Nostromo*
1905	Harkness, *George Eastmont: Wanderer*		Forster, *Where Angels Fear to Tread*
1906	Clarke, *Lancashire Lasses and Lads* Laycock, *Warren of Manchester* Tressell, *The Ragged Trousered Philanthropists* (in progress) Sinclair, *The Jungle* Andersen Nexö, *Pelle the Conqueror*	Labour Party founded 29 Labour MPs returned in general election	Galsworthy, *The Man of Property*
1907	Clarke, *The Red Flag* Conrad, *The Secret Agent* London, *The Iron Heel* Gorky, *Mother*		
1908	Harris, *The Bomb*		Bennett, *The Old Wives' Tale*
1909			Wells, *Tono-Bungay*
1910			Forster, *Howard's End*
1911		Seamen's and transport workers' strike *Daily Herald* started	

	Fiction discussed in this book	Events in labour history	Some mainstream English fiction
1912		Miners' strike	
1913	Carnie, *Miss Nobody*		Lawrence, *Sons and Lovers*
1914	Tressell, *The Ragged Trousered Philanthropists* (publ.)	Outbreak of war	Joyce, *Dubliners*

Index

Note: Only authors substantially discussed have their works listed.

Adams, Francis 62
Adderley, James
   Stephen Remarx 19-21
Allen, Grant ('Cecil
   Power') 15, 86, 159
   Philistia 11-13
Andersen, Hans 264
Andersen Nexö, Martin 2,
   232, 235, 249
   Morten the Red 233
   Pelle the Conqueror 231,
   234, 237, 242-3
Angiolilli, Michele 143
Arnold, Matthew 122
Ashraf, Mary 84, 263
Aveling, Edward 32

Bakunin, Mikhail
   Alexandrovich 124-5,
   128
Ball, Fred 245
Barltrop, Robert 233
Bax, Belfort 14, 69
Baxter, Dan 70
Bebel, August 14
Beecher Stowe, Harriet 30
Behan, Brendan 247

Behn, Aphra 30
Bellamy, Edward 246
Benjamin, Walter 99-100
Besant, Annie 34
Besant, Walter 28
Birrel, Olive
   Love in a Mist 21-4
Black, Clementina 3, 33
   An Agitator 29, 43-5, 98
Black, George 205
Blatchford, Robert 28, 50, 86,
   254-5, 258
Blatchford, Winifred 258
Boole, George 115
Booth, Charles 155
Bourdin, Marcel 123, 129
Braine, John 238
Bramsbury, H. J. 29
   A Working Class
   Tragedy 49, 59-63
Brecht, Bertolt 154
Brontë, Charlotte 30, 101
Brooke, Emma 3
   A Superfluous Woman
   39-40
   Transition 29, 39-43
Broomfield, Fred 226

Browning, Elizabeth 30
Browning, Robert 80
Bunyan, John 248

Caird, Mona 29, 35
Cameron (Gilmore), Mary 217
Canovas del Castillo, Antonio 143
Carnie (Holdsworth), Ethel 3, 94, 251-65
 General Belinda 264
 Helen of the Four Gates 264
 The Marriage of Elizabeth 264
 Miss Nobody 262-4
 This Slavery 264
Carpenter, Edward 50
Clapperton, J. H. 154
Clark, Manning 205, 213
Clarke, Charles Allen ('Teddy Ashton') 2, 4, 29, 64-5, 92, 94, 96-7, 198-200
 A Daughter of the Factory 180, 185-7
 Driving 175-6, 178-9, 183, 189
 Effects of the Factory System 175, 179, 190
 The Knobstick 81-6, 89, 173, 178-9, 185, 189, 195, 200
 Lancashire Lasses and Lads 176, 185
 The Red Flag 179, 181-4
Clarke, Eliza 177
Clynes, J. R. 179
Cobbett, William 89
Connell, Jim 50
Connolly, James 50
Conrad, Joseph 117, 122, 124, 213
 The Secret Agent 125, 128-33, 135, 142

Conway, Katherine St. John 182
Crompton, Samuel 176

Dawson, Julia 255
Defoe, Daniel 50
Dickens, Charles 50, 52, 91, 93-4, 162, 208, 244, 246, 248
Disraeli, Benjamin 107, 135, 169
Dix, Gertrude 3, 29

Edgeworth, Maria 30
'Egerton, George' (Mary Chavelita Dunne) 29, 159
'Eliot, George' 50, 94, 161
Engels, Friedrich 14, 160

Fawcett, E. Douglas
 Hartmann the Anarchist 136-40, 146
Fitzgerald, J. D. 205
Flaubert, Gustave 159
Fletcher, Alfred H. 94, 98
 Lost in the Mine 90-3

Garnett, Edward 203, 212
Gaskell, Elizabeth 30, 94, 107, 135, 169, 244
George, Henry 37
Gibbon, Lewis Grassic 121, 235
Gissing, George 28, 46, 69, 73, 153, 159, 240
Glasier, Bruce 50
Godwin, William 128
Goode, John 153, 159
Gorky, Maxim 2, 232, 237-8, 249
 Mother 231, 234, 237, 243, 245-6

Graham, R. B.
  Cunninghame 50, 70
Grand, Sarah 29, 35, 159

Habermas, Jürgen 1
Hardie, Keir 86, 182, 217
Hardy, Thomas 159
Hargreaves, James 175-6
Harkness, Margaret ('John
  Law') 3, 29, 153-60, 162,
  169-70
  Captain Lobe 157, 159
  A City Girl 157-8, 160
  George Eastmont 24-6
  A Manchester Shirtmaker 2, 157
  Out of Work 155-9
Harris, Frank 4
  The Bomb 144-7
Harte, Bret 203, 216
Haslam, James
  The Handloom Weaver's Daughter 99, 105-9, 198
Henry, Emile 143
Higgs, Mary 181
Hobart, H. W. 64-6
Hogben, John 160
Holdsworth, Alfred 264
Howell, Constance 3, 41
  A More Excellent Way 13-16, 29, 35-9, 154
Hudson, W. H. 213
Hutchins, Barbara 33
Hyndman, H. M. 14, 63

Irving, Dan 252

Jackson, T. A. 262
James, Henry 122-4
  The Princess Casamassima 133-6, 141
Jones, Gareth Stedman 79
Jones, Lewis 121

Kay, John 175
Keating, P. J. 29
Kelley, Florence 34
Kettle, Arnold 119
Kingsley, Henry 206, 211
Kollontai, Alexandra 34
Kropotkin, Pjotr
  Alexeyevich 14, 141
Kuliscioff, Anna 34

Lane, Annie 217
Lane, William 208, 211, 216-17
Lassalle, Ferdinand 14, 37
Lawrence, D. H. 86, 89-90, 213, 225
Lawson, Bertha 217
Lawson, Henry 1, 203-26
  Children of the Bush 204, 221-3
  The Country I Come from 204
  Joe Wilson and His Mates 218-20
  On the Track and Over the Sliprails 203, 208-10
  Triangles of Life 223-6
  While the Billy Boils 203, 207-8, 211-15
Lawson, Louisa 205
Laycock, Arthur 4, 94, 198
  Steve the Outlander 187, 190-1
  Warren of Manchester 187, 191
  The Young Gaffer 187-90, 195, 200
Laycock, Samuel 187
Lee, Peter 199
Lenin, Vladimir Ilyich 44, 234
Lerner, Gerda 31
Leslie, Emma 75-8, 94

How the Strike Began 75
The Seed She Sowed 75-8
London, Jack 232, 244, 246-7, 249
   The Iron Heel 231, 233, 235-7, 240-1
   The People of the Abyss 235
Lucas, John 111-12
Lukács, Georg 104, 154

Macarthur, Mary 255
MacGill, Patrick 170
Maguire, Tom 50, 64
Malatesta, Errico 140
Manning, Cardinal 78
Martineau, Harriet 74
Martyn, Caroline 182
Marx, Eleanor 32, 34
Marx, Karl 14, 37, 124, 211
Maupassant, Guy de 203, 212-13
Mayne, Fanny 73
Meacham, Standish 2, 198
Melchiori, Barbara Arnett 131
Michel, Louise 140
Mill, John Stuart 36
Mitchell, Jack 244
Moore, George 153, 155, 159, 162
Morris, William 14, 49-50, 144, 153, 189, 205
   A Dream of John Ball 49, 55-7
   News from Nowhere 49, 57-9, 78
   Pilgrims of Hope 2, 49, 52-5, 57
Morrison, Arthur 28, 153, 240
Morton, A. L. 58

Nechayev, Sergei

Gennadeyevich 125
Norton, John 205

Oakhurst, William 94
   The Universal Strike of 1899 78-81, 85
Ogilvie, Will H. 204

Parsons, Albert 145
Patterson, Emma 33
Peel, Frank 100-2
Petrie, Larry 216
Pierson, Stanley 6, 167
Plekhanov, Georg Valentinovich 237
Plant, Fred 4, 94, 198
   The Conductor's Sweetheart 195-7, 200
   Tamsie 197-8

Quelch, Harry 50, 65, 67-8

Reclus, Elisée 14
Richards, Grant 234
Roberts, Morley 140-2
Rossetti, Helen 140
Rossetti, Olivia ('Isabel Meredith')
   A Girl Among the Anarchists 140-4
Rossetti, William Michael 140
Rothstein, Theodore 70
Ruskin, John 106

Schiller, Friedrich 6
Schreiner, Olive 29, 159
Scott, Walter 99, 104-5, 107, 110, 113
Shaw, George Bernard 13, 153
   An Unsocial Socialist 2, 8-12

Shelley, Percy Bysshe 92, 128
Sillitoe, Alan 234, 238
Sinclair, Upton 2, 232, 235, 246-7, 249
  The Jungle 231, 237, 241-2
Snowden, Keighly 253
Spence, W. G. 214
Spies, August 145
Spinoza, Baruch 12
'Stepniak' (Sergei Mikhailovich Kravchinski) 115
Sterne, Laurence 66
Storey, David 238
Sykes, D. F. E. (and Geo. Henry Walker) 4
  Ben o' Bill's 99-105, 108

Tamlyn, John 64, 195, 198
  The Hermit of Cottondale 191-3, 200
  The Love of a Northern Farmer 191, 193-4
Thompson, E. P. 57, 100
Thompson, Francis 203
Tilley, W. H. 133
Tirebuck, William Edwards 3-4, 29, 92, 94, 96-7, 153, 159-70
  Dorrie 2, 161-3, 165, 167-8
  Miss Grace of All Souls' 16-19, 86-90, 162, 164-9
  Saint Margaret 164
Tolstoy, Leo Nikolayevich 173
Tonna, Charlotte Elizabeth 30, 74
Toulmin, Camilla 73
'Tressell, Robert' (Robert Noonan) 2, 121, 170, 232, 234, 243-9
  The Ragged Trousered Philanthropists 51, 59, 61, 65-6, 70-1, 83, 172, 231-3, 238-40, 247-9
Twain, Mark 224

Verne, Jules 136
Vizetelly, Henry 153
Voynich, Ethel L.
  The Gadfly 9, 115-19
Voynich, Wilfred 15

Walker, Geo. Henry (and D. F. E. Sykes) 4
  Ben o' Bill's 99-105, 108
Walker, Thomas 205
Watt, James 175
Wells, H. G. 97-8, 136
White, William Hale ('Mark Rutherford')
  The Revolution in Tanner's Lane 4, 99, 109-15
Whiteing, Richard 153
Whitman, Walt 70
Whittaker, Joseph 199
Wilkes, G. A. 215
Wollstonecraft, Mary 36
Woodcock, George 121, 123

Yeo, Stephen 3

Zetkin, Clara 34
Zola, Emile 151-2, 155, 158, 166-8
  Germinal 1, 50, 89-90, 123-8, 135, 137, 139, 153-4, 164-5
  Nana 162
  Thérèse Raquin 162